1

0

STAFFORDSHIRE

THE KING'S ENGLAND

Edited by Arthur Mee

In 41 Volumes

THE KING'S ENGLAND

STAFFORDSHIRE

By
ARTHUR MEE

fully revised and edited by
F. R. BANKS

Illustrated with new photographs by
A. F. KERSTING

HODDER AND STOUGHTON

Printed in Great Britain
for Hodder and Stoughton Limited,
St. Paul's House, Warwick Lane, London, E.C.4,
by Richard Clay (The Chaucer Press) Ltd.,
Bungay, Suffolk

INTRODUCTION TO REVISED EDITION

IN preparing the new edition of THE KING'S ENGLAND care has been taken to bring the books up to date as far as possible within the changes which have taken place since the series was originally planned. In addition the editor has made his revisions both in text and illustrations with a view to keeping the price of the books within reasonable limits, in spite of greatly increased production costs. But, throughout the book, it has been the editor's special care to preserve Mr Arthur Mee's original intention of providing something more than just another guide book giving archaeological, ecclesiastical, and topographical information.

In the case of every town and village mentioned in the King's England Series, it has been the intention not only to indicate its position on the map but to convey something of its atmosphere. And the biographical selections about people who are ever associated with that part of the country in which they lived, or who are commemorated in the parish church—which was such a popular feature of the former edition—have been retained and in some cases supplemented.

ILLUSTRATIONS

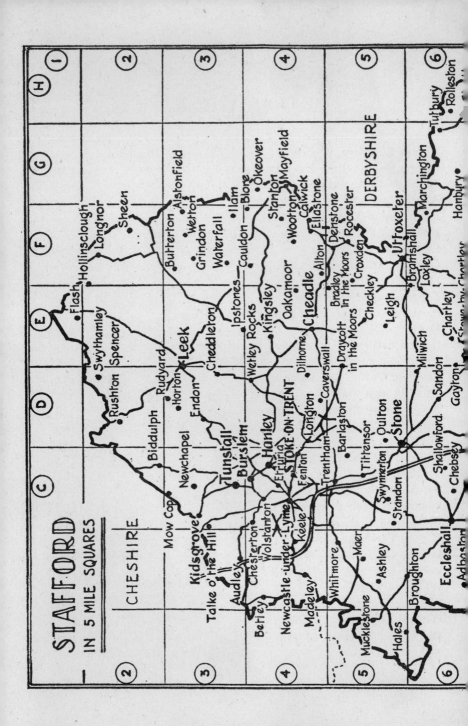

STAFFORD
IN 5 MILE SQUARES

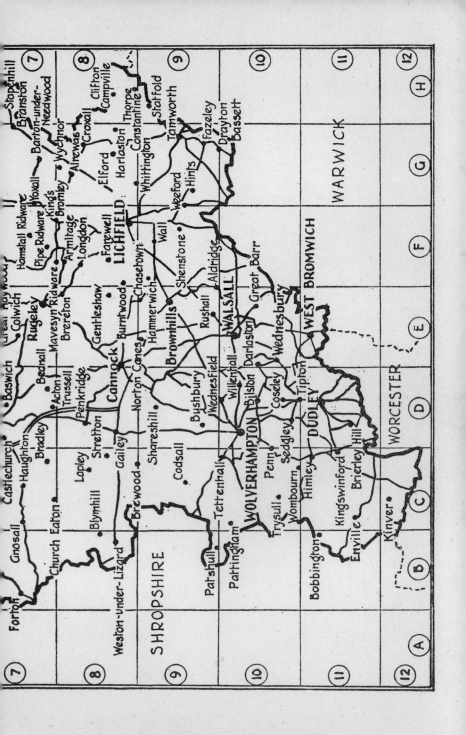

STAFFORDSHIRE

INTRODUCTION

THOSE who know Staffordshire only from its popular reputation may be apt to place a black mark against it as a traveller's county, for the Black Country lies within its borders, and the Pottery towns now known as Stoke-on-Trent form a great industrial area which grew up too fast for beauty to have its fair share in shaping it.

But it is true that the 740,404 acres of Staffordshire contain as pleasant and peaceful a countryside as we find anywhere in England. In the north the moorlands of the Pennine range come in with all their wild beauty, falling away into the less rugged grandeur of Dovedale and the dales and valleys of smaller streams carving their ways through the limestone. South of the county lies Cannock Chase, an expanse of 30,000 acres of heath interspersed by woodland which remind us that here was a wide forest hunted by kings, high-lying country above the valley of the River Trent.

Between the moorland and Cannock Chase lies undulating country through which the rivers flow slowly, the typical country of the dairy-farmer, not in any way monotonous, and rolling up to the borders of the Pottery towns.

Staffordshire, therefore, has much to delight the lover of wide open spaces, and though, with her 1,834,660 people, she is fifth in population but only seventeenth in size among our counties, there are great areas thinly peopled, for the busy towns contain more than three-quarters of her population.

The loneliest country in Staffordshire is the moorland north of Leek. Here walls of native gritstone take the place of hedges, and the grouse, the lapwing, and in summer the curlew, break its great silences. Mow Cop, crowned at 1091 feet by an artificial ruin, is on the border of Cheshire and famous as the site of the camp meeting at which the Primitive Methodist Society was born two years after Trafalgar. East of Mow Cop lies Biddulph Moor, the source of the Trent, and in a valley beyond, surrounded by well-wooded hills, is the beautiful Rudyard Lake on whose shores Lockwood Kipling asked Alice Macdonald to be his wife; they called their son after the place and so made its name renowned throughout the world. This lake, now popular for sailing, is nearly two miles long and its greatest width is over 400 yards; actually it is the reservoir for the canal dug to link the Mersey with the Trent towards the end of the 18th century. Perhaps it is odd to think that Rudyard Kipling was named after a reservoir.

A few miles east the ridge known as the Roches cleaves the sky at a height of over 1600 feet, the southern corner dropping to form one side of the beautiful valley of the River Churnet on its eastward course. Its valley is completed by the Morridge, a long ridge rising less abruptly to 1500 feet, but from Merryton Low, standing out 1603 feet high at the north, we look over the moors from which all the streams flow east to feed the Dove on the county boundary.

It is the Dove's famous tributary, the Manifold, which first gathers these streams together as they make their way through moorland rising 2000 feet and higher. This is the country which formed (with part of Derbyshire on the other side of the Dove) England's first National Park. All England knows of lovely Dovedale, half of which is in Staffordshire, though Derbyshire has the chief fame of it, but the valley of the Manifold, and the valley of its biggest feeder the Hamps, are less known, in spite of their wilder beauty and the ever-changing views which their frequent windings give us.

One dramatic thing happened here that helped forward the idea of the national park. The mineral railway has been transformed into a public walk, and we may saunter at will where until not very long ago the trains carrying great blocks of limestone would run. A great fortune had been spent on the Leek and Manifold Light Railway (not less than £68,000) but the line failed, and now the rails have been pulled up and the trackway is a walk where no wheels other than a bicycle's may come.

From its source near the village of Flash, in the extreme north of Staffordshire, the Manifold flows south, gathering from the moors small streams like the Blake Brook. At Hulme End its valley becomes impressive, though hereabouts are the remains of the deserted Ecton copper mines, which yielded such wealth in the 18th century that the duke of Devonshire is said to have built Buxton's famous Crescent from the profits of a single year. In the neighbourhood of Wetton Mill are several caves, and then come the bold rocks known as Darfur Crags, perhaps the most striking in the valley. Often in summer the Manifold here disappears underground, but when it does flow it soon comes to the Redhurst Gorge, famed for Old Hannah's Hole, a cleft from which a prehistoric urn has been recovered.

Remains of prehistoric man in far greater variety have been taken from Thor's Cave, an opening in a cliff towering over the valley. It is entered through an arch like the doorway of a Norman cathedral, and, within, two pillars of rock support the roof of the cave. Here in the middle of the 19th century a village schoolmaster found flint arrowheads, bone combs, bronze brooches and bracelets, iron adzes, Samian ware, and a Roman coin. Thor's cave had evidently been inhabited for centuries. Below it, nearer the river, is a smaller cave, called Radcliffe's Stable because Farmer Radcliffe hid his horse in it so that the horse should not be seized to carry one of the Pretender's Scotsmen towards London.

At the base of Beeston Tor, a limestone crag towering above the scene where the Hamps adds its waters to the Manifold, is St Bertram's Cave, in which Saxon jewels and coins of King Alfred were discovered. This cave, named after the saint whose shrine is at Ilam close by, was evidently a place of hiding from Danish marauders.

The River Hamps, like the Manifold, runs underground when summer comes to this limestone wonderland. It has risen near the lonely Morridge, and for the last two miles of its course lies under the shadow of Soles Hill, over 1100 feet high, now happily belonging to the National Trust. The Throwley estate, with its ruins of the Jacobean Old Hall, is bounded by this hill and the River Manifold, winding its way on to pass through the lovely grounds of Ilam Hall, also belonging to the National Trust. It was here that Johnson and Boswell came to see the river emerging after its course underground. Dr Johnson declared that the waters could not belong to the Manifold, but the gardener assured him that he had tested the phenomenon with floating corks. Passing close to Ilam's church, with its Saxon churchyard crosses, the Manifold flows into the Dove where it emerges from its famous dale.

From its source a little below Axe Edge in Derbyshire the River Dove has formed the boundary between that county and Staffordshire as it twists and turns in its deep valley. Beresford Dale, a wooded ravine taking its name from the Beaver's Ford at its lower end, has been immortalised in Izaak Walton's *Compleat Angler*. It is in the second part of that book, the part his friend Charles Cotton wrote, that we find the description of the Pike Pool with the needle rock which Viator declared was "one of the oddest sights he ever saw". Viator's host replied that young Mr Izaak Walton was so pleased with it as to draw it in landscape, in black and white, in a blank book he had at Beresford Hall.

The Fishing House built on the river's bank still stands to remind us of these two friends, whose initials are twined on a stone over the doorway. A companion stone is inscribed *Piscatoribus Sacrum*, 1674, but the friends little thought, as they stood watching the craftsman cut these words, that this delightful building would be sacred down the ages to thousands who would rather hold a good book than a fishing rod.

Charles Cotton loved this little paradise, where he was born in the

3

troubled days of Charles I. Weary of town life and its unpleasant traits after the Restoration, he would come here to rest and write and meditate, fishing with his older and wiser friend. In his poem *The Retirement* he writes of his native stream:

> Oh, my beloved nymph, fair Dove,
> Princess of rivers, how I love
> Upon thy flowery banks to lie,
> And view thy silvery stream
> When gilded by a summer's beam.

Through much wilder scenery the Dove next flows by Wolfscote Dale to reach land which, for many miles on one bank or the other, now belongs to the National Trust. At the hamlet of Milldale is the narrow Viator Bridge, an old packhorse bridge. "Why! a mouse can hardly go over it; 'tis not two fingers broad," says Viator.

Some four miles of exquisite loveliness now accompany the Dove —the Dovedale painted so often by the artist and sung by the poet. The Staffordshire side equals the Derbyshire side in beauty, though it is from the footpath on the Derbyshire side that we see most of its glory. Pinnacles of rock and limestone cliffs add quaintness and strength to the scene: Raven's Tor, Pickering Tor, Lion Rock (looking like a lion's head), Ilam Rock, Tissington Spires, and Dovedale Castles. The caverns of Dove Holes also give a touch of mystery to the dale.

The hills of Bunster and its Derbyshire rival Thorpe Cloud mark the end of the vale, and the river winds onward through a wider, more pastoral valley. On its banks stands Mayfield church with the grave of the daughter of Thomas Moore, who in Mayfield Cottage here wrote *Lalla Rookh* and the familiar poem beginning

> Those evening bells, Those evening bells,
> How many a tale their music tells.

Below Rocester, with the traces of a Roman camp, the Dove is joined by the Churnet, which comes through a deep ravine rich in woodlands from Cheddleton to Alton. The pinnacles of Alton Towers, as they rise above the trees of their beautiful grounds, and a 19th century convent on a rock not far away, recall the scenery in the valley of the Rhine. Beyond Oakamoor (where copper wire is made) no road runs up the valley, though from Froghall there is a canal with its towpath. The Churnet Valley is an ideal place for a nature reserve, and near Oakamoor one has been established at Hawksmoor Wood, under the protection of the National Trust.

It is in the dairy farmer's country of gentle hills and valleys that the tributary streams of the Dove now flow gently, and none bigger than the Tean joins it before it adds its waters to the Trent opposite Newton Solney, a village on the Derbyshire bank. The Trent is Staffordshire's longest river, rising below Biddulph Moor and flowing through the Pottery towns, which, however, long used the canals for their water-borne goods. Joined by the River Lyme, whose name is linked with the Newcastle on its banks, the Trent washes away any stains it may have received in the beautiful district of Trentham.

The story of Trentham reveals one of the evils of the industrial 19th century. Here lived the Leveson-Gower family, dukes of Sutherland, who gained great wealth from the canals and railways. The duke of 1840 commissioned Sir Charles Barry, architect of the Houses of Parliament, to rebuild the hall in the vast deer park through which the Trent flows, and a great building like an Italian palace arose; but as the years succeeded the river became more and more polluted, and in 1905 the family left the hall for good. The pollution is now abated and the magnificent park is a public pleasure-ground.

The Trent has now fallen 800 feet and on its journey across England to the Humber it will fall only 300 feet more, so that its flow henceforward is gentle. At Meaford Hall (since demolished) on its banks above Stone the famous Admiral Jervis, victor in the fight off Cape St Vincent, was born, and the charming house of Shugborough near Great Haywood, ten miles on, was the birthplace of the equally famous admiral Lord Anson, who made a voyage round the world which added much to the knowledge of his time.

Often would George Anson have crossed the long bridge spanning the river whose waters have here been increased by those of the Sow, which on its 18 miles from Broughton has passed through Eccleshall and Stafford and gathered up the River Penk and the Meece Brook. The bridge has 14 arches now, but in Anson's day it had 42, having been built over meadow and river by the earls of Essex for huntsmen on their way to Cannock Chase. The bridge is over a hundred yards long, but only four feet wide!

This Essex Bridge is perhaps the quaintest bridge in the county, but the longest and the finest crosses the Trent at Burton, having a length of over 1400 feet and a width of 50. On its way between these two bridges the Trent has received several small streams from Needwood Forest on its left bank, and on its right (as if to help it to become a wider boundary between Staffordshire and Derbyshire) the River Tame, which gives its name to Tamworth, one of the most important towns in England a thousand years ago. The Tame is a native of Staffordshire, rising near Wednesbury and forming the county boundary with Warwickshire for a few miles above Tamworth.

The Trent is thus the river into which most of the rain falling on the county finds its way, to be carried to the North Sea, but as the Pennines are the chief water-parting in the north of England, and have thrust a moorland spur into Staffordshire, we find a few streams making their way west. Perhaps the most interesting of these is the Dane, which rises on Axe Edge and prattles along the boundary with Cheshire, then makes its way to the River Weaver, and so into the Mersey. The Tern, on the other hand, for many miles dividing the county from Shropshire, is a tributary of the mighty Severn.

Except for the Trent for the few miles between Burton and the Derbyshire boundary, none of the rivers of Staffordshire is navigable for boats of any great size. This fact, and the forests, and the remoteness from the sea, made Staffordshire one of England's Cinderella counties for centuries, to be transformed almost within one man's lifetime into one of the most prosperous of all by the development of her coalfields. Even in 1801 less than a quarter of a million people lived here.

Prehistoric man did not settle here in great numbers, though the half-dozen hill forts he has left are in strong positions. Kinver Edge, 500 feet above the sea with magnificent views over the Cotswolds, the Malverns, and the Shropshire hills, is National Trust property, almost on the southern boundary of the county with Worcestershire. On Byrth Hill above Maer is the site of another big fort, and not far away, near Mucklestone (the most westerly village in Staffordshire), stand two prehistoric stones known as the Devil's Ring and the Devil's Finger.

The most important work of the Romans here is in three roads, Watling Street remaining to this day as one of the widest and best as it cuts almost in a straight line from east to west on the way to Wroxeter. Ryknield Street, a direct route from Derby to Worcester, crosses Watling Street near Wall, and here are to be found some of our most perfect Roman baths. They are National Trust property, and close by is a museum in which we see the Roman objects found here. Through the Potteries runs another Roman road, linking Chester with Little Chester, the forerunner of Derby, and along it we come across such Roman names as Chesterton and Rocester. Below the latter, on the Dove, is Uttoxeter, where in the marketplace Dr Johnson stood bareheaded in the rain, when he was 70, to do penance for refusing to help his father at a stall in his youth, a penance in which he showed something of the old Roman reverence for filial duty.

It was two centuries after the Roman legions had finally trod these roads that Christianity came this way. The Saxons had been slow in settling here, trickling in up the Trent valley and becoming known as the Mercians. Their powerful King Penda was the foe of Christian Northumbria, but his sons, converted to the new faith, brought missionaries home, and among them was the saintly Chad, who founded the see of Lichfield. For a few years at the end of the 8th century the see was raised to an archbishopric, an honour due to the influence of King Offa, whose name appears on our maps where there are still remains of Offa's Dyke, built to keep out the Welsh. Around Tamworth, where he had a palace and a mint, remains of another dyke made by Offa can still be seen. But of even greater interest in this town are the ditch and mound of its castle, for the castle was built by Alfred's warrior daughter, Ethelfleda, "Lady of the Mercians" and conqueror of both Danes and Welsh, and here she died after having made it possible for her nephew Athelstan, brought up at her court, to acclaim himself King of All Britain. Stafford also was founded by Ethelfleda.

No church built by Chad or his Saxon successors still stands, but we can still admire the elaborate carvings on churchyard crosses: Checkley has three and Wolverhampton has a particularly fine one. Some were fashioned before the coming of the Danes and others later. From a wall in Enville church look down a Saxon bishop and a Saxon priest, and on the font at Ilam are carvings of men and beasts which many attribute to a Saxon craftsman.

Norman architecture and sculpture is not impressive in Staffordshire, but dragons stand out from stones at Ipstones on the moorland and Kingswinford on the border of the Black Country. There are fine Norman fonts at Armitage, Bradley, and Pipe Ridware, but to appreciate Norman work at its best we should go to the priory church at Tutbury with its superb doorway, and to St Chad's at Stafford, with the magnificent nave that Orm built, recording the fact proudly in an inscription on a pier of the tower.

The iron hand of the Conqueror fell heavily on Staffordshire, for its inhabitants had made common cause with the north in rising against him in the early years of his reign, and had paid the consequences. As a result we find in Domesday Book a record of only about 3000 male inhabitants and hardly a mention of a church. During the next hundred years both churchmen and laymen must have entered the county in large numbers, for by King John's time every village had its church, and monasteries were being established in profusion.

Of the buildings raised by the great religious orders, only Lapley church and Tutbury are used today, having become parish churches at the Reformation. The tall west front and part of the south transept, together with remains of the beautiful chapter house of Croxden Abbey, form the only monastic ruin of any grandeur in Staffordshire, the 15th century tower of the priory church at Ranton claiming the next place; but of the famous abbeys of Burton, Hulton, Rocester, and Dieulacres, near Leek, hardly a stone remains in position, though they are to be seen in the walls of churches and farms.

Lovers of mediaeval architecture, however, will find many beautiful examples of this period in this county which held to the Gothic tradition even until Stuart times. The most perfect of all, of course, is Lichfield Cathedral, which with its reddish stone seems always to reflect the rays of the setting sun. Its three spires are a unique feature in this country, and careful hands have replaced stone by stone all those which time or vandal hands has spoiled, with the result that the cathedral appears today much as it did to its builders six or seven hundred years ago. While the choir is of the 13th century, the nave and the lady chapel are of the 14th and are perhaps the most perfect example of that rich style in all England.

In Weston-on-Trent church is beautiful work of the earlier period, while Clifton Campville, with its graceful spire, is an excellent example of 14th century building. The noblest church of the 15th century is St Peter's in Wolverhampton, which has rich panelling on its tall central tower and, within, a beautiful stone pulpit carved when the church was new and unique in the county. The finest oak pulpit, dated 1611, is in another big town, Wednesbury, and the pulpit, the reading desk, and the pew in which Izaak Walton would often sit at Alstonfield form a splendid group of woodcarving of the 17th century.

Timbered houses are not common, but the High House in Stafford and the five-gabled Haselour Hall near Harlaston are delightful survivors from Shakespeare's day, and from the early 17th century come the gatehouse at Tixall and Wootton Lodge, famous for its surrender to the army of Parliament without a stone being hurt. It was through Tixall gatehouse that Mary, Queen of Scots, passed to captivity in a house no longer standing, having met with the same fate as the houses at Tutbury and Chartley, her last prisons before Fotheringhay.

Holbeach House at Himley recalls the desperate end of the

8

Gunpowder Plot conspirators who sought to kill Mary's son, James VI and I. One of their number, Stephen Littleton, lived in its predecessor and in front of its fire a dozen of them tried to dry their own gunpowder after it had become wet when fording the flooded River Stour. An explosion wounded some of them, and all were either killed or captured the next day.

Littleton was not the only famous ruffian associated with Staffordshire. There are Gilbert Giffard, who spied on Mary, Queen of Scots, and perhaps concocted some of the letters that sent her to her doom; Jonathan Wild, son of a Wolverhampton wigmaker; and William Wood, ironmaster of that town, who was branded as a coiner and counterfeiter in Dean Swift's famous Letters. Wood was the great-grandfather of Mary Howitt, a girl of Uttoxeter who with her husband William wrote familiar verses of the trees and flowers and birds of Staffordshire. So two centuries before had written the Staffordshire youth Richard Barnfield of Norbury, whose most famous lyric, *As it Fell Upon a Day*, was long attributed to Shakespeare. To Charles Cotton we have already paid tribute, but in Shallowford we can visit the cottage (now a museum) of his friend Izaak Walton and remember that he left his farm about it to the poor of Stafford, where he was born.

As the county town was the birthplace of Staffordshire's Grand Old Fisherman, the city of Lichfield gave to the world the Grand Old Talker, Dr Johnson. We see him carved in stone (a poor king all unworthy of his fame) gazing on the old house in which his father sold books, and we meet him in spirit in many other haunts in this city—the Three Crowns where he stayed with Boswell, the Friary, and the Upper and Lower Stowe Houses, where he visited friends of a lifetime when he came back in his old age. It was in the neighbouring hamlet of Edial that Johnson set up as schoolmaster with David Garrick as a pupil, both having attended the grammar school at Lichfield, where yet lingered memories of Joseph Addison, who had become a pupil when his father was made dean.

A pupil at Lichfield earlier still was the saddler's son Elias Ashmole, the antiquary. His native city is almost as proud of the silver cup he gave it in 1666 as Oxford is of the collection we know as the Ashmolean. Ashmole took the king's side in the Civil War, but one of his bitterest foes, Thomas Harrison, was the son of a farmer of Newcastle-under-Lyme, and it was Harrison who brought Charles I from Hurst Castle to take his trial in Westminster Hall, and who called him a "man of blood". Arrested in his Staffordshire home at the Restoration, he showed on the scaffold a cheerful courage which greatly astonished Samuel Pepys.

Three years after Harrison's death another humble-born native of the county, Gilbert Sheldon, youngest son of a Stanton farmer, was made Archbishop of Canterbury. A noble and generous man, he built the Sheldonian Theatre at Oxford. Another charitable figure of that century was Thomas Guy, who went to school at Tamworth, lived as a miser and passed to his immortality as an astonishing philanthropist.

We now come to two names which are closely associated with the conversion of a big area of Staffordshire from agriculture to industry, the names of Wedgwood and Dudley. On the tomb of Josiah Wedgwood in Stoke, below his bust by Flaxman, we read that he "converted a rude and inconsiderable manufactory into an elegant art" and an important part of national commerce. Thomas Toft and others had been making pottery in the villages now absorbed by Stoke, and a Dutchman, Philip Elers, had settled near Burslem, bringing chemical knowledge from the Continent. To a factory at Fenton, where Thomas Whieldon was producing improved and decorated earthenware, Josiah Wedgwood went as a partner in 1752. He revolutionised the industry and 15 years later began his great works at Etruria. Josiah was not only a supreme craftsman but a business genius as well, and he arranged for James Brindley to bring the Trent and Mersey Canal by his works.

So the district became the centre of the pottery industry and the Six Towns (Stoke, Hanley, Burslem, Tunstall, Fenton, and Longton) thrived exceedingly. In 1910 they federated under the name of Stoke-on-Trent, which now has a population of over 276,000 and many other industries in addition to its numerous potteries, for coal, ironstone, and limestone lie about its soil as well as potter's clay.

Staffordshire has another extensive coalfield in the south as well as that in the north, with iron available to found great industries. Her vast forests were used as fuel by the earlier workers in iron; indeed the use of charcoal did not cease until the middle of the 18th century. But in 1619 a young man named Dud Dudley was summoned from his studies at Oxford to take charge of his father's iron-works at Pensnett in Worcestershire. He experimented with coal and secured such good results that his rivals drove him from the county. He set up a furnace at Himley, and another at Askew Bridge, near Sedgley, where he established a British record of seven tons of pig-iron a week. Dudley, however, was a pioneer before his time, and it was not for a hundred years that coal came into its own. Then above the coal measures arose those busy manufacturing towns which gave the name of the Black Country to this area, each town specialising in some branch of hardware—chains at Cradley, anchors and pumps at Tipton, bits and bridles at Walsall, traps and keys at Wednesfield, locks at Willenhall, tinplates at Bilston, locks, keys, and other ironwork at Wolverhampton, and tubes, axles, and stoves at West Bromwich.

Everywhere we see the winding gear at the pitheads, the great chimneys belching smoke and sparks, the ugly slagheaps, and the gigantic factories. Busy streets, innumerable railway lines, and a network of canals fill this crowded region, yet it has its quiet places and memorials, which we would not pass by.

Walsall has its statue of Sister Dora, and West Bromwich the Old Oak House, now a museum; Wolverhampton, biggest town of all, with over 266,000 people, has a splendid art gallery and other public buildings of distinction, while she has laid out 200 acres of parks and open spaces and has built garden suburbs which make her one of the most attractive towns in the Midlands. At Wolverhampton's gate is Bushbury church, very much as George Borrow describes it in *Romany Rye*, and a mile beyond is Moseley Old Hall, in which Thomas Whitgreave hid Charles II during his flight from Worcester. In the churchyard of Brewood lies Colonel William Carlos, who supported the king's head as he slept in the Boscobel Oak, which is only just over the border in Shropshire.

Staffordshire is indeed a county with a rich store of memories, with a past as well as a present and a great future. We may hope the famous Horn Dance will be danced in September for many years to come at Abbots Bromley, that the Crooked House near Himley will long amuse the passer-by, and that the natural beauties here abounding will be fostered and guarded by all who come this way.

Abbots Bromley. Little changes here, in this secluded village. It has old houses and older customs. From October 13 to Shrove Tuesday, its curfew tolls each evening at 8 o'clock; the Angelus is rung from November 13 to Christmas Eve at 6 a.m.; and the Shriving Bell is tolled on Shrove Tuesday at 11 a.m. Abbots Bromley has many charming old brick houses and delightful black-and-white timbered houses; older still is the grey-roofed market cross on its seven wooden pillars; but oldest of all is the Horn Dance, for which the village is widely famous.

Once perhaps part of a pagan religious festival, it is now danced on a Monday early in September by 12 people: Robin Hood on a hobby-horse, his Maid Marian, a jester, a boy with bow and arrow, two musicians, and six men wearing ancient reindeer horns. The dance is believed by some to mark certain rights of the villagers to privileges in Needwood Forest, which, hunting-ground of John of Gaunt and a long line of kings, spread here with a circumference of 25 miles, and was governed by laws of terrible severity. The vicar still holds the dance "properties", for in the old days a forest right won was important to priests and laity alike, meaning food and fuel.

Although much of the spacious church was rebuilt in the 19th century, it keeps its 14th century arcades and its clerestory and its aisle roofs, put up by 1500. The tower was raised in about 1704, and the chancel was added in 1850 by G. E. Street. On the north aisle wall is a brass portrait of John Draycote, who saw the county divided in its loyalty by the Wars of the Roses. The dance was already old to him, and he would not have been surprised to find its accompaniments, the reindeer antlers, in a chapel here. All about stretched the forest, and even after the ravages of the Civil War a census showed 47,000 great trees, said to exceed in size and value those of any other forest in England.

Bagot's Bromley, a mile away, had one of the ten parks within the forest bounds. Only the wet moat remains of the manor in which the Conqueror found the Bagots established. The Normans entered them in Domesday Book as taxable owners, and here they stayed for the next eight centuries, ancestors of the earls of Stafford and the dukes of Buckingham. One of their guests, it is said, was Mary, Queen of Scots, on her sad journey to Fotheringhay.

An obelisk in Monument Field tells of their departure in 1811 for Blithfield, two miles off; but a Bagot had already made that journey early in the 13th century, to marry the heiress and establish the line which after 600 years still has there a Bagot at its head. Bagot's Park, to the north, was long famous for its ancient oaks, some of which must have been two or three centuries old when the census of the forest was taken for Charles II. A 17th century glass furnace was unearthed in the park in 1966. There was once a Lord Bagot who, riding a poor horse in this magnificent domain, was asked by a friend why he did not sell £50,000 worth of oak, which he would never miss. "The Bagots are not timber merchants," he said. But many of the oldest trees have decayed in recent years, and have had to be felled.

Acton Trussell. The River Penk glides through it, and it now faces across the valley to the busy motorway. The little stream suits the village, where everything is on a small scale, the church not excepted, as small today as 600 years ago, except for the 16th century tower. Much is changed since then, but something remains that the priest would see when, at the end of an hour's good walk from Stafford, he reached here to serve what was then a chapel of St Mary's Priory.

When a renewal of the ancient fabric became necessary last century the parish summoned to the work one of the greatest of Victorian church builders, George Edmund Street, who gave London its Law Courts, and he turned to this tiny task from his most romantic work, the Crimean memorial church at Constantinople. He left what he could, preserving two fine original windows with Decorated tracery.

There is an alabaster tablet which brings to mind a family of Staffordshire poets. It is to Arthur Alsop, who was curate of this church and the allied church at Bednall from 1878 to 1880, serving under his father James Alsop, who was vicar here from 1867 until his death in 1880. On the death of James, Arthur Alsop served as vicar until his death in 1928 ended a faithful ministry of half a century.

The tastes of the two accorded perfectly: each was a devoted servant of his parish, and each loved literature; each, after preaching, catechising, and christening, after comforting the sick and succouring the needy, would retire to his study and his slippers, and there let imagination flower into poetry. Arthur Alsop saw his hopes crowned when one of his four sons, Philip, in turn proved a poet too. We may read more of these three generations under Bednall.

Adbaston. "Dear native Adbaston, remote from care," wrote its own poet, and remote it remains. But the village was not too isolated for the Normans; here they built their church, and here, in the 15th century church of today, are a Norman arcade and two of their deeply splayed windows, one on either side of the chancel. It is possible that the building of the 13th century chancel arch was witnessed by some of those who slept under the coffin lids built into the wall.

The oldest memorial in the church is a mediaeval tablet in the sanctuary floor with the engraved figures of Reginald Bradocke in a flowing robe and his wife in a tight-fitting gown and a horned head-dress. A wooden tablet over the south door tells us of William Wakeley, who died as the village Methuselah in 1714, a very old man—125 according to the tablet, though we need not believe it.

In the porch, since rebuilt, Charles Bowker Ash sat down in 1797, as a boy of 16, stirred by ardent love of this village to write his first elegy. Half a mile away is the brick farmhouse where he was born and left fatherless at three years old. By turns actor and surveyor, and ever a great walker, visiting every town of note in the country, he had always a song in his heart, and two volumes of poems he published in 1831 pleased and appealed to Coleridge.

The piece best remembered here is naturally that in which he chanted the beauties of his native village, declaring:

> *In thy sweet vales a balsam I could find*
> *When nought on earth could calm my troubled mind.*

He saw the landscape changing, but not all has gone. The rushes he loved on the moor are still a summer glory, and the old grange has yet the rustic charms that so endeared it to him.

Aldridge. It is now an industrial town, with large brickworks and other manufactures, but it still has in its keeping two stone figures of men who walked about the lanes 700 years ago, one perhaps the founder of the church, one perhaps a crusader. They lie under arches, Nicholas the priest in his robes in the chancel, and Sir Robert Stapleton in the south aisle in his knightly mail, with sword and helmet and lion defiant on his shield as when he may have fought the Saracens.

The church in which they lie was mostly rebuilt in the 19th century, but the tower is mainly of the 14th century, and the north arcade has echoed to the praise of nearly 20 generations. Near the door is a bread-box of 1694. In the church we come upon the memory of a parson (Edmund Tongue) who preached for half of the 18th century in this 17th century pulpit; and in the churchyard is the grave of one who sang in the choir for 60 years, William Prescott.

Alrewas. For centuries it was famous for its baskets, but this old village craft, like so many ancient traditions, seems unfortunately to have died out. The Trent runs past and the Trent and Mersey Canal runs through, and her waterways and her treasures give a special charm to the village life of Alrewas. Not least enviable of the village's possessions are the many delightful black-and-white brick and timber cottages, some of them with thatched roofs.

There was a Saxon church here when the Normans arrived, and in it, they say, Lady Godiva worshipped. It has gone, but its successor has a mediaeval tower and under this and on the north side of the church are the simple doorways the Normans used. The slightly pointed arches of the south arcade, rising from towering octagonal piers, may be late-Norman work. The north aisle and arcade (in the 15th century style) were rebuilt in the last century.

The font has been here 500 years, and worthy of honour it is, a fine example of Gothic fancy, guarded by four grotesque heads, perhaps a mediaeval device for scaring witches away. The chancel, which had already seen two centuries of services when the font was carved, has a 19th century clerestory to light it. On the north wall of the chancel is a faded painting showing a bishop with an attendant carrying his mitre, and an angel with a trumpet; and on the south side are three stepped sedilia and the piscina. The 19th century stone reredos has an unusual Crucifixion showing the two robbers.

The height of the nave demands a noble roof, and here is one of the 16th century, with fine timbers carved with clustered leaves. The chancel has 16th century stalls and bench-ends with poppy-heads; the pulpit is of 1639, and there are two ironbound chests, one of which has three locks.

Two brass monuments keep alive cherished memories: a small tablet to Henry Kent, whose 60 years of faithful service ended in 1916; a cross to Clara Selwyn, a young mother who died on a lonely Pacific island in 1877. She was the wife of a much-loved curate here, John Selwyn, who, son of the first Bishop of New Zealand and afterwards Bishop of Lichfield, came to England as a boy and developed at college into a magnificent oarsman, with no thought of church work. A return to the scene of his father's labours, however, roused him to a noble determination, and he gave his life to the people of Polynesia. It cost him his health and his young wife her life. Crippled and broken, he yet proved a great master of Selwyn College, Cambridge, where his influence remained long after his death, and here in Alrewas he is remembered for his curate days, when this fine Cambridge athlete preached on Sundays and on Mondays taught the lads to swim.

Alstonfield. This high-lying village of the limestone uplands has for its setting the splendid scenery of the Derbyshire border, with the winding valley of the Dove at its feet. Six great barrows house the dead who peopled the valley in the Bronze Age; and Saxon and Norman relics serve as stepping-stones across the later centuries.

The manor house with its tall chimneys is now a farm, but has on it the initials of John Harpur, who built it in the year before the Armada. There are the remains (a doorway and fragments of walls) of Beresford Hall, where Charles Cotton lived 300 years ago, writing his poems, translating Montaigne, entertaining Izaak Walton; and here is the famous Fishing House the veteran angler saw his young friend building.

Under its 15th century tower is the church to which they came, the church, with its chequerwork of limestone and gritstone, described by Cotton when he wrote the second part of Izaak's *Compleat Angler*. "What have we here, a church?" cried Izaak as he first saw it, adding, "As I'm a honest man, a very pretty church!"

In the churchyard, which is surrounded by yews and beeches, is set up a fragment of a Saxon cross with a serpent's head. In the south porch is another fragment with the most ancient portraits in the village, two Saxons at prayer, one wearing a short skirt with a belt and sword. A third Saxon stone, carved with plaitwork, is built into a wall, and there are remains of three mediaeval coffin lids in the north porch.

The Normans spared the Saxon crosses; the men who remade much of the church in the 16th century left the south doorway and the chancel arch the Normans built, and the 13th century windows and priest's doorway in the chancel. They left also the 14th and 15th century arcades of the nave. The church is rich in fonts, for there is another veteran indoors beside the modern one.

Among the 17th century seats is Cotton's own canopied pew, beautifully panelled, and carved with flowers, grapes, and sea-serpents, recently repainted. Cotton and Izaak would often sit in this pew, listening to sermons from the two-decker pulpit of 1637, handsomely decorated but with a text so economical that it makes us smile, for it is

Be faithful &c., and I will give thee a crowne &c.

We can picture the two famous friends walking from the church back to lovely Beresford Dale, and imagine the talk of Ben Jonson, Michael Drayton, Sir Henry Wootton, and the rest. Never was

17

Walton happier than when here; never would man more fully share the rapture with which Cotton wrote of the beauties of the river:

> *O my beloved nymph, fair Dove,*
> *Princess of rivers, how I love*
> *Upon thy flowery banks to lie.*

Brothers of the rod, they fished these waters with the ardour that fires their writings. Here is their tree-shaded Pike Pool with its lichened pinnacle of limestone rising from the water, a spectacle which so excited Walton that, describing it as one of the oddest things he had seen, he returned to the Hall and made a drawing of it in one of Cotton's books.

Many times he was here; the invitations he received and his answers to them are part of English literature. Cotton has pictured something of their simple life and habits:

> *How sweet are all things here!*
> *How beautiful the fields appear!*
> *How cleanly do we feed and live!*
> *Lord! what good hours do we keep,*
> *How quietly we sleep!*

The little Fishing House is still here, though it is now enclosed by a wood and difficult to reach. The pyramid roof was not complete in time for Cotton to see it, but together they sat here; a stone above the doorway is inscribed with their initials. It was a strange conjunction, the old London linen-draper born 10 years before the death of Elizabeth, and an aristocrat nearly 40 years his junior, a traveller, a man versed in the classics, and a master of modern languages, in whose father's house had gathered such literary giants.

It would have shocked the humility of Izaak Walton to be told that the brilliant young scholar who affectionately called him his father was to ensure his immortality by their friendship, even though he did, in 10 fruitful days, write the second part of the old man's *Compleat Angler*. As Walton's friend, Cotton's name will live in men's affections as long as the book is read.

But Cotton's fame is undying by virtue of his own performances. He was a true lyrical poet, as well as an inexhaustible jester, parodist, and creator of burlesque. Above all, he gave us a translation of Montaigne that is a masterpiece. We venerate Florio's stately version, for his was Shakespeare's introduction to Montaigne, but that of Cotton is a triumph of rich and racy English. He loved and understood the Gascon genius, and his work was a delight and recreation to him, as its reading is to us.

He inherited encumbered estates, was always impoverished, and had often to flee from his creditors to the seclusion of the hills, yet in spite of his travels and troubles he wrote untiringly translations, burlesques, essays on gardening, poetry, and finally his inestimable Montaigne. Born in 1630, he died in London in 1687 and was buried in St James's church in Piccadilly.

Alton. It is like the magic of Prospero, with something of the cloud-capped towers, the gorgeous palaces, the solemn temples, in its dreamland setting. With a silent sea of pines behind it, the stone-built village begins where the rocks end, above the deep and lovely valley of the Churnet. On one hill above the water, where a Norman castle stood, is a 19th century convent, looking on its precipitous rock like a Rhineland castle, 300 feet high; on a height crowning the other side of the valley is Alton Towers, the fairy-like palace in its peerless grounds. Ruined castle and lordly pleasure-house alike were homes of the Talbots; the two link 800 years of history.

The Talbots are not the only great names remembered here; before them were the Furnivals and the Verduns. It was Bertram de Verdun who first came riding up the valley eight centuries ago to build his great castle on the brow of the hill. Then, a man of law and war, he founded Croxden Abbey for the peace of his soul, joined Richard Lionheart's Crusade, and died in the Holy Land.

In later days nine Furnivals were lords of the castle, among them Gerard, who died at Jerusalem in 1219, Thomas the Hasty, who fell at Crécy, and John, whose heiress married a 15th century Talbot, and so carried the castle and village into the possession of that family. They did not at once settle at the castle, but John Talbot, the famous earl of Shrewsbury, so long champion of our arms across the Channel that they called him King of France, stayed here occasionally, bringing to the hilltop fortress strange tales of a girl in white armour named Joan, who had repulsed him from Orleans, and taken him, hero of 40 battles, prisoner at Patay, the first reverse to an English army since our triumph at Crécy. He no more doubted her being a witch than did Shakespeare, who makes this stout Talbot so great a figure in his play of *Henry the Sixth*.

Two more centuries of Talbot ownership passed, and then the castle was knocked to pieces in the Civil War. All that remains is a round tower with part of a wall. Divided from it by the old moat stands the chapel of the Convent of the Assumption, built by A. W. N. Pugin last century. Its alabaster reredos has eight finely carved saints in canopied niches; and its oak rood-screen, richly decorated with roses, has two angels with the Virgin and Child. Of the parish church Bertram de Verdun saw there remains only one Norman arcade, but the tower was up when the Talbots came 500 years ago; and the font bowl has for four centuries borne their arms.

It was at the close of the Hundred Years War that the Talbots established themselves at the castle; it was near the end of the Napoleon wars that they colonised the other side of the valley. In 1814 Charles Talbot, the 15th earl of Shrewsbury, came this way. From the centre to the circumference all he saw was his, the ruined castle, the lonely hill on which rabbits had converted a prehistoric settlement into a warren, and an old house named Alton Lodge. Like Kubla Khan in Xanadu, he forthwith "a stately pleasure-dome decreed". Taking 600 acres of wilderness, he spent the last 13 years of his life in changing it into an earthly paradise, and when he died his nephew carried on and completed the wonder of it all. For more than a century Alton Towers was one of the most famous of English houses, visited by thousands of sightseers. Until 1924 it remained a home of the Talbots, but it is so no more and is now partly derelict.

The grounds, laid out by the 15th earl, are unexcelled for beauty. The earl saw as saplings trees that are giants today. He planned and visualised, and his successor extended his planning, and today we see here one of the great sights of our countryside, a wonder of woodlands with shady paths and winding ways, great yew arches, an army of firs and beeches, sparkling lakes, fountains, and waterfalls, sudden peeps of lofty towers above and between the trees, and gardens of delicate loveliness and exquisite colour in summer.

There is a Chinese temple, a handsome bridge over a lake among cedars, a pagoda fountain on a delightful island, a cottage which was once the home of a blind Welsh harper, and many other interesting features. The Flag Tower, a five-storeyed stone structure 90 feet high, looks out over the glories of the Staffordshire hills and dales. The grand conservatory with its seven domes shines above seven terraces descending to the river's brim, suggesting to the eye the hanging gardens of ancient Babylon. It now contains an aquarium. Set in the heart of all this loveliness is the copy of the 4th century choragic monument of Lysicrates at Athens, with a bust of Charles Talbot, its inscription truly recording that "he made the desert smile". For amusement there is a boating lake, a sea-lion pool, a scenic railway and a new cable railway.

The magnificent battlemented house Charles Talbot built was enlarged by A. W. N. Pugin for John, the 16th earl of Shrewsbury. It proclaims its title of Alton Towers by its many towers and turrets. By 1852, when the 16th earl died, the cost of building the house and

The Butter Market and Goat's Head hotel

ABBOTS BROMLEY

The Horn Dance

The old manor house at Alstonfield

The remains of Alton Towers

laying out the gardens had amounted to over £1 million. The 17th earl died in 1856 without an heir and the estate passed to Henry John Chetwynd, 3rd earl and 5th baron Talbot, of Ingestre. In 1924 the estate was sold and the house began to fall into ruin, though the exterior still remains intact. The part of the interior that has survived contains refreshment rooms and an electric model railway claimed to be the largest of its kind.

Staffordshire is famous for its potteries, its ironworks, and its coal mines, but it had here one of the wonder houses of the kingdom, and its gardens, won from the wilds, are hardly surpassed by any private estate in Europe for the loveliness and diversity of appeal.

Armitage. With the Trent flowing at its feet, it has something of Rome underground, from which it has dug up spears and weapons of brass; it has a Norman church made new, and it looks in one direction to a modern priory and in the other to an ancient manor linking it with events in Shakespeare.

The church, crowning a hill above the river and the Trent and Mersey Canal, was rebuilt in 1847, with a nave and aisles in the Norman style and a chancel in the Perpendicular style. It retains an earlier tower, of 1632, and has a Norman font with 14 remarkable heads, arranged in pairs under a round-arched arcade. The doorway is carved with quaint animals, copying the original Norman doorway, the stones of which were removed and made into a cross, bound together in a cast-iron frame, now lying derelict in the churchyard. Among the memorials is the alabaster portrait of Captain Arthur Samson, the rector's son who, after winning the Military Cross in the First World War, fell while leading his company in action. The organ (encased in 19th century work) was built about 1769 by Samuel Green and is unusual in having a cornet stop.

Half a mile away, with its 19th century iron bridge crossing the river with one span of 140 feet, is Handsacre, from which we have a fine view of Cannock Chase. Among its trees stands the ancient brick-and-timbered manor, with water still in the moat, and the doorway still remaining from what was once an oratory.

From here in 1403 rode out Sir William Handsacre at the head of his retainers, intending to enrol with Hotspur and Douglas on their march to join Glendower in his war with Henry IV. At the same time his neighbour Sir Robert Mavesyn headed a contingent to fight for Henry, and the rival knights met by the Trent, where they fought a battle ending in the death of the lord of Handsacre and the march of the victor to Shrewsbury, where he and Hotspur perished on the field.

In a charming setting at Hawkesyard, a mile to the west of Armitage, is a Dominican priory, founded in 1894, with a college, a library, and a chapel that is a little gem of architecture. Under the vaulted roof of its beautiful chantry, rich with tracery, lie the founders, Josiah Spode (who had lived previously at the house here) and Helen Gulson. The stone chancel screen, pierced by graceful iron gates, is finely carved with many figures, and there is a handsome stone reredos with 39 saints and monks gathered about a statue of Christ. The chancel has 26 canopied choir-stalls, but the greatest treasure here is the rare organ-case, beautifully carved with foliage and four delightful cherubs. Formerly one of the glories of Eton College, it is a masterpiece of Grinling Gibbons, a prize of which the priory may well be proud. Part of the priory, named Spode House, is used as a conference centre and a residential college for adult education.

Ashley. The church has a disappointing exterior of 1861 and a much better interior, restored by G. F. Bodley in 1910. The early 17th century Gothic tower remains, with arches on three sides. An old yew in the churchyard is 12 feet round.

In the church are a brass tablet to David Kenric, a village boy who fought under the Black Prince, and the huge Renaissance alabaster tomb of Sir Gilbert Gerrard, who died a year after Shakespeare. He lies under an arch, a knightly figure in armour and ruff, with his wife, two sons, and six daughters. Attending them is a figure who might have come from the pages of *Ivanhoe*, the devoted black servant who died far from the land he loved after faithfully serving his master and mistress.

A beautiful monument of 1826, by Sir Francis Chantrey, shows us the figure of Thomas Kinnersley, who rests on his arm, lifelike, as he must have looked in the days of Trafalgar and Waterloo. Another wall-monument, of 1859, by Matthew Noble, has three delightful angels in memory of another Thomas Kinnersley. The more modern work of the church includes an elaborate gilded oak reredos with a Virgin and Child, by Walter Hare.

One of Ashley's rectors was John Lightfoot, the man who had Milton's tutor among his masters at Cambridge, and was a student of unsurpassed diligence. In order to be uninterrupted by domestic distractions he bought the field next to the rectory, and in it built a little study, a parlour, and a bedroom.

There he worked far into the night and slept in his little cubicle, completing the studies which made him the greatest Hebrew scholar of his age. He left in 1642 to take his stand for the Parliament, but so great was his fame that at the Restoration he became vice-chancellor of Cambridge University, of which he was deemed one of the brightest ornaments.

Audley. The Romans who built its Ryknield Street and had their camp two miles away left untouched the coal the hillside village mines today. Froissart, knowing as little of Audley as the Romans knew of its minerals, unwittingly gave it abiding fame in those immortal pages where the age of chivalry closes in a blazing sunset. In the church is a twofold link with his story of the Black Prince and his bravest knight at Poitiers.

Of the church of those days there remains the 14th century tower and nave arcades, and the sedilia and piscina in the chancel. The north aisle is of the 16th century, and the font is Jacobean. The rest of the fabric is of the 19th century, including the fine east window, which has on either side statues of SS Peter and Paul. In the chancel floor are tiles in imitation of the old ones at Tintern Abbey.

The chief treasures of the church are in brass and marble. A tombstone on the sanctuary floor has the figure of a vicar in cap, ruff, and surplice; he is Edward Vernon, founder of the grammar school in 1612. A portrait brass of 1628, on the chancel wall, shows us William Abnet, his successor. But it is an older brass and an older tomb that are the romance and glory of this place. The brass, with a Norman inscription, in the sanctuary, has the armoured figure of Sir Thomas Audley, son of the towering hero of Poitiers, the baron who vowed that no man should eclipse him in valour, and was given the post of honour in front of our army on the day of the battle. Froissart tells us that when the day was won the baron was carried, gravely wounded, to the tent of the Black Prince, who stopped and embraced him, saying, "Sir James, I and all the rest of us deem you the bravest knight in this battle, and to increase your renown I retain you for ever as my knight."

Here, it is said, is buried one of the men who carried him from the field to his tent. The alabaster effigy of Richard Delves lies on a sunken tomb in the chancel wall, his arms missing but his armour intact, a lion still at his feet. He was one of the four squires summoned to his tent by the heroic baron, who then and there divided among them the pension given to him by the Black Prince. In a niche outside the chancel wall is a mediaeval coffin slab.

Barlaston. Here, in the Trent valley south of the Pottery towns, are the famous pottery works of Josiah Wedgwood, transferred in

23

1940 from their original site at Etruria, near Stoke. Here visitors can see all the modern methods of production of stone, earthenware, and bone china. In the large model factory, which stands in a park-like setting, is a museum with 18th century and later Wedgwood ware, as well as examples of Josiah's own experimental pieces. The 17th century Barlaston Hall near by is now the home of the Wedgwood Memorial College, a residential college for adult education.

Barton-under-Needwood. Here is a peep of George Eliot's Loamshire, young in natural beauty, old in story and possessions. The village, with charming old brick and stone houses, and a timber-framed cottage or two, lies in the Trent Valley below the Forest of Needwood, a picture of charm with farms flourishing about it and looking up to a fine Tudor church whose history is like an act from a miracle play.

One of the rare examples of a church begun and completed in one lifetime, it was the gift of John Taylor, the most illustrious native of the village, one of triplets born to poor parents here and rising to wealth and eminence which enabled him to bestow the church as his blessing on the place which gave him birth.

Much today is as he knew it when he left his modest home here to help Henry VII and Henry VIII to govern England, and to deal as an equal with the haughtiest potentates in Europe. Here is still the curious three-sided apse he gave the chancel, and in it is a window with some of the glass he provided, showing a Crucifixion and crudely-shaped Apostles, colourful with rich blues, greens, reds, and purples. The nave has a fine timber roof, and on the tower is the date of building—1517.

The arch in the chancel wall was probably designed to receive John Taylor's bones. His initials are with the four shields over the nave arcades, and his coat-of-arms has three infant heads, his own and those of the two little brothers who came with him into the world to startle his impoverished father and mother.

On the site of Barton's church stood the cottage where John Taylor was born. For a quarter of a century Henry VIII found him a trusty servant, making him his private secretary and his spokesman at meetings of foreign envoys, himself delivering speeches Taylor had written, and taking him with him to the Field of the Cloth of Gold. He was at Henry's side when he met the sovereigns of France and Spain. Between his embassies Taylor had an important part in State affairs. A practised lawyer, equally at home in civil and ecclesiastical law, he was made Master of the Rolls, and was succeeded in that office by the notorious Thomas Cromwell.

Baswich. Now mainly a residential suburb of Stafford, it is chiefly known, perhaps, as a place which helps to fill our salt-cellars, but it is linked with moving and tragic events in our history. Bordering the little River Sow, to the north, is a farm on which we see an ancient stone wall, two Norman doorways, parts of windows, and remains of monastic buildings, the last relics of the 12th century Augustinian priory founded by Richard Peche.

Peche had an all unwilling share in the events leading to the murder of Becket. In the absence of the fugutive Primate he countenanced by his presence the coronation of the eldest son of Henry II, and, as coronations were the prerogative of the Archbishop of Canterbury, Becket came home indignant, excommunicated Peche and all the prelates concerned, and so virtually signed his own death warrant. In the year after the assassination Peche went to Canterbury to woo the priests to renew the services in the deserted cathedral, and as a personal atonement he built this priory here and dedicated it to the man he had offended. To this day the farm is called St Thomas's. When he came to die Peche directed that he should be buried in the priory.

Another notable figure who here sought shelter for his bones was Robert Ferrers, earl of Derby, married at Westminster as a boy of nine to a seven-year-old niece of Henry III. He grew up to challenge his royal uncle by standing with Simon de Montfort for public liberty, and sat in our first Parliament, but he was outlawed and dispossessed of his estates. Broken and impoverished, Derby turned his weary eyes to the priory, and here he mingled his ashes with those of its founders.

The church stands on a hill above the Penk, near its junction with the Sow, in a churchyard beautified by fine beeches. Of the mediaeval building the 13th century chancel arch survives; the tower, of the 14th and 15th centuries, has an upper storey raised in the 18th century, and the nave was rebuilt in brick in 1740. The chancel of this time was practically rebuilt again in 1967, when large transepts were added on the north and south.

The most remarkable feature of the church today is a huge squire's pew raised on pillars in the north transept (it was formerly in the chancel, along with one for his servants). On the pew is a prayer book of 1768, and below it is the 16th century tomb of John Fowler and his wife, recently restored and repainted, with 13 shields-of-arms of the Fowler family. In the nave is an old three-decker pulpit, and at the west end is an 18th century wooden gallery.

Bednall. The little church, rebuilt last century, has one striking feature, a west window with 25 figures. Among them are saints and Apostles, Aaron, Moses, Abraham, and Isaiah in company with Solomon, the two Augustines, and St Cecilia.

The vicarage was the home of the young Staffordshire poet Philip Alsop, whose father and grandfather ministered here from 1867 to 1928. Both were writers of verse, and Philip's father lived to see moving poetry born of the fine spirit of his son. When the war called, young Alsop, fresh from Oxford, joined the army and he wrote brave lines while sitting in the trenches before an attack on the Somme. Happily the poet was spared and came home to England.

James Richard Alsop, his grandfather, who died vicar here in 1880, was something of a character, claiming descent from a Norman family of Alsop-en-le-Dale in Derbyshire, and we have a picture of him conning over the sermons he had preached, finding them very good and publishing the best, and then sitting down to write little poems still remembered, full of kindly feeling, and likening simple well-doing to the unconscious beneficence of flowers, which, without senses themselves, "delight the sense of others".

Betley. Once a market town to which buyers came across the Cheshire border, it is now a village which markets elsewhere. It has many attractive whitewashed and timber-framed houses, and it has a pretty mere, partly in Staffordshire and partly in Cheshire.

Betley Court is a big 19th century house snug behind its high wall. Old Hall, a charming gabled and timbered 17th century building on a hillock, with great elms and sycamores to grace it, was long the home of the Egertons.

To them the village owes much of its 17th century church, which has a timber-framed clerestory and porches, and an 18th century Gothic tower. In the chancel kneels the alabaster figure of Ralph Egerton in the ruff and long cloak of Shakespeare's time, with his wife in a ruff and a tight-waisted dress, her daughter behind her. It was the next Ralph Egerton who rebuilt the chancel soon after the death of Queen Elizabeth I.

The most remarkable feature of the church is the use to which its timber has been put. There are few churches like it in this respect. Not only is the interior of the clerestory, like the fine roof, of oak, but also the beautiful pointed arches of the nave arcades, while 10 splendid oaks, their trunks hewn into octagonal pillars, carry the whole, an impressive and charming picture. The church has other old woodwork in the 17th century pulpit and a 14th century parclose screen.

Biddulph. It has one great house fallen into ruin and another in a scientific fairyland made from a swamp. It has an ancient tomb with legends of the centuries gathered about it. It has memories of crusaders and the mystery of the long ridge of Biddulph Moor, rising to over 1100 feet and giving birth to one of our longest rivers, the Trent.

Beginning its 170-mile journey here below the ridge, the Trent winds grandly down to green and pleasant lands, on by towns and hamlets and half a hundred bridges, and we are reminded that when hot-blooded men were riding from Staffordshire five centuries ago, some to fight for Hotspur and some for Henry IV, the fiery Percy and Edmund Mortimer, dividing the kingdom before they had won it, decided to straighten the river hereabouts. It is Shakespeare who tells us. "See," cried Mortimer, whose share was affected by its course:

> *See how this river comes me cranking in,*
> *And cuts me from the best of all my land*
> *A huge half-moon, a monstrous cantle out.*
> *I'll have the current in this place dammed up,*
> *And here the smug and silver Trent shall run*
> *In a new channel, fair and evenly.*

On the edge of the ridge, farther north towards The Cloud, is an ancient burial-place, a monument of unhewn monoliths called the Bridestones. It carries the legend that a Viking, having married a Saxon maid in the village, was slain with her soon after and buried here but in fact the burial-chamber is much older, dating from about 2000 B.C. It is now in private grounds and hidden by a new growth of shrubs.

We may believe that Crusaders who had fought the good fight lived to return to their native Biddulph, for outside the church are coffin-lids engraved with crosses, swords, and battle-axes. They form seats around the walls, looking on the churchyard with an octagonal cross which must have been set up not long after the last Crusader sheathed his sword.

The oldest possession of the church is the Norman font and the tower seems to be of the 15th century. Centuries have passed since the grey sandstone altar-rails were carved, and in old Flemish glass one of the windows has the Wise Men, Gabriel bringing the good news to the Virgin, with Christ, Abraham, and Isaac. A beautiful 15th century monument to William and Mary Heath has figures of Christ and angels.

What we have called a scientific fairyland here is Biddulph

27

Grange, a hospital for cripple children run by the Lancashire County Council. It occupies the magnificent grounds transformed from a swampy moorland last century by the horticulturist James Bateman, who became famous for his lectures, his orchids, and his gardens. Here he laid out a Chinese garden, an Egyptian garden, and a Wellingtonia avenue which attracted many pilgrims in his day and are still remarkable, a wonderland of beauty and novelty with pyramids of yews and plantations of pines.

By a fine box avenue and a ravine with a stream running through it stands the ruins which were once the home of the Biddulphs. Built in the reign of Elizabeth from stone quarried on the estate, Biddulph Old Hall was among the fairest houses in the county, until the Civil War brought tragedy and ruin. The Biddulphs were Royalists, and there is no sadder tale than that of the misfortunes attending them.

When the Royal Standard was unfurled at Nottingham in 1642, the Biddulphs drew the sword for Charles I. John Biddulph, owner of the hall, fell at Hopton Heath; his son Francis, a man in the early twenties who was already married and the father of children, committed the defence of the hall to Lord Brereton, and himself joined the Cavaliers fighting in Cheshire.

Lord Brereton deemed Biddulph Hall more defensible than his own home, Brereton Hall in Cheshire, and so brought with him here his wife and little child. The Parliamentary force sent against the hall was commanded by his uncle Sir William Brereton, who, finding it impossible to overcome the staunch garrison without artillery, brought up from Stafford a great gun called Roaring Meg. Constructed in time of peace, the hall was not intended to withstand bombardment, and Brereton the nephew, fearing for the lives of his wife and child, surrendered, and the hall was reduced to a ruin to prevent its again becoming a Royalist stronghold.

With his home destroyed, Francis Biddulph was soon denied the need for a new one, for he was taken prisoner when Chester fell to the Commonwealth, and was confined for two years at Eccleshall Castle. On being released, an outcast from his birthplace, he settled with his wife and children on a farm at Rushton.

His means still admitted of his maintaining a Roman Catholic priest and an Italian governess for the education of his children. The governess, locally famous for the beauty of her voice, and long remembered as Singing Kate, was the first of the Biddulph household to be attacked by the Plague of 1648. Biddulph rode 40 miles through the night in quest of a doctor, and wherever he called he left the deadly disease behind him. Death claimed poor Singing

Kate and some of the children, and terror caused his home to be shunned as a pest-house. Supplies became unprocurable, and the unhappy man had to go like a beggar to Congleton to beg for food.

Ruined and heartbroken, he turned from the county, leaving behind the wreck of the beautiful home in which he was born, and the Rushton farm where disaster in full tide had overwhelmed him. He made his way to London, where later his son John was married, but as to Francis himself the record fails, and we do not know his end.

Bilston. It comes into Domesday Book and was a market town for centuries before industry came to blacken this countryside. Bilston now has large foundries, making tubes and other iron products, as well as flourishing engineering works.

One of its sons was John Wilkinson, who has been called the father of the South Staffordshire iron trade. Born in 1728 at Bradley (on the outskirts of the town), he set up the first charcoal furnace for smelting iron ore and made other experiments as well as a fortune. His sister married Joseph Priestley, the discoverer of oxygen, and after a Birmingham mob had destroyed Priestley's property he was able to give his brother-in-law substantial help. Wilkinson died at Bilston, and they laid him to rest in an iron coffin at his seat near Ulverston, in north Lancashire.

Another famous son of Bilston was Sir Henry Newbolt, who was born in St Mary's vicarage (since demolished) in 1862. Who does not know his *Drake's Drum*, which has rung out on a thousand patriotic platforms and in ten thousand schools?

In the classical St Leonard's church, built in 1826 to the designs of Francis Goodwin, is a memorial to Mary Pearce, who died in 1836 and is said to have been descended from "three children of King Edward the First"; and there is a tablet reminding us of a very dark hour of the town. It was in 1832, when an epidemic of cholera broke out; 742 people died in six weeks. The nation raised £8000 to alleviate the distress, and £2400 of it went to build and endow a school to give free education to 450 orphans.

The Museum and Art Gallery, in Mount Pleasant, has examples of Bilston pottery and enamels, as well as exhibits illustrating local history and industries. The Greyhound and Punchbowl, in the High Street, is a 15th century timber-framed inn, a remarkable survival.

Blithfield. With a noble old hall, a church with many monuments, and memories of one of our oldest families, it has stirring

29

stories to tell. Beautifully set in the Blythe valley, the grey stone home of the Bagots stands among stately cedars, splendid old oaks, and glowing thickets of rhododendrons. It is impressive as the cradle from which sprang a long line of men linking us with events significant in our history as far back as Crécy.

One of the Bagots fought at Crécy and another at Poitiers. Another strides through Shakespeare with mischief in his wake and dread in his mind. A Bagot fought at Agincourt; one helped Henry VII to his crown at Bosworth Field; another shared the rout of Charles I at Naseby. They have witnessed repeated changes in our dynasty, and the passing of nearly 30 rulers of England, but ever a Bagot has succeeded a Bagot, and here they are today, delighting in this grand old home with its many great chimneys, its pinnacled porch doorway, and its host of windows.

The Hall is basically an Elizabethan house and was built by Richard Bagot, whose monument is in the church, but it was enlarged in the 18th century by Sir William Bagot and was Gothicised in about 1820 by William, 2nd Lord Bagot. It has a grand 17th century staircase, beautiful with carving, many portraits of successive generations of Bagots, and relics of the Stuarts they supported, including a cap of crimson satin, embroidered with gold and silver thread, that was worn by Charles I. In a room called Paradise are books and toys with which generations of Bagots have played.

On the lawn in front of the hall, the Abbots Bromley horn dancers perform each year on a Monday early in September. The valley of the Blythe below the house has been dammed to make a charming reservoir, completed in 1953.

Near the hall is the clerestoried church in which so many of the Bagots are buried. At its gate stand two yews between which generations of Bagots have passed to worship, to wedding, and to burial; and around the churchyard are many other old yews and oaks.

In the churchyard is a cross almost as ancient as the Bagots themselves, its modern shaft carved with a ship, some birds, and a crowned lion. Under an arched recess in an outer chancel wall is a much-weathered tomb with an effigy said to be that of Alfred de Blithfield, who preached here 700 years ago, a century before the tower was raised. The font looks old enough to have served in his day.

In the 13th century chancel is 14th century glass, some with ivy and oak pattern, and one light with a border of lions. The sanctuary window has striking post-War glass, and in a tower window are

16th century portraits of two of the wives of Sir Lewis Bagot. The fine woodwork includes not only 21 mediaeval bench-ends and a 15th century screen adorned with acorns and roses, but one of the most surprising things to be seen in a church—an altar-table which has been part of a farm bedstead! It is of oak, finely inlaid with roses and foliage, and is a handsome addition to the chancel.

The monuments are naturally the main interest here. In the chancel floor is an incised alabaster slab with the Tudor figures of Francis Aston with his wife and son. But it is by the Bagot tombs that we linger. The earliest is the alabaster Tudor tomb showing the finely preserved figure of Sir Lewis in a tunic, with armour on his legs and the full figures of two of his wives and the head of the third; here also are his 19 children. On a table tomb lie his eldest son and his son's wife, the son wearing a tabard and the wife a belted gown. A beautiful sculpture of 1596 is that of Richard Bagot, lying in armour with his helmet above him, his wife in a tight-waisted robe beside him.

Nearly 20 generations of Bagots have been lords of the manor, and the record of the family is truly a little volume of English history. Early in the 14th century, when feudalism was shaking the throne of Edward II who had knighted him, Ralph Bagot crossed the two miles separating his home from that of the heiress of Blithfield, married her, and established here a family which has since lived at the hall without a break. Like their famous oaks, they were tough and enduring, men bred to knightly feats, who figured in the great battles of the Black Prince, of Henry V, and on the stricken fields where the Stuart cause was lost.

By that time their name was lastingly inscribed in sinister characters on immortal pages of our literature. Sir William Bagot was, with Sir Henry Green and Sir John Bushy (Speaker of the Commons), the malevolent force being the throne when Richard II entered on the course which brought him to his doom. Bagot was especially esteemed at the Court, and it was from his house and in his company that the king rode to the lists at Coventry where Bolingbroke and Norfolk were summoned to meet in mortal combat.

Shakespeare gives us repeated flashes revealing the intimacy of the relations between the sovereign and his subject. After the suspended combat, Richard, seeking to justify Bolingbroke's banishment, describes in his picture of the exile's ride through London how

> *ourself and Bagot*
> *Observed his courtship to the common people.*

One of the four men to whom Richard left control of the kingdom on sailing to Ireland, Bagot escaped the fate of his associates when Bolingbroke returned, denouncing Bushy, Green, and Bagot as

> *The caterpillars of the Commonwealth*
> *Whom I have sworn to weed and pluck away.*

Frantic at the bad news awaiting his arrival from Ireland, Richard breaks off his soliloquies to enquire for Bagot and the others; but Bagot was already a prisoner in the Tower, from which he was released at the end of the year, to lapse into obscurity.

Elizabeth I gave the Bagots their baronetcy in 1590, and 190 years later the sixth baronet was created a peer, and the house produced, in the second baron, the man who was to write the family annals. There were now two bishops in successive generations. Lewis, brother of the first baron, a school-fellow of the poet Cowper, was successively bishop of Bristol, Norwich, and St Asaph, filling the three sees in nine years, and holding the last until his death.

A notable Bagot in Empire history was Sir Charles, who, beginning his career at 26 as Under-Secretary for Foreign Affairs with Canning, went to Paris as ambassador after the fall of Napoleon; then to the United States, where he had the distinction of establishing the neutrality of the Great Lakes, so that not a gun has since menaced either side of them. Next he was Ambassador to Russia with a difficult Tsar on the throne, and passed to the Hague, where he helped to create an independent Belgian nation.

He crowned his career in Canada, arriving there in 1841 when conditions were in a perilous state of flux. He won the sympathies of English and French alike, and by tact, good-nature, and patience, brought into being responsible self-government in the Colony. Lord Stanley disapproved the Governor-General's policy, and practically broke Bagot's heart by his censure; but history has vindicated Bagot. His health collapsed under the disappointment, however, and he died in Canada in 1843, a British warship bearing his body back to England.

Blore. Overlooking and sharing the natural loveliness of Dovedale into which it commands a splendid view, this hamlet of the limestone uplands has beauty of its own to show and a stirring tale to tell.

Blore Hall, a grey stone house now a farm, with mediaeval windows and traces of its moat about it, was long the home of the Bassets. Tall elms and stately sycamores flank the churchyard in which the 14th century tower rises above the 15th century church.

In the floor of the nave are the brass portraits of William Basset and his wife in the dress of the 15th century, he wearing a long cloak, she her cloak and veil.

Many Bassets are buried here, and in their chapel is an immense canopied tomb of alabaster raised in the 17th century by Elizabeth Basset to her father, whose inscription proudly describes him as a courtier and soldier, "witty, handsome, good, valiant, unparalleled, of pure blood from William's Conquest". William Basset lies in armour, his wife Judith in a long gown, a ruff, and a flowing head-dress; with them is the armoured figure of Elizabeth's first husband, Henry Howard, son of the earl of Suffolk, and two figures of Elizabeth herself in Van Dyck costume, one in mourning for her mother, and again kneeling in grief for the death of her husband.

Two years later she married William Cavendish, the first duke of Newcastle, and passed to the glories of Welbeck Abbey and Bolsover Castle, where she shared in two receptions of Charles I marked by such splendour as was said to have had hardly a parallel in England. For these visits Ben Jonson wrote two masques, *Love's Welcome at Welbeck* and *Love's Welcome at Bolsover*.

The 16th century chancel screen, with traces of its original colour, has fine iron gates, and is adorned with roses; the 16th century screen before the Basset chapel is splendid with grapes and roses. The oak benches and choir-stalls have been here 400 years. In a chancel window is 15th century glass of Christ wearing the Crown of Thorns, and of St Anne teaching the Virgin. The church has a Jacobean pulpit, altar and altar-rails, and a 15th century font.

Blymhill. Agriculture is still its parent industry, and the country-side has much of the charm that must have marked it when its famous botanist rector was exploring it last century.

A pretty road bordered by holly brings us to the church, which has been largely refashioned since the botanist parson knew it, but here is the fine tower which has been an impressive landmark for 600 years. In the churchyard is a grand yew which can be little younger, and the dial on a stone pillar has recorded centuries of sunshine.

In an outer wall is a recessed tomb, believed to be that of the builder of the chancel, which comes unspoiled from the 14th century. The oldest part of the interior is the 13th century south arcade, with fine arches on octagonal pillars. The work of refashioning was carried out by G. E. Street, and here we can see examples of his craftsmanship in stone, wood, iron, and brass. The chancel screen is crowned by a Crucifixion, beneath which are birds eating fruit.

The ten choir-stalls have seats with carved misericords. In the chancel, too, is a quaint mediaeval Nativity, carved in wood.

The botanist parson was Samuel Dickenson, of a family long conspicuous here. When his last sermon was preached in 1823 he had been 46 years rector, happy years for himself and the village, for he botanised with such success that his fame and skill were long a subject of local pride. Very pleasant were these fields and hedgerows to him.

Bobbington. A small village with 17th century and other old houses on the Shropshire border, its oldest living inhabitant is the great yew about 21 feet round behind the church. Though much restored, the church is mainly of the 14th century. A vine grows round the porch under the 19th century tower. A sculptured figure, perhaps Norman, greets us in the porch, and we pass inside the church to a Norman arcade. Here are a 13th century font and a crooked old chest hewn out of solid oak with two compartments and lids, covered with bands of wrought iron.

The tablet to Edward Corbett, who died in 1752, tells how he practised as a lawyer for 30 years in the historic court of Westminster Hall, more than a century before English justice moved to the present Law Courts in 1882. We read these good words of him:

> *Many He assisted in the Law,*
> *More he Preserved from it.*

Bradley. High farming has kept its hillside acres fertile through the centuries, and high fortune has kept safe for it one of the noblest of Staffordshire's treasures. The church, its gate by a magnificent chestnut, has gifts of beauty from the ages. The tower is 500 years old, and over it spreads a flourishing vine, while another vine covers the south wall of the church. The arcades in the nave and chancel rose splendid in the 13th century. The font is Norman, with an intricately carved bowl.

A 17th century alabaster wall tomb has the painted kneeling figures of Browne of Shredicote, a bearded man in a long cloak, and his wife in a tight-waisted dress, with a ruff and flowing headdress. Those who saw him to his last rest found time to write a rhyming inscription for his tomb, but not to mention his Christian name; he is merely "oraculous Browne". There is the head of a queen among the fragments of ancient glass in the nave; and the chancel screen, a fine example of modern carving, beautiful with grapes and roses, is worthy of the company it keeps. In the wall to the south of this are the mediaeval rood-stairs, a rarity in Staffordshire.

Bradley in the Moors. In 1750 this secluded hamlet (a farmstead and a few cottages) remade its little church, when the four vigorous yews in the churchyard, which were growing in Cromwell's England, were just getting into their stride for their journey down the centuries. There is a sundial on the tower, but only one thing here is older than the yews, a coffin lid which was already ancient before the old church came down and the yews were planted.

At first sight the tombstone to Anne Snape seems to be the patriarch of the churchyard, for the date 1307 accompanies the inscription:

> *Thus Death between us two has got*
> *And so hath broke a true love-knot.*

But there is a slip even in love, for the mason was 500 years out in his figures. His 3 should be an 8, and the year 1807.

Bramshall. Here is a gracious lady of the past, but the surroundings with which she was familiar are gone, and a 19th century church rises in the place of the old shrine she knew. An avenue of elms leads to the churchyard, which is surrounded by fine holly hedges, but all that remains of Bramshall's past are fragments of old glass with the heads and shoulders of a boy and girl, and the charming figure of Alice Tame, Lady Verney, in a white flowered dress and ruff.

Branston. Now practically a suburb of Burton, it looks across the Trent into Derbyshire and to the huge cooling towers of the new power station at Drakelow. The ponds left by old gravel pits here have become the home of numerous wildfowl, and a nature reserve has been created. A field study centre has been set up and the nature trails are followed by hundreds of school children. Branston itself is flourishing with industry: gravel works, cement products, and a large ordnance depot.

Among the trees crowning the hill to the north, beyond the Burton bypass and the Trent and Mersey Canal, is a property that belonged to Burton Abbey, the ancient summer home of the monks who made the abbey famous. It is Sinai Park, a moated and timbered 15th century house, now a farm, forming three sides of a square, and still very striking in its splendid situation above the valley of the Trent.

Brewood. This large village has material for a dozen Scott novels, for it has been the setting of centuries of romantic history.

It has in its story the thrill of Saxon forest life, the coming of the Normans, and the perfect love-story leading to the founding of the famous Giffard family, with figures shining in war and scholarship, suffering because they could not abandon their old religion, and suddenly producing one of the most astonishing villains in our annals.

We have visions of King John in purring pleasantry and in typical rascality; and we see our first Edward terrible in wrath. We move on through the ages and find a man who was prepared to die for Charles II; and we see Dr Johnson turning poor and sorrowful from the school that feared his scarred face.

Brewood was a royal forest until King John declared it disafforested and all its people free of the penalties attending the frightful forest laws. Then, repenting of his unwonted generosity, he made the place pay for the privilege he had already granted, a fact which was afterwards to count in saving the heir of the Giffards.

Where the gabled house called Blackladies now stands with its tall chimneys was a Norman convent of Black Nuns. Here in 1276 a stag started by Edward I in Cannock Chase was shot by John Giffard's arrow, and died in the fishpond. Charged before the Forest Court, Giffard was able to plead that the area had twice been disafforested by John, and so escaped the terrible punishment. He was fined, and the nuns, who had received some of the venison, were pardoned because they were poor, and "for the good of the king's soul".

Chillington Castle, where a young Norman Giffard wooed and won the heiress in the 12th century, has been replaced by Chillington Hall, which stands in a wooded park laid out about 1730 by "Capability" Brown and graced by a fine lake and by a magnificent avenue of oaks nearly two miles long. For 800 years the family has been here and in the park is a rough old wooden cross marking the site of a famous life-saving feat of archery which figures in its story. The house, partly rebuilt in 1724 by Francis Smith of Warwick, was extended on the north side in 1785 by Sir John Soane. It has elegant plasterwork and fine 18th century furniture and, in the hall is a 16th century fireplace by which Elizabeth I may have sat.

The grammar school founded by Edward VI still stands in the village, interesting because it was here that in 1736, the year of his marriage to his adored Tetty, Samuel Johnson came, a gaunt, towering figure with scarred features, his head and limbs agitated by uncontrollable movements. He sought the humble post of usher, but the master denied him, fearing lest he should become the butt of the school's derision.

Burton upon Trent Town Hall, with St Paul's Church

The king's bedroom at Moseley Old Hall, Bushbury

Caverswall Castle

Houses in the High Street at Cheadle

A fine 15th century tower and spire, 168 feet high, beckon us to the church. Somewhere in its churchyard lies Colonel William Carlos, who shared the perils of Charles II after Worcester, and, during the night of hiding in the Boscobel Oak, supported the head of the fugitive king as he slept. Here also is the tomb of the famous teacher Jeremiah Smith, who returned to the village in which he learned his A B C, after years as headmaster of Manchester Grammar School.

The church has a 13th century chancel, a 14th century north aisle, and 15th century nave arcades. The 14th century font was found in a garden several miles away. The reredos of 1911, with beautifully carved canopies, has a central picture of the Last Supper, and at the sides carved figures of John Baptist and nine saints and archangels. A curious feature of the 19th century south aisle is the group of five gabled windows, an effect gained by continuing the woodwork down from above.

The oldest of the monuments, in the south aisle, is the alabaster tablet engraved with the figures of a 16th century family, Richard Lane, his wife, and their 11 children. Here too is the storied brass tablet to Joan Leveson, who died in 1572, after having married three husbands. By an extraordinary mischance the brass wandered from the church and was built into the house of the stationmaster at Four Ashes over two miles away. In the same aisle are the coloured kneeling figures of the families of Edward Moreton, who died under Charles I, and Matthew Moreton, who saw the Restoration.

But the most important monuments are the painted alabaster tombs of the Giffards. First is Sir John Giffard, who died in 1556 and who lies with black hair and pointed beard in armour such as he wore at the Field of the Cloth of Gold, when Henry VIII rewarded him with a gift of Blackladies. With Sir John lie his two wives in close-fitting hats, necklaces, and long tight-waisted dresses. Round the tomb are ranged their 18 children, 13 of them as babies. Sir John died at 90, only four years before his son Thomas, who is here in armour like his father's, with black hair and pointed beard and with two wives, but with only 17 children.

Next there is another John, who, dying in 1613 after long imprisonment as a Roman Catholic, is shown short and stout, with black hair and beard, in fine armour inlaid with steel. By him is his wife, in the usual tight-waisted dress with necklace and ruff. Their 14 children are round the tomb, so that on these three monuments there are 49 young Giffards. Among John's children is Gilbert Giffard, the Iago of the family, who sold Jesuit secrets to Protestant

D

statesmen and Protestant secrets to Jesuits. On the fourth tomb are Walter Giffard, who died in 1632, and his wife; he was another son of John, stout and tall, with black hair and a pointed beard, and wearing armour.

The Giffards of Chillington Hall were already Counts of Longueville before three of them came to England with the Conqueror and were rewarded with English lands and titles.

In the 12th century Peter Giffard fought valiantly under Strongbow in Ireland. Rewarded with grants of land, he returned to England, and became possessor of Chillington and other Staffordshire properties. From that day to our own the Giffard line has not failed here. We can trace them down the centuries at peace with their tenants and neighbours, at war with the king's enemies, serving in Parliament, sheriffs of the county; warlike Normans thoroughly anglicised, always lovers of the chase in the adjoining forest, and often of learning.

It was not until the time of Sir John Giffard, who lies resplendent in the chancel of Brewood church, that the family resumed a foremost position in national affairs. Warrior and member of Parliament, standard-bearer to Henry VIII, he received the gift of the Black Nuns convent here. The great thing in Sir John's life is the adventure with the leopard commemorated by the old cross in the park. In common with other lords he received gifts of wild animals brought back from Africa and the East, and in 1513 had captive a splendid leopard, which one morning escaped from its cage and bounded across the park.

Sir John set out in pursuit, armed with his cross-bow and accompanied by his son. He followed hot-foot in the wake of the animal, which had by this time approached a woman with a baby in her arms. Fitting an arrow, he was about to shoot when his son checked him, saying to him in French, "Take breath, pull strong." The elder man did both, and as the leopard made its leap his arrow pierced it. News of the exploit became noised abroad, and the king granted Sir John a coat-of-arms showing the leopard's head, the bearded archer, his cross-bow and arrows, and, as a motto, the warning words uttered by the son.

The Giffards were Roman Catholics who, although they profited by the Dissolution, did not conform to the reformed religion, and, themselves guiltless, suffered in common with other Roman Catholics in the days when members of their church were constantly planning assassination and invasion. One who did not so suffer was Gilbert Giffard, figured as a child on a tomb in the church. His father, John Giffard, had endured imprisonment for his faith, but

Gilbert, born about 1561, and educated in safety by Jesuits abroad, consciously vowed himself to villainy. "Evil, be thou my good!" he might have said. Admitted to the most secret councils of the Jesuits he sold his information to Elizabeth's ministers, and calmly betrayed his Protestant paymasters to Spain.

Gilbert Giffard insinuated himself into the Babington Plot; it was he who devised the scheme of the beer barrels with false bottoms which contained letters sent to Mary at Chartley, and came back empty with her replies concealed in the same way. A more complete villain has rarely been produced in real life. When all was over he wandered away to France unharmed, and his death there in 1590 was not connected with his treachery.

He was the one moral and intellectual freak of the family. The Giffards never wavered in their loyalty to the Stuarts. Peter Giffard was 61 when Charles I raised his standard at Nottingham, but he garrisoned the castle here, and himself took the field with all his sons and nephews old enough to fight. The Giffards owned Boscobel, and the Penderels were in their service; it was the Giffards who made possible the escape of Charles II after Worcester.

The story of William Carlos, who was buried in Brewood church-yard, is told to every boy and girl at school; it is the story of the oak tree in which Charles II hid. Carlos was a member of a family which seems originally to have spelled its name Careless. He was a colonel in the Royalist army, and, on the advance of the King from Scotland into England, in 1651, he fought on his side at the Battle of Worcester.

When the field was lost, Carlos fled to Boscobel woods. Here stood the memorable oak, grown thick and bushy, and in it Carlos hid. Two days and nights passed, and then there came stealing through the woods a tall man dressed as a peasant. It was Charles, fleeing from Whiteladies, with a troop of horse hot on his track. Carlos invited him into his oak, and they hid together while pursuers beat the woods about them. So they remained for more than 24 hours, during which time Carlos made hazardous forays in search of food. A price of £1000 was set on the king's head, but his companion was one of the many faithful to him during his terrifying six weeks of hiding.

At length the fugitives parted, for Carlos was a known man, and his presence would have endangered the king. Five days after the battle he succeeded in escaping to France, where, after the arrival of Charles, he shared the pangs and privations of exile until the Restoration. On returning to England he was rewarded with a coat-of-arms, a third share of a tax on all the hay and straw brought into London and Westminster, and the office of inspector of livery stables.

Brierley Hill. On a hill indeed, it is a busy industrial town, with large iron and glass works, many steel and other metal works, brickworks and tileries, and a bacon-curing factory. The Central Library, in Moor Street, has a fine collection of glassware.

Crowning all is the church, built in 1765 and well restored in 1900. Among its stained glass windows is one of the Crucifixion given by John Corbett, the "Salt King" of Droitwich, whose grave is in the churchyard. One of the church's 18th century vicars was Thomas Moss, the poet who wrote the lines beginning

> *Pity the sorrows of a poor old man,*
> *Whose trembling limbs have borne him to your door.*

There are wide views from the churchyard, of the Clent Hills to the south, of the distant Malverns, of the prominent Clee Hills, Wenlock Edge, and the Wrekin.

Broughton. With a story of an adventure of Izaak Walton, an unusual 17th century church containing fine old glass, and a hall rich with Tudor beauty, it has a quiet fascination which fixes it in the traveller's memory.

The isolated and unspoilt church, a remarkable late-Gothic survival, its porch in the shadow of three veteran yews, was built in 1630 by Thomas Broughton, who lived at the hall, and whose crest is in the church.

The font is curiously placed, built into a niche in a pier under the tower, like a great stoup. The first parson to use it, William Ingram, dying when the church was new, has a quaintly worded brass inscription with these lines:

> *Here lies the first whom Death translated*
> *After this church was consecrated.*
> *True fight he fought, true race he ran,*
> *He was, he is, a blessed man.*

Splendid glass of the 14th and 15th centuries (much of it from the Netherlands) fills two windows in the sanctuary. One shows rich figures of David and three saints, with shields of the Delves and Broughtons; the other has two saints and the kneeling figures of Ellen Delves and her husband Sir John, who fought and fell in 1471 at Tewkesbury, one of the last battles of the Wars of the Roses. A third window in the sanctuary has old heraldic glass. The church still has the high oak pews of Stuart days.

The home of the Broughtons, now a Franciscan priory, is a fine gabled and timbered Elizabethan house added to about 1630. Among its fine carving are Tudor roses and grotesques as corbels, and some of the windows have 17th century Flemish glass with Bible scenes. It was from this charming house that Thomas Broughton watched his church rise, and saw that it was good.

After the Battle of Worcester there came for hiding at the house a Royalist refugee, Colonel Blagg, who had been entrusted by Charles II with one of the Crown Jewels. On stealthily quitting the house he left the jewel with his host, George Barlow, and he himself was captured soon afterwards and imprisoned in the Tower of London.

Izaak Walton, who was then 58 and had been living for a generation in London, never forgot that he was a Stafford man, and at this time he was on one of his periodical visits to his old home. Trusted in an unobtrusive way by the Royalist party, he came out from Stafford to Blore Pipe House while the incriminating jewel was in his friend Barlow's possession. Izaak took on himself the risk of carrying the dangerous gem away with him. To have been detected would have meant the Tower for him, but he passed on his way unsuspected. Blagg escaped from the Tower, and Izaak contrived to meet him and restore the jewel, enabling him at last to discharge his trust by carrying it to Charles in France.

Izaak Walton's part in this dangerous transaction was the one astonishing hazard in his long tranquil life, and the memory of it adds a zest and piquancy to the reading of his placid pages.

Brownhills. Joined for administrative purposes with Aldridge, this is a colliery town on the northern edge of the Black Country. It is of little interest in itself, but it looks up to the wooded heights of Cannock Chase, the road to which passes beside the Chasewater Reservoir with its sailing facilities, near Chasetown.

Burntwood. It has illustrious names in its story, names such as Darwin, Johnson, and Peel. It may be that literature owes it thanks for an ingratitude, for it permitted one of the greatest of Englishmen to languish in neglect where he might have prospered in inglorious obscurity; it let him fail and wander in poverty to build for himself a temple of immortal fame.

The ivy-covered red-brick church was built soon after Waterloo, on ground given by the father of Sir Robert Peel. It has modern furnishings and a bright war-memorial window. An old yew spreads its limbs in the churchyard, which has a view towards Cannock Chase. Nearly two miles away, towards Lichfield, behind a belt of lofty trees, stands Maple Hayes, a fine house famous for the Botanic Gardens laid out by Erasmus Darwin, and celebrated by him in verses famous for their prediction of steam locomotion and mechanical flight.

It is a more enduring place in literature that Burntwood owes to its neighbour Edial (to the south-east), where still stands the 18th century hall regarding which the *Gentleman's Magazine* published a famous advertisement in 1736:

> *At Edial, near Lichfield, in Staffordshire, young gentlemen are boarded and taught the Latin and Greek Languages by Samuel Johnson.*

Here he came, a bridegroom of 27, with Tetty as his bride, a widow of 47. He was "lean and lank, so that his immense structure of bones was hideously striking to the eye", deeply scarred, his hair "straight and stiff and separated behind", and given to convulsive starts and gesticulations that excited surprise and ridicule; she was stout, florid, and painted, flaring and fantastic in dress, and affected in speech and in behaviour.

Only three pupils answered the advertisement, David Garrick, his brother George, and a boy named Offley, but for 18 months Johnson kept the school going for them, little dreaming that his Davy would one day tell the story of his "tumultuous and awkward fondness" for the wonderful Tetty, and mimic the gait and gestures of the weird genius who was to make him a great master of elocution and enable him to restore Shakespeare unmutilated to the stage.

Convinced that schoolmastering was his great chance, Johnson formulated a system of teaching the classics which he thought must eclipse all its predecessors, yet he found time to write here nearly the whole of his tragedy, *Irene*. It was with this as his sole literary asset that in March 1737 he closed the door of the house behind him, and, with Garrick for his companion, set out for London, "when I came with twopence-halfpenny in my pocket, and thou, Davy, with three-halfpence in thine", as he used fondly to recall.

Who shall say that if Staffordshire had sent her sons here to be educated by him Dr Johnson might not have missed his immortality? She neglected him and drove him to the pitiless capital to live on eightpence a day when he had it and to starve for 48 hours at a time when he had not, but in spite of all to write and talk his way to fame.

Burslem. Standing above the Trent, it is a little kingdom of industry surrounded by coal, ironstone, and the precious clay and marls which for more than two centuries it has been converting into crockery. The Mother of the Potteries, it is the "Bursley" of Arnold Bennett's "Five Towns", and with Tunstall, Hanley, Fenton, and Longton forms part of the county borough of Stoke-on-Trent; but as the birthplace of Josiah Wedgwood it will always remain to the world an individual town, made famous by his labours.

No town and no industry has ever owed more to one man than Burslem and pottery owe to Wedgwood. When he was born in 1730 Burslem was a poverty-stricken little place, making the crudest earthenware. Dragging a maimed limb after him for most of his life, he effected such a revolution that Burslem wares attained almost world-wide celebrity.

The town grew rapidly, without beauty or symmetry, and it bears the ill-favoured impress of its infancy; but behind the grim walls of these works, like pearls in the rough shell of the oyster, are realms of enchantment where mounds of clay and marl are blended, shaped and moulded, baked and fired, painted and glazed, and given abiding beauty. In these works we forget the dull streets of Burslem and lose ourselves in wonder.

Fittingly the town's noblest building is the Wedgwood Institute, built in 1863, with a school of art and science where Sir Oliver Lodge and Arnold Bennett were students. On the front are terracotta panels designed by John Lockwood Kipling (the father of Rudyard Kipling) and showing various processes in the making of pottery; above are the figures of the months, with mosaics and signs of the zodiac, each month in its own arch. Over the porch, with one of his vases in his hand, stands the Father of English Pottery, and in the porch are portraits in relief of John Flaxman, whose genius developed in making exquisite designs for Wedgwood's famous ware; and of Bentley and Priestley, names highly honoured in Staffordshire.

The parish church of St John, near Waterloo Road, is not a comely building, but it has its low 15th century tower, and in the chancel are two fine examples of Wedgwood, a beautiful figure of Christ in black, and a Wedgwood plate reproducing the Descent from the Cross by Rubens. It is here in memory of Enoch Wood, who made both the plate and the statue. In the neighbourhood a few of the old "bottle ovens" have survived.

At Smallthorne, about a mile east of Burslem, is the interesting Ford Green Hall, a 16th century house, partly timber-framed, that has been restored as a period museum of furniture and domestic objects.

The Roman Catholic church of St Joseph has a romantic story of the glass in its 22 windows. Among the congregation were past and present students at the School of Art, whose director suggested that they should design and make the lights. Twelve gifted volunteers gave their leisure to the task, designed and cut the glass, assembled and leaded it, and completed a work of beauty which, apart from saving the young church thousands of pounds, is in the opinion of some experts equal to mediaeval craftsmanship.

The undertaking, highly creditable to all concerned, was quite in the spirit of Wedgwood, who held that art and craftsmanship form a natural partnership. One of the men who grew up under his influence was Noah Heath, Burslem's potter poet.

Burton upon Trent. For a thousand years it has watched the river flowing by, and for long has played its part in history, with a 7th century saint to bless it, an 11th century abbey to shield and foster it, and a 16th century grammar school to teach it. It has been destroyed by fire, shaken by earthquake, and swamped by the bursting river; it saw the Barons' War and the Civil War, and it raised a million-pound building for making machine-guns in the First World War.

Once a centre of the clothing world, war destroyed that great industry, but for two centuries Burton has been the home of brewing. It is said that even in the 13th century an abbot of Burton was using water from the wells here for brewing, and it is this clear water which has led to the saying that nature meant Burton to brew. We may prefer the clear water, but we are bound to be impressed by the wonderful growth of this industry.

It was in the 18th century that Burton brew started to become world famous. The first brewery was established in 1708, and one company quickly found customers overseas, Peter the Great and the Empress Catherine of Russia among them, and Burton beer was drunk in Danzig to celebrate the departure of Napoleon. William Bass founded a business in 1777 producing 2000 barrels a year at first, which now sends out barrels by the hundred thousand. At one time there were nearly 20 breweries; these have been reduced by amalgamation to six, but between them they produce about 3 million barrels a year. Some of them are established in factories like great arsenals, and there are kindred firms dealing in malt, yeast, and food extracts.

The immense establishments of the maltsters, the coopers, the makers of machinery, and all the apparatus of the industry depend on the brewing, and to serve these many firms there is an unparal-

leled number of level crossings in the public streets, where we feel
like a trespasser in a vast dock siding, for trains pop in and out and
cross the roads like trams. But there is more than industrial Burton
to see. The town has fine wide thoroughfares with pretty peeps of
the river, which is a joyous summer picture.

Opposite the town hall is the bronze statue of Michael Bass whom
his old friend Mr Gladstone made Lord Burton. He left the town
rarely enriched, in part aided by his father, but mainly by his own
gifts. To him Burton owes its bridge, its town hall, and the churches
of St Paul's and St Margaret's, as well as clubs and other social
centres. He died at 72, and his fellow townsmen raised this monument in front of the handsome 19th century town hall.

The museum and art gallery, in Guild Street, is the repository of
an interesting collection of British, Roman, and Saxon relics, including urns, shields, bosses, buckles, and brooches, as well as finds
from the abbey here and a fine group of birds and animals. The
most interesting mediaeval original in the museum is one of Burton's
15th century knights, an alabaster figure in chain mail who was
once buried where the monks chanted mass at the abbey.

Of the abbey itself, founded before the Norman Conquest and
endowed with over 70 manors, nothing remains. It lay behind the
town's great market, on the site of the parish church of St Modwen.
We could not but recall in imagination the scene of 700 years ago,
when Nicholas of Tusculum was here as papal legate at the abbey,
with King John cringing for the return of his crown, securing by his
servility the lifting of the Papal Interdict and the support of the
Pope in defying Stephen Langton. From the abbey, and the scene
between these three, it was but a short journey in time and space to
Runnymede and Magna Carta.

The grammar school, founded by a 16th century abbot and made
new last century, is a brick building near Lichfield Street. The
stone bridge, 470 yards long and carried on 32 arches, was erected
in 1864 in place of the bridge which had served the town from
mediaeval times. But the original was rich in history. Generations
of monks wore its surface smooth. During the Baron's War it rang
with the clamour of battle, when Edward of Lancaster held it for
three days against the forces of Edward II; then, outflanked by a
crossing at Walton, upstream, he reduced the unhappy town to
ashes, and went his way. The bridge survived, and over it in 1586
passed one of the saddest figures in history. Mary, Queen of Scots,
detected at Chartley in the act of plotting the assassination of
Elizabeth, rode across the bridge on her way to her trial and execution at Fotheringhay.

The parish church, St Modwen's, rebuilt in 1719–26 by William and Francis Smith, of Warwick, stands on a gentle slope by the Trent, where we picture the monks diligently fishing on Thursday for Friday's dinner. The only relics from the previous church are the font, of 1662, and a 16th century chest. An elaborate 19th century wall-monument to Thomas Salt has three seated women and two children. The old burial-ground, near by, has been laid out as a Garden of Remembrance.

Burton has interesting 19th century and later churches. St Paul's, built in 1874 by Lord Grimthorpe and J. M. Neale, near the town hall, is like a cathedral in miniature, with a central tower and with oak and iron screens and other fittings by G. F. Bodley, who built the church at Hoar Cross. St Chad's, in Hunter Street, north of the Derby road, was completed in 1910 and was Bodley's last church. Holy Trinity Church, in Horninglow Street, leading to the bridge, has a tall tower and spire, and here is lovely mediaeval glass from the earlier church, with sunshine setting on fire its reds and golds, and bringing back to its greens, purples, and blues the colours its makers created long ago.

Remote as may have been its century, this glass is still too modern to have been seen by the founder of the first church here, for the earliest Christian settlement at Burton was two centuries before Alfred. St Modwen, the founder, was the daughter of an Irish prince when Ireland was keeping alight the torch of learning in the Dark Age of Europe. After many adventures she established a little convent here 1300 years ago. Many religious houses sprang from the convent, but Modwen passed on to aid her brother in Scotland, and there in 700 she died. Three centuries later her body was brought here and laid to rest, with a Latin inscription meaning:

By Ireland life, by Scotland death was given,
A tomb in England, endless joy in Heaven.

The translation of her remains to the scene of her fruitful labours must have been effected by Wulfric, the Mercian earl who founded the abbey. His great building succeeded hers, which the Danes had destroyed; they were to destroy him, too, for he fell in battle with them near Ipswich in 1010. Around the great abbey the town grew to become a seat of learning and the birthplace of an important historical work written by the monks, the Burton Chronicle. All this was a long while ago, but it is pleasant to find an industrial town of modern expansion treasuring the story of its past as Burton does.

One of its sons, Isaac Hawkins Browne, literature would remember even if Burton forgot. Son of a rich vicar of Burton, he went from

Cambridge University to the Bar but did not practise, devoting his time to literature and Parliament. Perhaps nobody now reads his serious poems on design and beauty and on immortality, but his witty parodies of the six leading poets of his age, published as *A Pipe of Tobacco*, greatly admired in their day, were the ancestor of a numerous progeny. He was declared by Dr Johnson to be of all conversationalists the most delightful with whom he was ever in company, and that from the prince of talkers is a very trumpet tribute of fame. Johnson, talking to Boswell and Bennet Langton, paid his friend this further compliment: "We must not estimate a man's powers by his being able to deliver sentiments in public; Isaac Hawkins Browne, one of the first wits of this country, got into Parliament and never opened his mouth." A thousand speeches of his own could hardly have assured him greater fame than these two judgments of our English Socrates.

Bushbury. The houses of Wolverhampton's suburbs have crept out to it and have almost reached the village church, but fortunately the growth of the town will never affect the historic building in this neighbourhood—Moseley Old Hall. A vital link in one of the most exciting episodes of English history, it is now in the keeping of the National Trust.

Here, after dusk on the evening of Sunday, September 7, 1651, came Charles II, his cause lost at Worcester and he himself unable to escape across the Severn into Wales. Across these fields he came with six men to the back of the house, entering by this door still on its hinges. Thomas Whitgreave, the squire, did not recognise him, with his hair cut short and his face stained with walnut juice.

In the house we can see the panelled bedroom with the bed in which the king slept, the attic windows where the squire's three sons kept watch for the Roundheads, and the hiding hole where Charles was hidden when the soldiers actually came to make enquiries. All these are much as they were, but the outside of the hall is different, its Elizabethan timbers now encased in brick. The king got safely away from Moseley, and after the Restoration he showed his gratitude by granting a pension to the squire and his son.

In the much-restored 14th century church of Bushbury is a memorial (in the south aisle) to Thomas Whitgreave, who lived on until 1702, and there are other things to see: the strangely carved font, the carved beams of the chancel roof, and the much-worn figure of a priest in the chancel, believed to be Hugh de Byshbury, founder of the church. There is a silver plate 600 years old, and a fine Elizabethan chalice.

George Borrow came with his gipsy friends to a service here in 1825 and described it in a chapter of *Romany Rye*. The trees in the churchyard, the benches for the poor, and the little chancel door were all remembered by him.

Butterton. It lies at the heart of a noble moorland picture, and builds itself up of stone hewn from the hills around the River Manifold.

The village has some 18th century houses, and just below it the road from Grindon actually runs along the bed of a stream. Just to the east lie prehistoric barrows, which they call lows here; and from these have come spearheads and articles of adornment buried with those who wielded and wore them. The church, rebuilt in 1871, stands at a height of over 1000 feet, and has a prominent tower and spire. It has saved the 14th century font, with traceried panels, from the previous church.

Cannock. Who has not heard of its famous Chase, a great tract of moorland with deep valleys, masses of bracken, brown streams, birch woods, and hills crowned with pines? Once the hunting-ground of kings, it has been in olden days a wild and desolate country where wolves were heard and outlaws sought refuge.

An old town and the centre of a rich colliery area, Cannock has a charming marketplace, with noble limes sheltering a green, a haven of peace in a busy world. A boy who played here was buried in Westminster Abbey. He was Henry Francis Cary, famous for his fine translation of Dante. Though born in Gibraltar, in 1772, he spent much of his childhood here, living in a house near by, since demolished.

A mediaeval cross keeps company with the church, the tower of which has watched Cannock growing bigger for 500 years or so. On the tower are the arms of Humphrey de Stafford, who fell at the Battle of Northampton, in 1460. The rest of the church was rebuilt, in the Decorated Gothic style, in 1752.

Here it was, before the church was made new, that Henry Sacheverell, the much-hated and despised champion of the High Church and Toryism, preached many of his violent sermons, the kind of sermon that was afterwards to bring about his trial for sedition and libel, to cause tumult and riots, and finally the burning of his sermons by the hangman.

On the old Watling Street, a mile and a half south-west, is a quaint inn, half brick and half timber, for three centuries known as the Four Crosses. On a beam over the window is a Latin inscription meaning

You would weep if you knew you had but a month to live. You laugh when perhaps you have not a day.

High up on Cannock Chase, near Pye Green, is one of the tall Post Office towers for television and radio telephony. Near Broadhurst Green, farther north, is a German military cemetery, consecrated in 1967, with the graves of 4929 Germans who died in the two World Wars, and a hall of honour which contains a remarkable bronze by Hans Wimmers.

Castlechurch. It has a little company of houses near its church and castle. Just over a mile from Stafford, its church is of the 19th century, except for a tower built 500 years ago with a 17th century sundial engraved in its stone. An avenue of old yews shades the pathway to the porch. Inside are four windows with figures of the Evangelists and outside is the grave of Thomas Mulock, whose daughter wrote *John Halifax, Gentleman*.

Long before we come to the village we see what is known as Stafford Castle standing above the trees on a hill. It is Staffordshire's young ruin, a house begun about the time of Waterloo and never finished. It is a ruin on a ruin, for it stands on the foundations of a castle destroyed in Cromwell's day, a pathetic pile, slowly crumbling. The hill is worth climbing for the marvellous view stretching beyond Staffordshire and Shropshire into the mountains of Wales.

Cauldon. It is all stone, its houses built of stone quarried for centuries at Cauldon Low, while weapons of the Stone Age have been found in what is called Big Low. In the churchyard of the small but attractive 18th century stone church is a gravestone with an inscription saying, Here lieth Margaret Manifold, aged seven times seven years old.

Cauldon is now dominated by its huge limestone quarry, from which much of the stone for building the new motorways was taken. The quarry has eaten into the northern slopes of the lonely Weaver Hills, sometimes called the "last of the Pennines" because they are the southernmost of the limestone uplands. From the grassy ridge of the hills there is a charming view over the deep Churnet valley to Alton Towers and across the Dove into Derbyshire.

Caverswall. It has memories of a man who defied a king, of an immortal admiral, and a famous writer. The writer was Robert

Buchanan, son of a journeyman tailor. Gifted and versatile, he wrote dramas, novels, and poems in all moods, some of great tenderness and beauty.

Here he must often have looked with wondering eyes at the noble towers of Caverswall Castle, now a convent and guest house, with its red stone walls half-hidden by great elm trees. The first castle was built 700 years ago; the present house, possibly designed by John Smithson, the architect of the magnificent Bolsover Castle, in Derbyshire, is almost like a fortress in its massive strength, corner turrets, and fine windows. It was raised by a man who might have foreseen that he must build for defence as well as for beauty.

He was Matthew Cradock, who, about the time the *Mayflower* sailed, saw the walls of his new home rising on what had degenerated into a farm. One of the founders of Massachusetts (where Winthrop was elected governor because Cradock did not arrive to fill the post) he helped the colony with money and provisions, but was kept occupied at home by events leading to the Civil War. It was he who stood up in the Long Parliament and declared that if Charles I fortified the Tower he would see to it that London paid no taxes. Matters were nearing a crisis when he died suddenly in 1641, leaving his new home to serve as a fortress for the Parliamentary forces.

The parish church has still its 14th century tower, its 13th century chancel, and 17th century semicircular arches borne on pillars set up when the old castle was new. The pulpit and two finely carved pews may be the work of the craftsmen who made the Jacobean altar-table. In the chancel are an alabaster tablet with the arms of Matthew Cradock and Sir Francis Chantrey's exquisite sculpture of Lady St Vincent, who has knelt here since 1816, veiled, with clasped hands, her coronet beside her. She was the wife of Admiral John Jervis, Lord St Vincent, who saved us from invasion, quelled an alarming mutiny in the fleet, and purged the Admiralty of the hordes of knaves who were robbing the Navy and the nation. A stern, relentless man, he was buried a few miles away at Stone.

Robert Buchanan, born here in 1841, was one of the vigorous spirits of last century. His father was a newspaper writer who had started life as a tailor at Ayr, and he took his son back to Scotland, where he was educated at Glasgow University. At 19 Robert came to London with his friend David Gray, a weaver poet who lived just long enough to see one of his poems set up in type. Poverty oppressed them both. Robert became a journalist, writing for the *Athenaeum* and for *All the Year Round*, edited by Charles Dickens. He thus made many illustrious friends, keeping some all his life, but losing more by his fiery independence of character, which at times became perversity.

He established himself as a poet with his *Undertones*, followed by a volume of *London Poems*, revealing a deep and tender sympathy with the unhappy and unfortunate. In these, as in all his best poems (notably a beautiful love story, *White Rose and Red*), he showed fine narrative power, and a rare mastery of melody.

The perversity of his nature showed itself in a satirical poem, signed Caliban, in which he attacked Swinburne and other poets, who replied with vigour. He then wrote a famous article on "The Fleshly School of Poetry", in which he hotly assailed the Pre-Raphaelites. Rossetti answered this with "The Stealthy School of Criticism", and a long battle of words followed, ending in a libellous letter by Swinburne for which Buchanan recovered £150 damages. Five years later, however, he admitted that his criticisms had been exaggerated and he dedicated his novel *God and the Man* to Rossetti, "the old enemy".

He wrote a great deal of poetry, some of it with deep feeling and power; in a lighter vein he wrote of love, sweeter than hearing or seeing, sadder than sorrow or death:

> *The love that comes to the palace,*
> *That comes to the cottage door:*
> *The ever-abundant chalice*
> *Brimming for rich and poor.*

In 1876 he began his career as a novelist, producing year by year work of power and imagination. He had worked in the grip of a bitter personal tragedy, his beautiful wife dying after a long and painful illness. She had shared with him from the age of 20 all the hardships as well as the successes of his life. Her sister Harriet Jay was an actress, and with her help Buchanan now turned his novels into plays and wrote many other dramas which met with success both here and in America. In spite of boundless generosity to friends less fortunate than himself, he seemed on the way to fortune, when suddenly he lost all his savings in an unlucky investment and was made bankrupt. In the same year he was attacked by paralysis and a few months later, in 1901, he died at Streatham in south London, a poor man after all his labours.

Chartley. It has been a stage for drama among the most thrilling in our history, the parts played by queens, nobles, and high-born desperadoes, with the Spanish king in the background; and with plot and counter-plot as astonishing as the wildest fancies of fiction.

51

Old houses with grand timbers look out on the glories of a park of nearly 1000 acres, but there is no church; the interest centres on the manor house and the hilltop ruins of the 13th century castle. With old elms about them, here are two round stone towers, their walls 12 feet thick, pierced by narrow openings for the discharge of arrows, and bearing an engraved cross proclaiming that the builder bore his part as a Crusader.

He was Ranulph, sixth earl of Chester, who, while this castle was rising in 1220, was also building Beeston Castle in Cheshire. With Ranulph in Palestine, as everywhere, was his brother-in-law William de Ferrers, earl of Derby. They were together at the deathbed of King John, and witnessed his will. At Ranulph's death the castle passed to the earl and remained in his family until 1461, when Sir Walter Devereux married the heiress of Chartley, leaving her here when he went to fight for Richard III and to die by his side at Bosworth Field.

His son brought here as bride the heiress of the great house of Bohun, which had given Thomas of Woodstock a wife and Henry IV a queen. Devereux was father of the man from whom descends our oldest viscounty, and grandfather of the first earl of Essex, who, married to Lettice Knollys, cousin of Queen Elizabeth I, was called by the queen the rare jewel of her realm, and the bright ornament of her nobility.

By this time the castle was replaced by a manor house which in the 18th century was again replaced by the grey stone house hidden among the trees. Here, while Essex was breaking his heart in Ireland, Elizabeth came on a visit to her cousin Lettice, liking her entertainment so well that she stayed ten days. Essex dying the following year, the royal favourite Leicester married the widowed countess, and was responsible for the introduction to Court of the young earl then growing up as a model of grace, learning, and valour, though not of wisdom, he who was hero for a time of the queen and the nation alike.

When the earl was 18 his home was chosen, against his will, as the prison of Mary, Queen of Scots, who was brought here during the Christmas season of 1585. Within a month Gilbert Giffard appeared on the scene, a plausible villain of 24, educated abroad, and secretly in the service of the Roman Catholics as well as of Elizabeth's watchful ministers, betraying each to the other.

He came here to Mary with French credentials, declaring his will and ability to convey letters to her, and to transmit her replies in turn. Unaware that Walsingham knew and approved of his coming, Mary trusted him fully, and he carried out his bargain to the extent of smuggling letters to her and from her; but before they left his hands all were copied, and duplicates forwarded to Walsingham.

Giffard was the intermediary between Mary and the conspirators in the Babington Plot. His method was to secrete letters for her in a box hidden in the false bottom of a barrel in which beer was supplied to her. On delivery the beer was drawn off, the box secured, and its contents read by Mary, whose replies were placed in the box, which was then carried out in the empty cask. As soon as the letters reached his hands Giffard translated them from their French cipher. But he not only gave Walsingham copies, he also contrived to let the Spanish Ambassador in Paris know the contents, and through him Philip of Spain, who pronounced the plot a holy enterprise and promised that it should have his support in men and money.

In the barrel came Babington's letter informing Mary of his scheme to murder Queen Elizabeth, to release and crown Mary, and to rouse all Roman Catholic England on her behalf, a task in which he was to have the assistance of a Spanish army of invasion. Mary replied, approving the plan and urging immediate action. As she had been an accessory in Scotland to the murder of her husband Darnley, and had married his assassin, so here at Chartley she was accessory to the plot against her cousin, and was reported to be willing, in case he killed Elizabeth, to marry Babington.

In August 1586 Walsingham struck; Babington and his 13 fellow conspirators were arrested and executed. Mary was seized and imprisoned while her apartments here were searched, her cabinets forced, and all her correspondence impounded. Within a few days of the terrible penalties on the conspirators Mary left Chartley, and in September 1586 began the journey to Fotheringhay which was to end at the place of execution five months later.

Twenty years afterwards James I came here and made merry in the scene of his mother's imprisonment. After Mary's departure the house reverted to the young second earl, but he was little here; his wonderful career, which kept him mainly in court and camp, ended in his execution when he was only 34. He left a widow, who had been the wife of Sir Philip Sidney, and an heir, Robert Devereux, the third earl, destined to become the first General of Cromwell's Army. He died in 1646, and the estate passed to Sir Robert Shirley, whose son was created Lord Chartley by Charles II. Queen Anne added the earldom of Ferrers to the title, and it was the fourth earl Ferrers who brought disgrace to the Chartley home by murdering his steward. Dressed like a bridegroom, he drove to Tyburn in 1760 in his own landau, drawn by his own horses, and

E

driven by his own coachman, and there, in the presence of 200,000 people, he was hanged.

Some 20 years later the house was destroyed by fire, and the present structure took its place, so that the crusader's castle has, in its ruins, outlasted the hall which succeeded it as the setting of so much history. The Shirleys, a family of great antiquity, continued in possession until the opening of this century, when, for the first time since the Conquest, the estate was sold.

There are still here mighty trees Queen Elizabeth saw, but of the renowned herd of Chartley cattle there is no sign. Among the most famous herds in existence, the Chartley cattle were white, with black ears and long branching horns, descendants, it is said, of the great British Aurochs domesticated by the Romans. For a thousand years they ranged the great Needwood Forest. Soon after Ranulph had built the castle the present park was enclosed and the cattle fenced within its boundaries; and here for 700 years they remained, never wholly tamed, one of the wonders of the countryside. Then, while the estate was still in the hands of its last Shirley owner, tuberculosis attacked the herd, and only a few escaped. These passed into the safe keeping of the duke of Bedford at Woburn Abbey, and there we must seek the remnants of one of the most ancient and famous of all our cattle herds.

Chasetown. Lying to the north of the Black Country, it is a place that lives on coal, but its outlook is not black. This town of 19th century development has a justifiable pride in the lovely country at its doors, stretching up to the wooded heights of Cannock Chase. Nearer at hand, the large Chasewater Reservoir, built originally to feed the Staffordshire and Worcestershire Canal, has become a favourite resort for sailing and other water sports, and international motor-boat races are held here.

Cheadle. With millions of tons of coal below and miles of magnificent countryside above, Cheadle is rich. It is an old market town with thriving textile industries; its market cross, raised on six steps, is a link with the Middle Ages. It has a beautiful group of timbered and gabled Tudor houses, a row of 18th century shops, and a 19th century church whose most notable possessions are an old oak chest with two locks and the 17th century altar-rails.

The splendid Roman Catholic church, built of red stone, is one of Pugin's masterpieces, completed in 1846, in the Decorated style. Its spire, rising 200 feet, is seen far off, and its west door is guarded by rampant lions heavily moulded in brass. Inside is a wealth of colour and ornament: there is a Doom over the chancel arch, the ornate chancel has a gilded altar-screen, and the baptistry has a brass screen of fine workmanship. In the north aisle is an exquisite 15th century triptych of the Last Days of Our Lord, by a Flemish craftsman.

A mile away to the north-east stands Hales Hall, built by the granddaughter of Sir Matthew Hales. It has noble trees and an avenue of old yews.

From Cheadle we come up the wooded valley of the Churnet to the lonely spaces of Hawksmoor Nature Reserve, mostly given to the National Trust by John Beech Masefield, to whose memory a gateway was opened by his famous kinsman, John Masefield, the poet. The reserve of 250 acres of woods, moors, and marshes is the home of many birds and animals, a rare spot for wild flowers, ferns, and rhododendrons.

Chebsey. In this quiet place near the river Sow are fragments of Saxon England; one of the 11th century in the churchyard, the shaft of a cross decorated with knotwork; others in the church, thought to be bits of a cross the Normans may have saved when they began building a church here.

Some of the Norman work is still standing, including a window north of the chancel and a simple doorway now built up, on the north of the nave. The south doorway, the chancel arch and the massive arcade are of the 13th century. The tower, 500 years old, has an outside stair turret, and a bell that was ringing before the Reformation.

Checkley. The little river Tean flows murmuring to the Dove; the smiling fields, the splendid trees, and the snug hedgerows carry the eye to the hills swelling on the horizon. Apart from the traffic along the busy main road to Stoke, little has changed in this beautiful country since the mediaeval villagers built their church, one of the most interesting churches in Staffordshire.

It is the venerable mother church of a wide area, with a churchyard as impressive as anything of the kind Staffordshire has to show. Here are three weathered shafts of Saxon crosses about five feet high, an astonishing heritage for a village churchyard. On one are three figures claimed to be bishops slain in a battle between Saxons and Danes at the hamlet half a mile away still called Deadman's Green.

Above these Saxon relics rises a grand 15th century tower from a massive 13th century base. On an outer wall is an old stone sundial. A prettily vaulted Jacobean porch guards a fine 14th century doorway with ballflower ornament. The high and beautiful interior, with a 17th century clerestory and timber roofs, has a late 12th century arcade with its arches pointed, a second arcade which has been here 700 years, and a remarkable Norman font carved with an ass and palm trees.

To this font may have been brought for christening the 13th century knight who lies in worn armour in the chancel. A Tudor alabaster tomb here shows Godfrey Foljambe in armour and ruff, and his wife in a close-fitting hat, ruff, and belted gown. In the lofty 14th century chancel are traceried windows which have rose-decked stone bosses and contain Flemish glass 600 years old. The colouring is sober, the drawings of the figures primitive, yet imaginative and impressive. In the east window are four saints and a 13th century bishop, and below, with the Crucifixion, are St Margaret and her dragon, Abraham and Isaac, the scene of the murder of Becket, and Henry II doing penance for the crime.

Other chancel windows have the Virgin and Child and two saints; Moses with the tables of the law, and SS John and Simon. In yet another, with much heraldic glass, are delightful roundels with the occupations of the months: February for netting, March for pruning, April for planting, May with its flowers, July for the hay-cutting, another month for the harvest, and finally, for October, the fattening of the swine. With a reaping machine in place of the scythe, the pictures might characterise the march of the months over these fertile fields today.

Three 16th century choir-stalls have richly carved poppyheads with roses, animals, and figures wearing headdresses suggestive of Red Indians, whose habits and attire could hardly have been known by the carvers. There can be no mistaking the significance of the initials A.D. on the poppyheads; they stand for Anthony Draycott, rector here and chancellor of Lichfield, a sore scourge of Protestants in the reign of Mary Tudor. Round the south chapel is a fine old screen, its linenfold enriched by heraldry.

Cheddleton. It lies on a hillside amid charming scenery near the River Churnet. A red stone lychgate of the 19th century brings us to the church with a tower of Queen Elizabeth I's day, a chancel and south arcade 600 years old, and a north arcade a century older. One of its glories is a group of fine windows, two with the touch of great artists in them—a St Cecilia by Rossetti and three fine trumpeting angels by Burne-Jones. In the nave is a mediaeval brass eagle lectern, brought from Belgium. The 14th century chancel has stepped sedilia and a piscina, and a rare treasure, an oak panel in the reredos with painted figures carved by a craftsman 400 years ago. The panel, probably Flemish work, shows the burial of Christ. In one of the choir-stalls a brass tablet tells us that Fred Wilshaw sat there as a chorister and choirmaster for 56 years. In the church-yard is the restored shaft of an old cross set on three steps.

In the valley of the Churnet are large paper-mills that were first established here 150 years ago. In the valley, too, farther upstream, is an older mill, the only working flint-mill in Staffordshire. In the 18th century, potters began to add flint to their earthenware composition to improve its whiteness. Flint being a very hard substance, it needed to be ground very finely, and to make it easy to crush it was burnt in special kilns and then ground with water on a pan-mill, where large stones were driven round over a pavement of smaller stones. The mills were first powered by waterwheels, but later steam was introduced. The mill was restored in 1969 as an industrial monument and is to form a museum of the ceramic milling industry.

Church Eaton. The greatest possession of this attractive village is its church in memory of St Editha, whose well is near High Onn, more than a mile away.

Norman masons built the tower and 15th century builders added the spire. The long arcade comes from the 13th century. A fine window with tracery nearly five centuries old fills the east wall of the chancel. Its 19th century glass has nine scenes from the life of Christ, portraits of bishops, and St Michael, all from the hands of the artist who filled the old windows of the tower with new portraits of the patron saint.

In the churchyard is the marble tomb of Arthur Talbot, who preached in this place for 54 years last century.

Clifton Campville. Its treasures are gathered in the remarkably fine and spacious church, perhaps the most satisfying parish church in Staffordshire, standing proudly near the place where three counties meet.

Much of the church was built in that noble period of English architecture, the 14th century, and it was then that the vaulted tower and spire were raised to a height of 189 feet, both lovely and slender, the spire set off with flying buttresses, the tower with a lofty arch to the nave and large windows in the Decorated style. The north transept, a century older, has a chapel with a vaulted roof under a priest's chamber, the fireplace and the 13th century windows still here.

The church is rich in screens, with three of the 14th century, one of the 15th, and one of the 17th. The gates of the 15th century screen were fixed 200 years later, in 1634, and on them is the name of the rector who saw them brought into the church. The eight stalls, nearly 500 years old, have finely carved misericords adorned with leaves and grotesques. The nave has an unusual queen-post roof.

Fading away on the wall of a recess in the south aisle are portraits of a mediaeval knight and his lady, perhaps Sir John Vernon and Maud Camville, receiving a blessing from Our Lord. On a brass in the south chapel is a lady, thought to have been the wife of Sir Richard Stafford, shown in the height of fashion 600 years ago; it is a palimpsest, with another figure hidden on the underside. In the chapel, too, is an old chest hewn out of an oak tree. On a marble wall-monument is a woman weeping for John Watkins, who was rector here for upwards of 40 years until 1833; and among other monuments is one by Rysbrack with a casket between two pillars in memory of Sir Charles Pye of 1721, and one with an urn in memory of Sir Richard Pye of 1724.

More striking is an alabaster table-tomb in the south chapel with figures of Sir John Vernon, a lawyer of Henry VIII's day (he died in 1545), and his wife. He wears a bonnet and long gown, and she is in a square hood and flowing dress, a knife, a purse, and beads at her side. Round the tomb sit seven monks, some with books and others with rosaries, and at the head are a son and daughter kneeling at prayer. In a recess in the nave, in a stone coffin with an engraved cross, it is thought that the founder of all the beauty round about may have been buried.

Codsall. It is now best known for its large Royal Air Force Station, developed during the Second World War, but Codsall itself is an expanding residential village, a few miles from Wolverhampton. In the grounds of Oaken House are two giant wych elms, one about 22 feet round and one 24. Two other giants are yews in the churchyard, one 15 feet round; both have weathered centuries of storm, and with them on a short pillar and three steps is a sundial which has marked years of sunny hours.

The high-lying church, rebuilt in 1848, has a tower 600 years old and a doorway 200 years older, its zigzag moulding and carved capitals finely preserved. Inside is the brightly painted and gilded tomb of Walter Wrottesley, Sheriff of Staffordshire in Charles I's day. We see him with his head on his helmet and a gauntlet at his feet, his five children gathered round him, one of the sons in

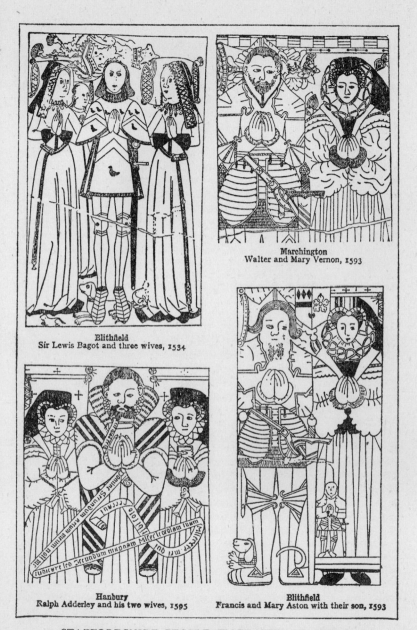

Elithfield
Sir Lewis Bagot and three wives, 1534

Marchington
Walter and Mary Vernon, 1593

Hanbury
Ralph Adderley and his two wives, 1595

Blithfield
Francis and Mary Aston with their son, 1593

STAFFORDSHIRE PEOPLE ENGRAVED IN STONE

armour and two in red tunics. The daughters wear black dresses with golden collars and cuffs.

On the wall near the south door is a Dutch Delft-ware plaque presented by the Protestant churches of the Netherlands in gratitude for the hospitality shown to the Dutch servicemen during 1940–47.

Pendrell Hall, a 19th century house at Codsall Wood, on the road towards the park at Chillington Hall, is now a residential college for adult education.

Colwich. It lies in beauty by the Trent, with the wooded hills of Cannock Chase rising beyond the valley. It thrills us with memories of one of our most ancient families, and recalls the fame of one of the soldier builders of the British Empire.

To the east of the village, in a spacious timbered park beyond the river, is Wolseley Hall, the home of the Wolseleys since the days before the Conquest. It has much fine woodwork, including a staircase said to have been carved by Grinling Gibbons. Here, say the Wolseley records, the line was already established when, in the 10th century, King Edgar gave the family its present lands as a reward for destroying wolves, with which the county was over-run.

Many of the Wolseleys rest in the old parish church, whose churchyard gives us a superb picture of the river winding through the fields and of the distant glory of the forest heights. With a handsome 17th century tower, the church has a 13th century arcade and much work of the following century, though the 28 canopied choir-stalls are of the 19th century.

The great possessions of the church are the Wolseley and Anson monuments, but there are others of interest, among them a tablet to James Trubshaw, who is buried here. The son of a Colwich builder, he worked for William Beckford in building Fonthill Abbey, built three fine halls, bridged the Derwent at Derby, set upright a church tower in Cheshire which was five feet out of plumb, and, crowning achievement (said by the great Telford to be impossible), crossed the Dee at Chester with a bridge of a single span 200 feet wide, which was then the widest arch in Europe.

Under a Gothic arch is a wall-monument in the chancel with engraved figures of Christ, an angel, and two wounded soldiers, above the tomb of Lady Chetwynd, who ended a life of good works in 1860. The glass includes a memorial window at the west end to Major William Hodson, hero of Hodson's Horse, whose astounding feats in India included the capture of the King of Delhi. He was killed in 1858 by a shot from an unseen enemy hidden in a house at Lucknow. His father was vicar here for 22 years of last century.

The Wolseley memorials represent only a few of the members of this ancient family buried here. The first with a monument is Sir Robert, who lies on a 17th century tomb in long breeches, tunic, and cloak, with two angels and two girls holding skulls above him. Born a subject of Queen Elizabeth, he suffered confiscation of his estates during the Civil War, and died poor in 1646.

His heir Sir Charles made his peace with the Commonwealth while still a youth, and became deeply attached to Cromwell, sat in two of his Parliaments, was called to his House of Lords, and was one of the committee which urged him to accept the Crown. A scholar and a gardener, Sir Charles was the father of 15 children. There is a tablet to his son Sir William, who was drowned during a thunderstorm by the bursting of a mill-dam while driving in his carriage. His coachman escaped, "being carried by the torrent into an orchard, where he remained fast until the flood abated", but Sir William and his four horses were overwhelmed.

Sir Charles's youngest son Richard fought in Ireland, where he acquired property and founded the Irish branch of the family which in 1833 produced one of the bravest soldiers of the century, Field-Marshal Wolseley, whose arms and banners are on the north aisle wall, though he is buried in St Paul's Cathedral. Few men have had a more remarkable career than he. Joining the Army at 19 he fought through the Burmese and Crimean Wars, and in the Indian Mutiny and the Chinese War of 1860, while still in his twenties. In Canada he commanded the Red River Expedition, adding the province of Manitoba to the Dominion.

He met Gordon in the Crimean trenches, and remained his devoted friend up to their last parting, which was when Gordon left Charing Cross in a tall hat and frockcoat, with nothing in his purse but the odd money Wolseley gave him. It was not his fault that he arrived with his relief expedition too late to prevent the death of Gordon at Khartoum. As Commander-in-Chief Wolseley reorganised the British Army, completed 48 years of service, and died after 13 years of happy retirement, enlivened by the writing of an appealing autobiography. He invented the name of Thomas Atkins for the private soldier.

Wolseley lies in St Paul's with Nelson; with the Wolseleys here at Colwich is buried Lord Anson, forerunner of Nelson. In the locked north chapel is a monument by Westmacott showing an angel reaping corn in memory of Thomas Lord Anson, who died in 1818, and a wall-monument with a graceful figure of a weeping

woman to Lady Anson, who died in 1843, though to the greatest
of the line, the immortal voyager, who was brought here to his
burial in the vault in 1762, there is but a modest tablet in the
chancel.

The Ansons had been long in Staffordshire before establishing
themselves at Shugborough at the beginning of the 17th century. It
was here, where never sea wind sang, that young George Anson con-
ceived his passion for an ocean life, and from here that he went to
join his first ship. His immortal expedition, described by his own
pen in one of our sea classics, brought out the magnificent character
of the man, his wisdom and courage, his discipline and humanity.
It was Anson's account of the loss of one of his sailors in a storm
which inspired Cowper's poem on a castaway, in which are the
lines:

> No poet wept him; but the page
> Of narrative sincere,
> That tells his name, his worth, his age,
> Is wet with Anson's tear.

Anson left no family and his barony became extinct, but he was
succeeded in his estate by a nephew, and from him descend the
earls of Lichfield.

George Anson, born here in 1697, developed early the romantic
passion for the sea that had animated Drake and Hawkins and
Raleigh; and from 14 onwards he served as a volunteer, at one time,
as acting lieutenant in the frigate *Hampshire*, being under Peter the
Great, who had been given command of the English ships sent to
the Baltic. Service against the Spaniards took Anson in 1723 to
South Carolina, and his popularity in America is attested by the
fact that Anson County is named after him. He had his first holiday
for 19 years when peace brought him home in 1735.

In 1739 there occurred the war fomented by the story that an
English captain named Robert Jenkins had had his ear cut off by a
Spanish captain at Havana. Into this war plunged Anson, sent in
the *Centurion*, with five other ships to round Cape Horn and harass
the Spanish shipping along the coast of Peru. His ships were in a
deplorable condition. The food was scanty and unwholesome, and
his 2000 men included invalids from hospitals, infirm pensioners,
and men who had never hauled a rope or handled a gun. Such was
the little fleet that staggered out to cross the world. At the mercy of
wind and waves, Anson lost himself, unable to find the longitude of
Selkirk's island, Juan Fernandez, where he wished to recruit his
men and save his sick. His ship had been used in 1736 for the suc-

cessful demonstration of John Harrison's marine timepiece for finding the longitude, but that instrument lay rusting in London while Anson, steering east and west in search of the island, lost 80 precious lives!

Yet Anson continued, until his ships were reduced to the *Centurion*, and his men to 200; capturing Paita and various prizes, and anchoring at the island of Tinian to recoup. There a storm carried his ship away, and Anson was a thousand miles from civilisation with only a little 15-ton prize to save him. For three weeks he laboured to lengthen this craft, and one day the *Centurion* came sailing back to the island, and in her he sailed to China.

He stayed at Macao, repairing for five months, then set sail for Manila, where a Spanish ship hove in sight, a galleon heavy with treasure, which was captured, with 500 prisoners. Anson finally reached England, by way of the Cape of Good Hope, in June 1744, slipping through a French fleet in the fog to do so. His log laconically records the sequel:

July 2. Fresh gales and cloudy; sent away treasure in 32 wagons to London, with 139 *Officers and Seamen to guard it.*

It was a treasure indeed, "1,413,843 pieces of eight, and 35,682 ounces of virgin silver"; over two millions sterling in our currency.

Anson's voyage round the world is the classic of the 18th century, a tremendous feat ranking with Drake's, and to the same end. Honours crowded upon him; he died a rich man at Moor Park, Hertfordshire, and was brought back to his birthplace to be buried in the tomb of his kindred.

Croxall. With a mound near the church to remind us of its Saxon days, it is a little place of great names and great memories, the resting-home of a woman celebrated in song by Byron, and of a man who helped to decide one of the puzzling problems of the literary life of last century.

To the south-west of the village, beyond the River Mease, is Oakley, a three-storeyed farmhouse which 500 years ago was the manor of Sir John Stanley, whose family was to produce the first earl of Derby. Sir John was often the host of Edward IV. Croxall Hall, a fine gabled brick house with spacious windows and tall chimneys, was for generations the home of the Curzons, who are buried in the church, and after them of the earls of Dorset.

The church, standing above the river, south of the hall, and overlooking a wooded dell, has 14th century windows on the south side of the nave, under a blocked arcade, and unusual 15th century windows on the north side. A 15th century tower stands on a base as old as Magna Carta.

In the floor of the 14th century chancel is a remarkable series of tombstones to the Curzons. The oldest shows Thomas and his wife, he in the plate armour and pointed helmet of the Wars of the Roses, she in a long dress and a high-crowned hat. John Horton lies in armour such as was worn by the men who fought at Agincourt; his wife, a Curzon, has a long belted gown, and with them are their six children. George Curzon wears plate armour; his wife has a ruff and a richly brocaded dress.

The figures of William and Elena Shepherd, engraved in 1500, have suffered sadly, and little John Howes, under the tower, wearing his christening robe, has been as harshly treated by time since they laid him here in 1554. The most beautiful thing in the church is the Chantrey monument to Eusebius Horton of Catton Hall (over the border, in Derbyshire), showing her two daughters standing by the grave of their parents, each seeking to soothe the other's grief.

But the monument for which this church is famous is the wall-monument with two little angels above an inscription to Sir Robert Wilmot-Horton and his wife Anne, who survived him 30 years. He is the man who had a leading part in the burning of Byron's Journals, and she it is who "Walks in Beauty like the Night".

Born at Osmaston in Derbyshire, he was a cousin of the poet, his mother being a daughter of the famous Admiral Byron. Lord Byron first saw Lady Wilmot-Horton at a ball wearing a black robe starred with spangles, and her beauty so stirred his imagination that that very night he wrote the famous stanzas *She Walks in Beauty*, which open his series of Hebrew Melodies:

> *She walks in beauty, like the night*
> *Of cloudless climes and starry skies;*
> *And all that's best of dark and bright*
> *Meet in her aspect and her eyes:*
> *Thus mellowed to that tender light*
> *Which heaven to gaudy day denies.*
>
> *One shade the more, one ray the less,*
> *Had half impaired the nameless grace*
> *Which waves in every raven tress,*
> *Or softly lightens o'er her face;*
> *Where thoughts serenely sweet express*
> *How pure, how dear their dwelling-place.*

And on that cheek, and o'er that brow,
So soft, so calm, yet eloquent,
The smiles that win, the tints that glow,
But tell of days in goodness spent,
A mind at peace with all below,
A heart whose love is innocent!

Byron's brief domestic happiness and its tragic sequel centred about the time this poem was written. In that year he married; 12 months later he parted from his wife and infant daughter, never to see them again. In the protracted negotiations which followed Wilmot-Horton had a conspicuous private share. His rôle was delicate, for he was a friend of the unhappy wife and the champion of his cousin, Byron's stepsister, Augusta, to whom the injured wife ascribed much of her unhappiness.

Byron gave Tom Moore the manuscript of his memoirs, to be published after the poet's death. Moore sold them to John Murray for 2000 guineas, on the understanding that they could be redeemed, unpublished, on the repayment of that sum, during Byron's lifetime or within three months of his death. Read by various people of discretion and understanding, the memoirs were declared gross and scandalous, and ruinous to the reputation of persons then living. Wilmot-Horton, acting in the interest of Augusta, was among the most active in staying publication, and was present in Murray's drawing-room when, after a stormy debate, the manuscript was solemnly burnt and Moore refunded the money.

Croxden. It is possible that here, amid the finest monastic ruins in Staffordshire, lies the heart of the worst king England ever had, whose body lies in all the glory of Worcester Cathedral. In a charming valley, with a stream flowing to meet the River Dove, are the beautiful ruins of Croxden Abbey, founded in 1176 for monks of the Cistercian order by a Crusader, Bertram de Verdun, who built Alton Castle and is believed to have been buried in one of three stone coffins which lay behind the high altar.

Lovely in decay, the abbey is in a fair setting. Of the 13th century church there is still standing the fine west front, the walls perhaps 40 feet high. Here are three exceedingly tall lancets above a magnificent doorway with clustered pillars. The high walls of the south transept, and the west front of the chapter house, with a beautiful arch between windows once overlooking the cloisters, all of the 13th century, are still defying wind and rain. There is still something to see of the parlour, where conversation was allowed, the monks' dormitory and the rere-dorter, or latrine, and near by is the 14th century guest house. A road runs through the site of the church, and stones from the abbey are built into the near-by farmhouse. One of the monks was William de Shepesheved or Shepshed, whose 14th century Chronicle of the Abbey is now in the British Museum.

Perhaps some who come to this peaceful spot think of King John, who died in his misery not far off. It has long been said that he was ministered to on his deathbed by the monks of Croxden, though the claim has also been made for the monks of Croxton Abbey in Leicestershire. Is it in the shadow of these venerable stones, we may wonder, that the heart of England's worst king lies humbled in the dust?

Denstone. There is nothing old here, but everything new is beautiful, for Denstone has several times won the award for the best-kept village in Staffordshire. The church, built by G. E. Street in 1862 for Sir Thomas Heywood, has an elaborate font adorned with angels and windows with a series of 20 scenes from the Life of Christ. Denstone College, a public school founded in 1868, has one of the most magnificent views from any school. Its handsome buildings, with a company of firs on a hilltop, look over the glory of the Churnet Valley to the Weaver Hills. There is a fine bronze statue of St George by Alfred Drury, a memorial to the Old Boys of the school who died for peace; and in the great hall is a portrait of Sir Thomas Heywood, whose gifts to the school will long be remembered. The chapel has a Mother's Window from the workshops of Christopher Whall.

Dilhorne. As delightful as anything for miles around is the village, below the edge of the moorland hills a few miles from Cheadle; and very pleasing is its church, with stones bridging the centuries from the 12th to the 19th. The base of the tower is said to be Norman, and it is the only tower in Staffordshire with eight sides. The nave arcades are of the 13th century, the chancel of the 15th century, but the aisles and clerestory were rebuilt in 1810. The altar-table and rails are from Charles I's day, the parish chest here is probably older, and the font has been here since the Normans were building the tower.

Draycott in the Moors. Generations of Draycotts lived at Paynsley Hall, a fine old house south of the River Blythe and reached by a stony road. It was a Draycott who shut the door of the house in the face of the Roundheads, so that they broke in and held it for the Parliament; it was a Draycott who opened the door to the conspirator Anthony Babington. It was an Anthony Draycott who was rector here in Mary Tudor's day and became notorious for his cruelty to Protestants. He suffered persecution in his turn when Elizabeth came to the throne, spending his last years in prison. Here he is said to be buried.

For 700 years Draycotts were worshipping in the hillside church, which was rebuilt in the 19th century, except for the 13th century tower and north chapel. One of them (possibly the founder who may have seen the tower built) lies carved in stone, his cross-legged figure in armour, his sword ready. The upper part of the tower was rebuilt in about 1628.

Engraved in alabaster in the north aisle is the worn portrait of Sir William Draycott, who left money for the poor housekeepers of the village in 1517. On an alabaster tomb in the north chapel is a 17th century figure of Richard Draycott with his son and two daughters, all under arches, and finely preserved are the painted figures of John Draycott of 1600, a knight ready for battle, and his wife, she wearing a closely fitting hat and a ruff. Here also is a handsome alabaster monument to John Fitzherbert, wearing armour and two necklaces, his wife with him in the fashionable dress of Mary Tudor's day, and their 12 children (11 of them daughters) in a row. The church has a Jacobean altar and an oak chest hewn out of a tree trunk. In the churchyard is a yew with a hollow trunk 18 feet round.

Drayton Bassett. Few people know this village, near the Warwickshire border, but everyone has heard of its famous son, who was buried here at the dramatic ending of his great career in the middle of last century. Honoured for all time, and one of the most remarkable of our 19th century statesmen, the nation mourned him as a father. His statue stands in London facing the Parliament in which he served the people nobly, but it is here that he is buried.

A fine beech and other trees are old friends of the church Sir Robert Peel built. The 15th century tower is all that is left of the building where for centuries the Bassetts of Drayton used to come; a powerful Staffordshire family 500 years ago, their lands passed to the Countess of Essex who is said to have been visited here by Elizabeth. The church was built nearly 150 years ago in the days of great prosperity for the Peels, the father being the founder of a cotton factory and a pioneer of modern business methods. He was an able politician, too, and the author of a book on the National Debt and national prosperity. An advocate of reforms which brought about great changes in factory life, he is remembered for giving

London workhouse children a chance to be useful citizens. He died at his house which he built here and has a stone monument in the church. His funeral sermon was preached by a rector who had been here 30 years then and was to preach for nearly another 30 years before his long day was done.

His son, the great Sir Robert, has a marble tablet under a beautiful canopy; and Drayton Bassett is proud to be the shrine of so great a man, statesman, reformer, repealer of the Corn Laws, and great English gentleman. He used to come to this church, and it was on going home from here one Sunday that his father told him the strange story of the child at Fazeley close by, who fell from an attic window of the inn without hurting himself.

Sir Robert Peel's house, Drayton Manor, has gone, pulled down in 1926, but visitors can still enjoy the beautiful gardens Lady Peel loved so well. They are now converted into pleasure-grounds, with two boating lakes, a zoo and many amusements for children. The house was the one Lady Peel loved best of all, and here Sir Robert longed to be with her. In the midst of a busy life which produced a hundred thousand public documents in our archives, he would leave his desk in Downing Street to shop for her or to find her seeds and plants.

He wrote to her one day that he had been all the morning occupied about her cloak, and had had a long consultation about it with the tailor; and he wrote again: "You shall have the packet of seeds; the violet has been watered." At another time, just returned from executing her botanical commission, he wrote: "I found a Stephanotis and a plant which bears a yellow flower and grows over the house. The blue campanula was not so easy to find."

"Home, sweet, home," he wrote again, "I long to be back. I turn away from the fifteen little black teapots I see on the table before me and think of our little round table, my Julia opposite to me, and little Julia and Bobby dividing the biscuits."

He had lived at Drayton since he was 10, and once as he was going to Parliament from his London house he wrote home to his wife, "I cannot mention Drayton without bitterly lamenting that I am away from all I hold dear. I am just going to that wretched place I left last night heartily wishing I might never enter it again." If he could love her more he said, the sight of others and their odious ways would make him do so.

Sir Robert Peel was born near Bury in Lancashire in 1788. His father, a wealthy cotton manufacturer, sent him to Harrow, where Byron was one of his form-fellows, and to Oxford, where he acquitted himself with distinction. Handsome, eloquent, and witty, he was withal incurably shy except with intimates, and Wellington, complaining later of difficulties at Court, lamented, "Peel has no manners and I have no small talk."

Entering Parliament at 21, he was Chief Secretary for Ireland for six years and Home Secretary for five, bringing into existence our Metropolitan Police Force, whose members were called Peelers and Bobbies after him. His new force was received with fierce opposition in some quarters and was actually declared a preliminary to a stroke by which Peel was to set Wellington on the throne!

After long resisting Roman Catholic Emancipation, Sir Robert Peel supported it, so alienating the Old Tories without conciliating the Whigs, and during his first Premiership he was equally opposed to Reform. Prime Minister again from 1841 to 1846, he faced his task with a broad and open mind. "Work," Dean Jackson had urged him, "work like a tiger or like a dragon (if dragons work more and harder than tigers)"; and work he did, 17 hours a day, his family almost strangers to him. He loved his home but saw too little of it. Although he had an able Chancellor of the Exchequer, he himself as Prime Minister introduced two Budgets.

Upon him rested the responsibility for a great reversal of policy in the national interest, the repeal of the Corn Laws, of which he had consistently approved. He saw famine in Ireland, and want and discontent in England, and, holding that his duty to the nation was greater than his duty to his party, he dared to propose repeal and himself introduced the measure abolishing the duties. His party was split asunder, but as he left the House on the night of his resignation in 1846 a silent multitude awaited him, and, with bared heads, escorted him home as the saviour of the country.

During the last year of his administration he was bitterly attacked by Disraeli, in a speech as dishonourable as any ever delivered in Parliament. Peel listened, *with a letter in his pocket from Disraeli begging for office*, and, great gentleman that he was, he kept the secret. But that night he entered his secretary's bedroom and said, "Never destroy a letter; no public man who respects himself should ever destroy a letter." That was all.

His last four years were spent as a private member in support of Liberal Free Trade policy, and his life ended tragically in July 1850. He went out riding on his horse and was thrown, being taken home to die on the day after a speech which John Bright declared to be a speech of peace, "that beautiful, that most solemn speech".

Dudley. It stands with its proud castle on a hill in the Black Country, a town which has thrived for centuries on the riches of the earth. Around it are found all the materials necessary for the great industry of smelting iron—ironstone, limestone, fireclay for lining furnaces, and the thickest seam of coal in the kingdom. For many generations the furnaces of the smelters consumed the forests near by, until in Stuart times a young man found that coal could be used instead. He was Dud Dudley, summoned from an Oxford college to manage his father's ironworks at Pensnett. Today the town of Dudley gives us not only raw iron, but iron and steel manufactures of every kind and size from a nail to a railway bridge.

We cannot wonder at any place losing its beauty amid slagheaps and the waste mounds from mine and furnace; and in winning its industrial reputation Dudley has lost much. But it has not lost its chief treasure and its greatest interest, the ruined castle on a hilltop high above the chimneys. No one can travel hereabouts without being drawn to it, for it is seen all over the Black Country and beyond.

Perhaps there was a fortification here in Saxon times. Certainly it was one of the Conqueror's men who raised these earthworks which have been the foundation of the castle ever since, for they come into Domesday Book. What buildings the Normans had here we do not know, but the inner walls of the great gatehouse are theirs, as is the motte or mound supporting the massive Keep, and a Norman arch is still visible in one of the walls of the buttery.

The castle has a great courtyard reached only by passing through three gatehouses, the last of which has a barbican or outer work. The courtyard is bounded by a 14th century curtain wall sometimes eight feet thick, with a long line of ruined buildings running about halfway round the wall. Starting from the battlemented keep, with its massive drum towers, we pass in succession the 17th century stable block, the impressive inner gatehouse, the 14th century chapel with its big yawning window and its vaulted cellar, the remains of the Great Chamber, just as old, and the Tudor hall with its gaunt mullioned windows. Next come the buttery, with a beautiful two-storeyed bow window, and the shell of a building with two great gables which once included the kitchen and some of the bedrooms. Bringing this long line to an end are two more buildings which would be chiefly used by the servants, the first with a tall staircase turret, and the second yet another gatehouse that has lost its gables.

The keep is chiefly of the 14th century, and is not only a fine stronghold, but a wonderful viewpoint from which we can look into seven English counties and even into Wales. On the ruined walls are two Russian guns captured at Sebastopol. The great gatehouse was also raised upon its Norman core by 14th century hands; and so immensely strong had it become a few decades later that the enemy who sought entrance here was confronted once by a drawbridge, twice by a portcullis, and three times by great doors.

During its 800 years the castle has seen more than one great family come and go. From the end of the 12th century to the beginning of the 14th it belonged to the De Somerys, one of whom, Sir John, built the curtain wall, finished the gatehouse, and began the keep. He seems to have ruled the neighbourhood in what we may call gangster fashion, extorting money and labour from everyone in exchange for the protection he could give. After the De Somerys came the De Suttons, who built the chapel and added the barbican to the gatehouse; and then, generations later, came their descendant John Dudley, son of that Dudley who appears unpleasantly in our history books among the unscrupulous agents of Henry VII.

To this John Dudley, who became Duke of Northumberland, we owe much of the charm the castle has, for it was he who refashioned all the domestic buildings in the Tudor style, employing as architect Sir William Sharington who had made himself a fine house out of Lacock Abbey in Wiltshire. They are very remarkable buildings for their time, simply and finely made, the forerunners of the splendid country houses of the Elizabethan Age. How many of his days the Duke spent here we do not know, for he was prominent in the country's affairs in those short years of Edward VI. He strove to set on the throne Lady Jane Grey, his daughter-in-law; and the reign of Mary Tudor saw him executed at the Tower, where he is buried with Anne Boleyn and Catherine Howard.

Not many years after his death Queen Elizabeth came this way in all her majesty, a special withdrawing-room being set aside in her honour. The Civil War saw the end of the castle as a fortress, but the beautiful domestic buildings were hardly touched until they were brought to ruin in the 18th century by a terrible fire which raged for three days. It is said that red-hot lead from the roof streamed down the hillside, setting fire to the long grass and terrifying the town.

The outer grounds of the castle, the upper part of which can be reached by a chair-lift, are now occupied by Dudley Zoo, with a fine collection of animals (elephants, lions, tigers, bears, giraffes, apes, and so on), of reptiles, and of flamingoes and other interesting birds. Far down beneath the castle are the strange limestone caves where for many years the solid rock was quarried and carried away by water.

The Town Hall, in Priory Street, is a fine building of brick and stone opened in 1928, when its entrance hall was consecrated as a war memorial. The Council House, near by in Priory Road, was built in 1935 by W. A. Harvey and H. G. Wicks. The Museum and Art Gallery, in St James's Road, behind, has a collection of paintings and a fine new gallery illustrating the geology of the district. This includes maps and diagrams of Wren's Nest, an outcrop of the Wenlock limestone north-west of Dudley, created a geological nature reserve in 1956.

The churches have not the attraction which great age brings, yet there are things to see in several of them. St Edmund's, built in 1724, has on its walls marble portraits of a magistrate and of a surgeon who was 65 years in the town. The Roman Catholic church, built in 1842 by A. W. N. Pugin, has a brass portrait of a 19th century priest in his robes. St John's, at Kates Hill, built in 1840, has a wonderful view of the castle and a marble font in memory of one who was vicar for 62 years. And St Thomas's, built in 1818 by William Brooks in a Regency Gothic style, with a spire rising 175 ft., has an elaborate font, a mass of fine carving with Biblical scenes, rich canopies, and angel figures. The cover is fashioned as a tower and spire, and has eight tiny figures under canopies.

But if Dudley has lost all its ancient churches it has still the ruins of one of them, in a park below the castle on the west. Here after some 700 years are still standing some walls of the church belonging to a Cluniac priory founded in the 12th century. The walls have seen strange sights since the monks left them, for during the last century a tanner was living and working in what had been a sacred place. He was followed by a thread manufacturer, and later by people who ground glass, polished fire-irons, and made fenders.

The priory had its connections with the men who were lords of Dudley. Here in 1273 they laid Roger de Somery who owned the castle and obtained the king's permission to fortify it. And here about 200 years later they laid one of the greatest of the long line of Suttons, the sixth Lord Dudley, who was celebrated as a statesman and who saw, at the end of his long life, the opening years of the Tudor Age. He was the grandson of Sir Walter Blount, who comes into Shakespeare with Falstaff and Hotspur, and before he was 28 they had made him Lord Lieutenant of Ireland.

Through all the troubled Wars of the Roses he lived, and in his will we get an interesting glimpse of the funeral ceremony of a rich man in those days. Here at the priory 24 new torches were to be lighted during the service. Every priest was to have fourpence and every singing-man threepence, and as soon as he was buried a thousand masses were to be said for his soul at a cost of £16 13s 4d. His "goodly monument", which was to cost £20, was eventually taken away from the priory and lay for many years in an older St Edmund's church.

This great town of iron has every reason to remember those two 17th century ironmasters, Dud Dudley and Abraham Darby. Their lives overlap, their work was related, but each toiled independently of the other and took his secret to the grave. Dudley was one of the 11 illegitimate children of the fifth earl of Dudley, who sent him to Oxford and in 1619, when he was 20, recalled him to take charge of his ironworks here.

In the midst of abundant coal Dudley, in common with the rest of the industry, was using charcoal to smelt iron. Our forests were vanishing so quickly that the bulk of our iron was imported from Spain and Sweden. Dud Dudley succeeded in using coal for smelting, first coking his fuel, it is believed. At Pensnett, at Cradley, and elsewhere he met with great success; but floods destroyed some of his works, rioters ruined others, charcoal-using rivals persecuted him with lawsuits, slanders, and injuries, and then came the Civil War.

Dudley followed the fortunes of Charles I, fought in many battles, fortified cities, cast iron artillery, was captured, sentenced to death, escaped on crutches, and then, penniless and broken, secured support and cautiously resumed his work as an ironmaster. With the Restoration he failed to regain the patents granted earlier to him, but, poor and slighted, went to his grave in 1684 with the knowledge that he alone possessed the secret which could make his country supreme in iron-producing.

Abraham Darby was born in 1677 at Wren's Nest, a Quaker farmer's son, and was put to kiln-building. With Dudley dead and his secret lost, the country was still burning wood for iron-smelting and importing its ore from abroad, together with the iron pots and pans used for cooking in palace and hovel. Darby made fruitless experiments in iron pot-casting, then went to Holland, source of our supplies, and learned the Dutch method.

Returning, accompanied by skilled Dutch workmen, he established a flourishing foundry, first at Bristol and later at Coalbrookdale in Shropshire. At first he used only charcoal, but later he coked the best available coal, improved the draught of his furnaces, and succeeded beyond all hope in producing pig-iron in unprecedented quantities, and converting it into excellent pots, pans, kettles, door-frames, weights, pestles and mortars, and a wide range of implements for farm and industry.

73

He died in 1717 at Madeley Court, leaving a great business to the care of the ignorant guardians of his two little sons. Disaster followed and the founder's son, the second Abraham Darby, had practically to re-discover his father's methods. His son, the third Abraham Darby, carried the work to triumphs unimaginable to the originator, for, taking control in 1758, when only 18, within a year he constructed the first iron bridge ever erected, spanning the Severn at Ironbridge, near Coalbrookdale. He died in 1791, leaving an England that no more burnt her forests for the smelting of iron.

Eccleshall. For centuries the home of the Bishops of Lichfield, five of whom are buried in the church, this small town has an old market but is three miles from the nearest station. The bishop's fortress-palace is only a remnant, but its church remains one of the glories of the county, with Saxon and Norman speaking from its stones, but with nothing to show that during the Civil War it was a Commonwealth stronghold.

The town has seen a sad day in the life of one of our queens. Here in 1459 came Margaret of Anjou, consort of the hapless Henry VI, fleeing from the stricken field at Blore Heath, where the second battle of the Wars of the Roses had resulted in the capture of the king. With her was their only child, the little Prince of Wales, who was to live to be murdered by Richard of Gloucester after the battle of Tewkesbury.

The Bishops of Lichfield, who are said to have lived here from the time of the Saxons, had their manor house on the site where Bishop Walter Langton built the castle, a mighty structure whose wide moat, now a garden, is still crossed after 700 years by his beautiful two-arched bridges.

Round the castle and the church centred the life of the town until the Civil War came. Bishop Wright garrisoned the castle for Charles I, and died after having withstood a siege; the Parliamentary forces made the church their fort, without damaging it. Towards the end of 1643 the Cavaliers gained the town and shut up the Commonwealth men in the church, but hot on their heels came Parliament men from Stafford who captured the Stuart reinforcements and ultimately the castle itself. The old episcopal fortress was dismantled, but late in the 17th century it was restored as a fine house which continued to be the home of the bishops until last century, when it was dismantled.

The magnificent clerestoried church, reached through a modern lychgate, stands as a record of the ages. In the flower-bordered churchyard, under a granite cross, is buried John Lonsdale, a much-loved Bishop of Lichfield for more than a quarter of the 19th century. The stones of the south wall of the chancel are grooved by the metal tips of arrows sharpened on them by men who helped to make the bowmen of England the military lords of mediaeval Europe.

The great 15th century tower, nearly 100 feet high, rises above the west end of the nave, where it is supported by three beautifully moulded arches on clustered pillars. It stands on a 13th century base. Under the tower is some Norman moulding, but the oldest treasures are the carved Saxon stones in the tower, in the south arcade, and, finest of all, in the 13th century vestry, where a stone shows two men, one thought to be an archbishop and the other St Chad, in the act of mounting the horse on which he rode 1300 years ago. Much 13th century work remains in the church, including the chancel and the nave arcades, with floral capitals, and other parts are of the 15th century.

The monuments include those of five Bishops of Lichfield; the weathered figure brought in from the churchyard may be a sixth. The earliest is the 16th century tomb in the south-west chapel with the engraved figure (half of it is missing) of Richard Sampson. Chaplain to Wolsey, friend of Erasmus, lawyer, ambassador, he earned the dubious distinction of standing high in the favour of Henry VIII by assisting him in the divorce from Catherine, and in the proceedings which sent Anne Boleyn to execution.

A finer character is recalled by the engraved figure on the tomb of Thomas Bentham in the north-west chapel, lying in his robes as he was known in the years just before the Armada. His figure is repeated on the side of the tomb, with his wife and four children. A great scholar, ejected by Mary Tudor from his fellowship at Oxford, he fled to Switzerland, but returned and bravely sustained the London Protestants throughout the days of their persecution. With his two wives in tight hats and long robes, kneeling under arches in the wall above him, lies William Overston, in his bishop's robes, his head on a Bible. He was bishop during the Armada, and at the death of Queen Elizabeth I had to encounter stubborn opposition to the reformed doctrine.

The next bishop, after the weathered stone figure under the tower who may be Bishop Wright, was laid here after two centuries; he was James Bowerstead, who died in 1843, and his alabaster figure lies in the chancel under a Gothic canopy, wearing his mitre, and with his crozier in his hand. The last of the group, John Lonsdale, whose monument is in the churchyard, was one of the noblest of the line, a model of learning, humility, and tolerant commonsense. He ordained in this church 646 clergy and 567 deacons, and ended his long life dramatically in the midst of his work. As an old man of 78 he presided at a diocesan gathering and died in his chair immediately after.

At Slindon, two miles away to the north, is a delightful little red stone church of 1893, with a figure of St Chad in a niche over the south door, charming vaulted stone roofs over the chancel and below the crossing tower, and an alabaster reredos with a carving of the Last Supper.

Elford. It is a little casket of wonder, splendour, and history. Though Elford Hall, built on the site of the house in which Henry VII slept the night before Bosworth Field has gone, the monuments of those who lived here, the Stanleys, the Smythes, and the Howards, are in the church.

The village, a storied gem of the beautiful Tame valley, has charming old red-brick and whitewashed timber-framed cottages with roses rioting over porches, and a splendid avenue of limes, a living aisle, leading to the church door.

The church has a tower of 1598, but the rest of the building was made new last century. Within it is a gallery of mediaeval glory, superb sculptures wonderful in beauty and eloquent with history. Magnificent examples of mediaeval carving, they were faithfully restored in 1849 by the skilled hand of Edward Richardson.

The 19th century work forms a worthy setting for this rich heritage. Under a fine oak canopy the font has eight angel heads. The pulpit has panels showing the Crucifixion, Christ walking on the sea, and Christ entering the Temple. A delightful feature is the carving on a chancel capital. During the restoration the architect found that a swallow had realised the words of the Psalmist and near the altar had "made her nest where she might lay her young"; and in this charming picture in stone a mason has perpetuated the incident, showing the bird alighting on the nest, where with open beaks the young ones await her.

There are two brasses to rectors in the chancel: one (in the floor) a portrait of John Hille, dressed in the long cloak he wore in 1621, and a tablet to Francis Paget's 47 years last century. Old Flemish glass in an aisle window has Joseph with his staff and a Madonna kneeling before a bishop. In a modern window under the tower kneel Matilda Camville, Matilda Vernon, Matilda de Arderne, Cicely de Arderne, and, in their tabards and cloaks, Sir Richard Stafford and Sir Thomas Stanley, names linking us with the past.

The famous monuments are themselves milestones. The earliest is the alabaster tomb on which lie the effigies of Sir Thomas Arderne, who fought at Poitiers and died about 1400, and his wife Matilda. He wears plate armour and has on the front of his helmet the words Jesu Maria. The sword in his hand is richly chased, and his gauntlet has a diamond pattern. Like his wife he wears the SS collar of the Lancastrians. She has a Plantagenet bonnet, a cloak, and a flowing robe, and her hand is clasped in his. At the sides of the tomb are 22 small statues, 12 shield-bearing angels and 10 mourning kindred.

On another tomb lies the magnificent alabaster figure of Sir John Stanley, who died in 1474. The statue, 15th century sculpture at its best, shows him in armour, his head resting on a helmet with the crest embodying the Stanley legend of a child saved by an eagle; every link of his sword-chain perfect, a tiny face clear and winsome on its buckle, and the border of his tunic is richly adorned. It was his brother who was gaoler of Good Duke Humphrey's wife, accused of attempting the life of Henry VI by witchcraft; it was he who by tradition at Bosworth, with a diadem picked from a thorn bush, crowned Henry VII on the battlefield, the beginning of the dazzling Tudor dynasty.

Perhaps the most appealing of all these splendid works is the effigy of Sir John's little grandson, a curly-headed boy of about 1460 in a long robe, holding a ball in one hand and pointing with the other to his temple, where he was fatally struck by the ball when playing tennis. Latest of the monuments is the alabaster tomb of Sir William Smythe, who died in 1525. He lies in armour between two wives in flowing gowns. The first, wearing a three-cornered hat, was Annie Staunton, daughter and heiress of Margery Stanley, sister of the little boy killed at play. The second, in her coronet, was Lady Isabella Neville, niece of the earl of Warwick, the King-maker.

It was a tremendous chapter of history that closed in the grave with the Lady Isabella. Reared in the home of one of our proudest nobles, she shared the wildest vicissitudes of fortune; her father and the Kingmaker fell at Barnet, and their bodies were exposed for two days at St Paul's Cathedral, to convince the country that the formidable brothers were really dead. Then the proud lady we see here was beggared by the confiscation of her father's estates, and her eldest brother, the heir, because of the poverty to which the family was thus reduced, was degraded from his rank, being declared incapable of supporting his title. Few women have known such crushing sorrows and reverses as she who lies here serene in her coronet.

Ellastone. Immortalised in literature, it is a delightful village with houses looking into Derbyshire across the River Dove, and the Weaver Hills rising behind them to over 1200 feet.

It is of "George Eliot" (Mary Ann Evans) that we think here, for she loved this place and made it the scene of many of the incidents in *Adam Bede*. This village was her Hayslope, Loamshire was Staffordshire, and what she called Eagledale was the romantic Dovedale, not far away, with all its charm of cliff and wood. The village inn she wrote about is here still (though now an antique shop) and Donnithorne Chase was perhaps Calwich Abbey or Wootton Lodge, a mile and a half away.

George Eliot's father, Robert Evans, who spent his early life here, was the Adam she portrayed so vividly; her uncle Samuel was the original of Seth Bede, and Samuel's wife gave the novelist the idea of the story when recounting an incident in her career as an Evangelical preacher. Her grandfather's house remains, and though the famous workshop where her father was a carpenter has suffered an unhappy change there is something to recall the early chapters of *Adam Bede*. Samuel Evans's house has been much rebuilt, but Ellastone is a place for George Eliot's readers to wander in, its folk still much as she portrayed them, and a score of its houses the very picture of the one in which Mrs Poyser lived. In the churchyard we find her grandfather's tombstone.

The church in company with three fine yews has a tower of 1586 and a chancel finished two years later in Armada year; the rest was rebuilt in the 19th century. In the chancel is a medallion portrait of the Rev. Walter Davenport Bromley, a friend of the poor last century, whose ancestor let Wootton Hall to Rousseau for a year; and in the north chapel are a stone to Bernard Granville of Calwich Abbey, the only neighbour Rousseau made friends with, and a tomb with the broken figures of John Fleetwood and his wife, who first turned the abbey into a home 400 years ago. Both have lost their hands and faces and feet, and the knight's legs have gone, but he still has his armour and a weapon each side of him, and round his tomb are the family shields-of-arms. John died in 1590 and is not buried here, but his son Thomas built this memorial tomb and was himself buried under it.

The story of Calwich Abbey begins in Norman England when an Augustinian monastery was founded here beside the River Dove. We can trace the old fishponds, and here is a yew they may have planted, but the monks themselves were driven out in 1530, and

John Fleetwood converted their abbey into a home and set an antiquarian writing:

Calwich being a cell or house of religion, now a Lancashire gentleman is owner thereof, who, as I have heard, hath made a parlour of the chancel, a hall of the church, and a kitchen of the steeple.

In 1603 Richard Fleetwood was reigning at Calwich, and in the Ellastone church register we read of his marriage to a girl of six, whose first child was born and buried here before she was 13. A few years later James I sold Richard a baronetcy in return for money for soldiers in Ulster, and Sir Richard, now turned Roman Catholic, decided that Calwich was too small, and had built for him the stately Wootton Lodge, still one of the finest houses in the county.

His son Thomas remained quietly at Calwich through the Civil War, though the rest of the family got into trouble by fighting for the king, and thus he was allowed to keep the third of his estate which had not already been forfeited because of his religion. But the early 18th century saw the last of the Fleetwoods of Calwich, and Bernard Granville arrived, pulled down the old monastery house, and built himself a new one by the stream, which he broadened into a lake.

A morose bachelor, he planted trees and added to his house and garden till Calwich was known as the prettiest place in Staffordshire, and in spite of his taciturn temper, which became more extreme the older he grew, many were the famous guests who visited him here. Handel came often, and played on the organ he designed for his friend, to whom he gave a manuscript copy of his works in 38 volumes.

Then, in 1766, came Jean-Jacques Rousseau, to spend a haunted year at Wootton Hall near by, and to make friends with the only neighbour who could speak French with him. When Mr Granville closed his country house for the winter Rousseau so missed his friend that he filled the time by writing his immortal *Confessions*. As for the grumpy old bachelor, he missed the Frenchman equally when, crazed with fear of imaginary persecution and treachery, Rousseau fled back to France.

But there was one woman who was glad to see the last of Rousseau, and she was Mr Granville's sister, the matchless Mrs Delany, for she eyed with alarm Rousseau's gallantry to her favourite niece Mary Dewes, and the girl's obvious pride in the attentions of the great man, and certainly Rousseau's letters addressing her as the beautiful shepherdess of Calwich were a change from her Uncle Bernard's, which began *Dear Madam* and ended *Your most faithful humble servant*!

Mrs Delany loved Calwich, where she spent whole summers even after her marriage to the Irish don which so offended her brother. She chats about the house in letters which we may read today, as we may also see in the British Museum the wonderful collection of paper flowers which this great dame of the 18th century started to cut out when she was 74.

More glowing accounts of the house were written by Anna Seward, who came here when the bachelor's nephew had inherited Calwich. But in the 19th century it passed out of the hands of the Granvilles, and down came the house which had known the inimitable Mrs Delany and her devoted Irish husband, the immortal Handel (his gruffiness softened here), and Rousseau with his furtive restless eyes.

Endon. It is the village of a man who claimed to have danced more days than most of us, and famous for its ceremony (unique in Staffordshire) of dressing the well on the Spring Bank Holiday week-end, when the ceremony begins on the Saturday (at 2 p.m.) with a service in the church, after which a procession is made to the well and the new well-dressing "queen" is crowned.

The church, high up with miles of beautiful country to see from its churchyard, is mostly of the 19th century, but has an earlier tower. It has also a fine east window of 1893 by Burne-Jones, glowing with colour showing Mary Magdalene, Christ holding the world, and St John. The churchyard is the resting-place of old Will Willett, who enjoyed his hour of fame for having (as he said) danced for 12 days and nights in 1752. The truth was that his dancing began on the evening of September 2, when England altered the calendar and dropped 11 days, and ended on the morning of the next day, September 14.

Enville. Looking out over village roofs the 19th century tower of Enville is built in the style of Somerset's famous towers, attracting us up the hill to the old and beautiful things in the church. Oldest of all are two fragments of Saxon work in the wall, a bishop in a niche and a figure standing on a grotesque head. This figure is holding a type of fan used in the Eastern Church.

The bold arcades of the nave are Norman, and the rest of the church was rebuilt in the 14th century. Some fine carving is seen on the four old misericords in the chancel. One has musicians, another a scene of bear-baiting, another a horseman caught in a falling portcullis, and the other a man and woman praying with beads and a book. The arm-rests are carved with faces and animals. Oak panels in the 19th century reredos are inlaid with woods mentioned in the Bible.

The carved figure in the chancel is of Roger de Birmingham, a 14th century priest who rebuilt it, and when the church was restored last century and his tomb was opened, they found his skeleton with some traces of his vestments and a cup and paten. Still here after nearly four centuries are the alabaster figures of Thomas and Anne Grey and 13 children, he with his long pointed beard and she with her pet dog pulling at her skirt. In a window above them (in the south aisle) are some figures in mediaeval glass: the Virgin, St John the Baptist, St Michael with the Dragon, and St James.

Two other memorials will interest the traveller in Enville. One is to Thomas Amphlett of 1763, a young merchant in the East India Company, who was barbarously massacred in "the confusion of the times"; the other is a tablet to William Wrighte, who died two years later, the youngest son of that Sir Nathan Wrighte who was Lord Keeper of the Great Seal of England. Three stone coffin lids are lying in the churchyard, and part of the mediaeval cross still stands, with the flat, raised tomb of Peter Lafargue, a Huguenot refugee of 1711, close to it.

To the south of the church is Enville Hall, a 19th century Gothic house in lovely grounds designed by the poet Shenstone, whose brother was married at Enville. A mile or so away to the northeast is Highgate Common, part of the largest unenclosed stretch of land in Staffordshire after Cannock Chase, and a splendid vista of heather and bracken in summer. By the roadside at Highgate Farm is a superb giant of old England, a spanish chestnut about 26 feet round.

Etruria. It is in the heart of the Potteries, between Hanley and Newcastle-under-Lyme, a gloomy and somewhat sinister world of chimneys and spoil heaps, but it is the birthplace of much that is beautiful, and the Sovereign of England is lord of the manor.

Here in 1766 Josiah Wedgwood founded the famous pottery works still carried on by his descendants at Barlaston, where they moved in 1940. Here England's master potter built a village for his workmen and gave it an Italian name under a mistaken impression that a famous classical vase he admired and imitated was Etruscan. Here Wedgwood built up his business and made his name a byword for excellence throughout the world. Here he made his wonderful reproductions of the Portland Vase, one of the great Roman treasures of the British Museum. Here he perfected the processes which, combined with his excellent taste and technical skill, were to make his pottery the finest in the land.

Etruria Hall, built in 1770, where Wedgwood lived nearly a quarter of a century, happy in his work and in his friends, is still standing, although it is now the offices of a mining company. It saw the passing of the great Josiah in 1795 and the birth of his famous son Thomas, who has been called the first photographer, chiefly remembered for his discovery of the use of light for making pictures. But he is also remembered as a generous friend of genius, and generous were the tributes which genius paid to him. Sydney Smith knew of no man who appeared to make such an impression on his friends, and to Wordsworth he gave "an impression of sublimity". Thomas Campbell spoke of him as "a strange and wonderful being full of goodness". He died a few months before Trafalgar, and we come upon him at his grave in the old church of Tarrant Gunville in Dorset.

Farewell. We greet this quiet hamlet with delight and bid it farewell with regret. Its name means the fair or clear spring, and an enchanting scene it is, with a sparkling stream hurrying to the green meadows past the little church among the trees. The church, descendant of a Benedictine priory founded by a 12th century Bishop of Lichfield, was transformed in brick in about 1747, but has kept its 700-year-old chancel, the old altar-rails, and four 13th century oak stalls. The reredos has a painting of the Crucifixion in memory of a daughter of Henry Binfield, vicar of this fair farming community for 40 years. The splendid Hall, on the hill above, is of the early 18th century and has an oak staircase and grand oak panelling.

Fazeley. An industrial village on the eternally busy Watling Street, it has a church built by Sir Robert Peel, the great industrial pioneer who, in dedicating his famous son to the service of his country, gave his own name immortality. The church, in the early Gothic style, has an east window of three lancets with figures of Paul and the Evangelists in memory of Cyprian Thompson, vicar for half of last century.

It was here one winter's day in 1825 that a child of three, leaning from the attic window of the village inn, fell to the pavement but was hardly hurt. On hearing of it Sir Robert Peel, the Prime Minister, was greatly interested and related the story in a letter to his wife.

Fenton. The city of Stoke-on-Trent has swallowed up its streets, but not its fame. One of the busy pottery centres, it is also noted as the birthplace of Whieldon ware, the beautifully coloured and glazed pottery fashioned here in the 18th century by Thomas Whieldon, master of Josiah Spode. In addition to its numerous china and earthenware factories, Fenton has engineering works, collieries, and chemical works.

This home of skilled craftsmen was also the birthplace of an artist who has been called the greatest of the idyllic painters of England. George Heming Mason, son of a master potter, was born here in 1818. At 25 he set out on a Continental tour with his brother Miles, eventually settling in Rome and taking a studio. A change in the family fortunes forced him to seek a career with his brush and he managed to eke out a frugal existence at portraits.

When the Italian war broke out his brother Miles joined Garibaldi's army and he himself helped to nurse the wounded, narrowly escaping being shot as a spy during the siege of Rome. However, better times were in store and Mason rapidly became a successful artist. In 1858 he came back to England, married, and went to live at Wetley Abbey. His first painting after his return was the *Wind on the Wold*, once in the possession of his great friend Lord Leighton and now in the Tate Gallery. Henceforth the Staffordshire countryside was to be his inspiration, and the genius that had blossomed under blue Italian skies was to flower in the grey but softer air of his native land.

Flash. This small and remote village, in an exposed position and often cut off by snow-drifts in winter, is the highest in England, standing at 1525 feet on the edge of the moors extending south from Axe Edge, in Derbyshire, and looking out over the head reaches of the Dove and the Manifold. Its plain church, founded in 1744, was rebuilt in 1901. Across the hills to the north-west, and reached by a moorland track, are the Three Shire Heads, where a bridge crosses the Dane at the point where Staffordshire, Derbyshire, and Cheshire meet.

The village gave its name to the term "flash", meaning counterfeit money. In the last century the Three Shires Bridge was a haunt of coiners and other law-breakers, and as the police in any county could only act within the county boundaries, the crooks could easily escape capture merely by crossing the bridge into the next county.

Forton. This secluded village is near the Shropshire border, nestling below a hill crowned by an old cone-shaped building called the Monument. The church has a 14th century chancel and a sturdy 15th century tower joined by a nave and arcade rebuilt in 1723, when, however, the 14th century north aisle was retained. There is a fine tomb with alabaster figures of Sir Thomas Skrymsher, lord of the manor, who lived at the Hall, rebuilt in brick in 1665, near by, and his lady. The knight is in armour, his head on a helmet, she is in a loose gown, and their nine children are with them. He is said to be descended from one of the Magna Carta barons.

There is a brass inscription to Mark Whitmore, who sang in the choir for 68 years. All through the Crimean War, the South African War, and the First World War he was singing here. A window with the Adoration of the Kings pays tribute to Sir George Boughey, who preached here for 45 years in Mark Whitmore's time.

The churchyard has an ancient yew 17 feet round, and a glorious view over a branch of the Shropshire Union Canal, with a stream winding its way through the fields towards Aqualate Mere and the deer park of Aqualate Hall. The Mere, over a mile long and 700 yards wide, is the county's biggest lake, a jewel of shining silver with an emerald setting where the herons nest.

Gailey. It has given its name to three reservoirs, the Gailey Pools, which serve the Staffordshire and Worcestershire Canal. As lovely as natural lakes with their fringe of rushes and trees, they are the haunt of many water-birds, but their shores are now noisy with motor traffic, for here the modern motorway (the M6) crosses the A5, following the Roman Watling Street. By another cross-roads is the small 19th century church, with a carved oak pulpit and a brass tablet to Mary Elcock, a nurse for 50 years.

But it is a doctor we remember here, for at Kinvaston close by Robert James, a famous 18th century physician, was born. At Lichfield he was a schoolfellow of Dr Johnson, who was to praise his skill in ungrudging terms. "I enjoyed many cheerful and instructive hours (he said) with companions such as are not often found—with one who has lengthened and one who has gladdened life: with Dr James whose skill in physik will be remembered, and with David Garrick."

Dr James is best known as the inventor of a powder famous in its day for the treatment of fevers. Oliver Goldsmith took some during the attack of fever from which he died, a fever which Dr Johnson thought was really increased by financial worry. Poor Goldsmith's apothecary believed the powder aggravated his condition and a bitter controversy ensued. It did not, however, dim the popularity of Dr James, and the powder was given to George III in his pathetic mental collapse long afterwards.

Gayton. This small and tranquil village, near the Trent valley, has an old church rather badly treated by the 18th century builders, who gave it an ineffectual brick tower and built a wall into the north arcade. The chancel was added in the 19th century, but the church has kept its fine Norman chancel arch, with zigzag ornament, and a 13th century arcade; the plain font is also Norman. In the nave are some old patterned tiles and in the chancel is a battered figure of a 600-year-old lady.

In the churchyard are many yews, one perhaps 300 years old.

Gentleshaw. It stands high up on the commons of Cannock Chase, 700 feet above sea-level, with widespreading views east to the spires of Lichfield and the Trent Valley, south to the Clent Hills beyond the Black Country, and south-west towards the Clee Hills and the Welsh border. The church, built in 1837 and extended eastward in 1901, has an oak reredos with stone panels of the Crucifixion, the Annunciation, and the Resurrection.

Beaudesert Hall, which once proudly looked through the trees in a hollow of its great park, was formerly a palace of the bishops of Lichfield, but had been for many centuries the home of the Pagets. It was dismantled in 1935, except for the library, with its tall Tudor chimneys, and part of the estate is now a permanent camping ground for Scouts and Guides.

Near one of the park entrances, on the edge of Cannock Chase, is a hill of over 800 feet crowned by a great earthwork called Castle Ring, one of the most striking Iron Age hill forts in England, with a glorious view said to extend into 11 counties.

Gnosall. This large village has a collegiate church which after 800 years of change is still one of the finest in Staffordshire, a stately building with much that is massive and a little that is delicately beautiful, all the grandeur given it by the Normans, and grace added in the 13th and 15th centuries. Norman masons built its oldest walls and the four arches of the central tower. There is Norman work in the transepts, with a fine triforium and two arches on the south side. The west end and the nave arcades are of the 13th century, a transept door is of the 14th, and the clerestory is of the 15th century. The 14th century flowing tracery of the east window contains fine glass of 1918 forming a war memorial.

The central tower is of the 15th century above its Norman arches, and was perhaps built by the men who raised the south chapel and its arcade to the chancel. In this noble place are the monuments of a child and a soldier, the child's in a recess of the chancel, the

G

knight, in the south chapel, dressed in crusading mail, his head on a pillow, his feet on a lion. The church has an old dug-out chest, with three locks, and a modern font made from a block of alabaster.

A grand old servant of the church was John Till, whose name is in enduring brass. He preached here for the first time in 1845, and was still preaching here when the 20th century came.

Great Barr. Its church was rebuilt in 1677 and much restored, in the early 14th century Gothic style, about a hundred years ago. In the south chapel is a painting of the Virgin and Child, sombre yet appealing, by Alessio Baldovinetti, an Italian artist of the 15th century who was skilful also at mosaic work. He invented a new way of mixing colours but it was not a success, and some of his pictures have come down to us in bad preservation.

Over a mile north-east of the church is Barr Beacon, perhaps the proudest possession of this little place, for it is the Staffordshire and Warwickshire war memorial and belongs to the public. Rising to over 700 feet, it is a glorious stretch of windy ridge, capped by beeches and a lookout platform with a toposcope. Here we can stand while our eyes range over England from Lichfield Cathedral and Sutton Park to Dudley Castle and from the Lickey and the Clent Hills to Cannock Chase and to the Wrekin in Shropshire.

Great Haywood. This attractive village, now avoided by the main road through the Trent valley, has old houses in its winding main street, but its chief sight is Essex Bridge, built over the Trent by the 17th century earls of Essex as a short cut to Cannock Chase. It is low and narrow, with grey walls and recesses over the buttresses, safety-zones for humble folk who might be crossing when the noble lords came riding by. Years ago the bridge had 40 arches; today there are only 14, but it is still the longest pack-horse bridge in England.

On the other side of the river is the beautiful park of Shugborough, on the site of a palace of the Bishops of Lichfield, and the seat since 1624 of the Anson family, later earls of Lichfield. This graceful and charming house was begun in 1693 (the centre block is of this time), but it was greatly extended by wings on the north and south sides built about 1748 for Thomas Anson, who had succeeded to the property in 1720. He was a founder member of the Society of Dilettanti, established for the encouragement of Greek classical art, and the elder brother of Admiral Lord George Anson, who was born here in 1697, sailed round the world, and came home to be buried in the neighbouring church of Colwich. The house was altered in the Regency style after 1790 by Samuel Wyatt for the first viscount Anson, who was succeeded in 1818 by his son, created the first earl of Lichfield. On the death of the fourth earl, in 1960, the property was offered to the Treasury, in lieu of death duties, and transferred to the National Trust, though the fifth earl continues to live in part of the house.

The house contains fine portraits by Reynolds, including one of Admiral Lord Anson, and by other English masters, as well as beautiful 18th century English and French furniture, much of it collected by the second Lord Lichfield. The 18th century stable-block now houses the Staffordshire County Museum, a fascinating collection illustrating many aspects of the county's domestic and social life, history, and industry. The rooms include a brew-house, an old laundry, and an agricultural gallery, and here too are the 18th century travelling coach used by the earls of Lichfield and the state coach of the earl of Shrewsbury, made in 1887.

In the park enclosing the house are some interesting garden buildings, among them a Chinese House designed by an officer of Lord Anson and built about 1747, but most noticeable are the four large monuments by James "Athenian" Stuart, based on drawings made by him at Athens. These include a triumphal arch, copied from the Arch of Hadrian and commemorating Admiral Lord Anson and his wife, of whom there are busts by Peter Scheemakers.

Grindon. This isolated village stands high up in the moorland country, among the lonely hills and friendly valleys, above the deep-set valley of the River Hamps, much of which is in the keeping of the National Trust. Its church of 1831, sometimes called the "Cathedral of the Moors", stands at a height of 1050 feet, with a distinctive spire soaring far above the sycamores bordering the churchyard. It has amusing gargoyles, a font adorned with roses and tracery, and angels bearing up the chancel roof. Relics of the previous church are two coffins and a battered Norman font, under the tower. A memorial in the church commemorates those who lost their lives in 1947, when an aircraft crashed on the moors while bringing food to the village, then cut off by heavy falls of snow.

Hales. High among the hills near the Shropshire border is Hales, so old that it is thought to be on the site of a Roman camp. Here a Roman certainly lived, for his house has been found in recent times. The Normans are said to have built Tyrley Castle hereabouts, though little remains of it; but still standing in pleasant grounds with a fine yew hedge is Hales Hall.

By noble beeches on a hillside stands the 19th century church; but it is a rough stone cross in a field a little way off that we come to see. Known as Audley's Cross, after Lord Audley who was in command of the Lancastrian Army, it was set up on a big pedestal in the 18th century, and stands on the site of the Battle of Blore Heath, the second great fight of the Wars of the Roses. Here in September 1459 Richard Neville, earl of Salisbury and father of the Kingmaker, came to blows with the Lancastrians. Neville had 5000 men and the Lancastrians twice as many, but the little army defeated the big one, victory going to the men of the White Rose.

Near Blore, a hamlet over half a mile north-east, in what is known as Buckingham's Field, began an adventure which gives the district another niche in history. It was here, when fleeing from the Battle of Worcester, that George Villiers, second of the evil dukes of Buckingham, fell from his horse and broke an arm. Taken to Armsdale, he was sheltered and nursed by a kindly woman in a cottage which still stands. Before he had recovered Commonwealth soldiers arrived seeking him, but the ready-witted woman saved the duke by hiding him in the oven where her bread was supposed to be baking.

Hammerwich. It remembers a man who gave us our Hospital Sunday, and the servant of our greatest talker. The cottage hospital was built in memory of Thomas Barber Wright, originator of Hospital Sunday; and in the church registers is the name of Charles Bird of Burntwood, who died in 1801 and was proud to the end, we think, to tell he was servant to Samuel Johnson in those hard days spent at Edial Hall in 1736.

The prominent early Gothic church was built in 1872. In a case on a wall is an old bassoon, played by the village blacksmith when he led the church choir in the last century. From the churchyard, with the stump of an old yew 12 feet round, we look over miles of fine country in the neighbourhood of Lichfield, the Trent Valley, and Cannock Chase, and into Warwickshire.

Hamstall Ridware. Great treasures are to be found in this small village among the meadows near the River Blythe, one of the three villages named Ridware from an old word for river-folk. Its mediaeval cross on three steps has been restored as a war memorial, and its Elizabethan manor house, now a farm, has a fine 17th century gateway, a brick tower, and dovecotes with the holes still in them for pigeons to come in and out.

Near by is the church on a gentle slope above the river. It has

13th century arcades, 15th century aisles, and a tower begun 600 years ago, its spire half as old. In the tower hang four bells, one with a Virgin and Child; and over the tower arch is a deeply splayed window in a Norman wall. The walls of the chancel have stood 600 years, and on either side of the reredos here are quaint mediaeval paintings on wood.

Much old glass shines in the windows. There are nine apostles in 16th century glass, and three belonging to more modern times. In the south chapel are two 14th century women, one a queen; and more precious still are a few fragments in the north chapel, for they are thought to be of the 13th century. Both chapels are enriched with screens two or three centuries old, one showing two boys stealing apples.

On the south aisle wall is an inscription to one who must have been descended from a race of mighty men, Thomas Stronginthe-arme, who died in 1778. On the table-tomb of Richard and Joan Cotton, of 1502, are painted the shields of their eight sons and six daughters, each shield having an eagle and a portrait, with little histories of the children above. One tells the brief story of the brief life of William, who was clerk to the King's auditor and died in London when he was 20.

One other treasure found here is a beautiful 14th century chalice and paten dug up in 1817. It is now on permanent loan to the Victoria and Albert Museum in London. More than a mile south-west, near the Trent, is Pipe Ridware, with two old yews by the 19th century church, and in the church a splendid Norman font with interlacing bands.

Hanbury. It has in its church a sculpture gallery of members of the aristocracy of Staffordshire—Hanburys, Agardes, Adderleys, and Egertons. Under a richly decorated arch in the north aisle is Sir John Egerton, in tunic and breeches. He died in 1662, and was a staunch Royalist, a worthy son of his father Sir Charles, lying curly-haired in the chancel since 1624. Sir Charles, like his son, was axe-bearer in Needwood Forest, and his monument shows him in armour with a round shield.

Ralph Adderley wrapped the drapery of his couch about him in the chancel as long ago as 1595. With him on his alabaster tomb are the incised figures of his two wives in Stuart dress, and his 15 children. The Agardes here, behind the chancel arch, are of the 17th century, their painted monuments with busts of a husband and wife and daughter, the man in a cloak and frills, his wife and daughter, two Puritan ladies, with broad black hats. Perhaps the monument

89

Hanbury treasures most is the tomb of Sir John Hanbury, a cross-legged knight in armour with his sword and shield. Sir John finished his fighting days in 1303, and his sculptured form, probably of local craftsmanship, is the oldest alabaster figure in England.

The church in which these proud folk lie is of the 19th century, but has arcades 600 years older, and a font at which Sir John Hanbury may have been baptised. It has a modern alabaster case with a cross on each side. Scenes from the Life of Christ adorn the chancel walls. In a niche outside the tower is a fine statue of St Werburgh holding a staff and book, a copy of a carving at Lichfield Cathedral. St Werburgh, a niece of Ethelred, King of Mercia, was prioress of a Saxon nunnery here of which no stone remains. Chester owes its Cathedral to her, for after her burial here her body was removed to Chester and the cathedral begun as her shrine.

From the churchyard, with its old yew, on the edge of a steep hill, we look out over the valley of the River Dove far into Derbyshire. Below the hill to the north-east are the modern gypsum mines of Fauld, the successors of the alabaster workings for which Hanbury was famous in the Middle Ages.

Hanley. It gave us Arnold Bennett, who has immortalised it in his stories of the "Five Towns". One of the largest and busiest of the Pottery towns, and the principal shopping centre, it has little beauty of its own, though it is for ever sending fine things to the ends of the earth.

In the excellent City Museum and Art Gallery, built in 1956 by J. R. Piggott, are many treasures, among them a collection of Roman and mediaeval pottery found in the district, a throwing wheel of 1785 used by Josiah Wedgwood, and a fine range of Staffordshire pottery figures.

The hilltop parish church of St John, in Town Road above the Market Square, comes from the 18th century. From the churchyard there is a view across the industrialised Trent Valley to the prominent spire of Wolstanton. In the church is an inscription to Ino Middleton, its first rector, who died just before Trafalgar after being here for the astonishing period of 64 years, followed by Robert Ellis Atkins for 46 years. It would have been possible for the first of these rectors to have known a man who saw Cromwell and for the second to have known a child living on into the First World War.

It was at Shelton Hall (long demolished) that Elijah Fenton, one of the laziest of all Englishmen, was born in 1683. The youngest of 11 children of an attorney, he went to Newcastle Grammar School, published a volume of poems when he was 26, became a friend of

Pope (for whom he translated four books of the *Odyssey*) and wrote a life of Milton. Dr Johnson said he would lie in bed and be fed with a spoon, and even Pope, who wrote the epitaph for him, declared that he died of indolence.

Enoch Arnold Bennett, novelist, playwright, and miscellaneous writer on life and books, was born at Hanley on March 27, 1867. A plaque at the corner of Hope Street and Hanover Street marks the site of his birthplace. He spent his early years at No 205 Waterloo Road, Cobridge, towards Burslem, a house that has now been arranged as a Bennett museum.

Bennett's best books picture the ordinary life of his early surroundings. After some years experience in a lawyer's office he went to London and, joining the staff of a weekly paper for women, brightened it by natural writing which showed a wide range of shrewd observation. It was a short step from miscellaneous journalism to the writing of stories, short and long, and before he was 30 he had attracted many readers by his types of character representative of his native district. His *Old Wives' Tale* gave him a standing in fiction that seemed to promise lasting renown. It was true to life in a remarkable degree. *Clayhanger* kept the promise open, but its successors did not sustain it.

Heroically industrious, and determined to take the world by storm, Bennett launched out into fiction covering a wide range of subjects and style, into drama in which he gained considerable success, and he also wrote a number of small books giving hints for personal management of life, until he was one of the best known of living writers, wealthy and outwardly successful in a high degree. But his career was somewhat of a tragedy from the point of view of admirers of the *Old Wives' Tale*.

The life of no man is more open to the whole world than that of Arnold Bennett. He kept a diary which has been published, and in conjunction with his books it shows him clearly as he saw himself. He gained what he sought to gain, but his gains were those of a rather vain materialism. In essence he was a son of the Potteries and from them inherited a sense of humanity suggesting a noble use of his sensibility in literature. He was a marvellously acute observer and a clever writer in a vein that every reader could understand. But while Bennett, with his keen observation of life, was telling people how to manage their lives he had no ideal for his own life worthy of his abilities. His aim was to be an artist in fiction, and he became Frenchified in spirit by study of French models. The vain shows of wealth consummated his ambition. He found his paradises in the best hotels and the proud possession of a luxurious yacht.

Bennett was a clever man but not a great man, and he lost his way because he never realised what constitutes human greatness, though he had gleams of a true humanity. He lived for his work, and laboured in making himself a misfit in Vanity Fair. He died in London in 1931.

Harlaston. To the west of the village is the timber-framed Haselour Hall, a charming picture with five gables and transomed windows, in a lovely setting. Inside is a priest's hiding-place and a wonderful oak chimneypiece, with muzzled bears that have been climbing poles since 1610, and panels showing the Battle of Hastings and a boar hunt. In the private chapel, which has stood since the 14th century, are grand old oak beams and an east window with three saints.

The attractive little church of this small village above the River Mease was rebuilt in the 19th century, except for part of the 13th century tower, which still keeps an old timbered bell-turret, itself supported inside the church by massive timbers.

Haughton. It has old cottages, a charming hall with timbers that have weathered all the storms since Tudor days, and a church refashioned in the 19th century by J. L. Pearson, but with a 14th century doorway and windows 400 years old. And Nicholas Graviner's tower is still standing, while on a tomb-slab, in the church where he preached until about 1520, is Nicholas himself, his portrait engraved in alabaster, two angels supporting the cushion at his head.

In the church is a beautifully panelled old oak chest, and an altar-table made from a cedar which fell in the rectory garden. The unusual stone altarpiece was designed by Pearson. One of the windows has the striking figure of a fighter pilot—Clement Fletcher Royds, RAFVR, who was killed in action in 1945.

For well over a hundred years the rectory was the home of the Roydses. Edward, who came in 1822, was followed in 1837 by Charles, who was laid to rest in the churchyard in 1879. Gilbert followed him as rector until 1922, a century after the first Royds preached his first sermon here; and after him came Thomas, the fourth Royd, who carried on until recent years.

The oldest of all old things hereabouts is on the way to Castle-church and Stafford—Berry Ring, a prehistoric earthwork of about seven acres.

High Offley. This small village lies in quiet country to the north of the Shropshire Union Canal, its only link with the outside world from the late 18th century. We come uphill to a church with stones that have weathered 700 winters and with a wonderful view across Shropshire to the mountains of the Welsh border. The east window of the south aisle is of the 13th century, the deeply splayed west window a few years older. There is a Norman arcade with round arches on round pillars, and the tower, 17th century above and Norman below, has a pointed arch into the nave. Of four bells in the tower one is of the 15th century, and another has the prayer:

God save the church, our Queen and realm,
And send us peace in Christ. Amen.

It came with its prayer in 1601; in 1603 it tolled for Elizabeth I. The three windows on the north of the nave have colourful post-War glass.

Himley. Close to the park gates of Himley Hall, a plain mansion of 1827 built by William Atkinson for Lord Dudley and now a training centre, stands the little 18th century church, ugly with plaster outside but with an attractive interior. Its oak screen and panelling are excellent Georgian work; and it has a graceful lectern of brass given in memory of Edward Davies, rector here for 41 years until 1886. The font was given by village children.

About a mile away, among the coalpits and brick works south of the Dudley road, is a remarkable inn, the Glynne Arms, better known as the Crooked House. Crooked it is, for the mining operations underground have caused one end of it to sink several feet into the ground and it is now propped up by massive buttresses. It is certainly one of the most astonishing sensations to walk about this house. Astonishing things they will show you, too. One of the grandfather clocks is leaning absurdly sideways, and another touches the wall at the bottom and has to be more than a foot away at the top if it is to go.

Holbeach House, half a mile south on the Stourbridge road, is the modern successor of a famous house in which the Gunpowder Plotters had their last refuge, and the home of one of them, Stephen Littleton. The 12 conspirators arrived here tired and dispirited two days after the capture of Guy Fawkes. Sir Everard Digby saw that they were in a hopeless plight and went to hide in the woods, followed by Stephen Littleton and two others. The rest stayed and were besieged by the Sheriff of Worcestershire, who ordered the house to be set on fire. Catesby and three others were shot dead as they dashed from the building; four were captured, Digby and his followers were soon found, and, with the remainder of the gang,

93

executed in London. Part of the old house remains, with two secret hiding places the plotters doubtless knew and intended to use, one behind a fireplace, the other next to the kitchen chimney.

Hints. This small village lies in attractive rolling country south of Watling Street, and here a strange relic was dug up one day in the 18th century—a lead pig weighing 150 pounds, with a Roman inscription. The loveliest corner is the churchyard, superbly kept with a lawn like velvet and beautifully situated on a slope down to thick woods in the steep little valley of the Bourne Brook. It is a charming place to be at on a summer's day.

The war memorial stands on the base of the mediaeval church-yard cross, a fine linking-up of the centuries; but the inscription to the fallen in the church takes us back far beyond mediaeval times, for it comes from Thucydides, and was put here at the suggestion of a farmer. These are the words:

These men dared beyond their strength; they hazarded beyond their judgment; and in the utmost extremity they were of an unquenchable hope.

The church itself, of variegated stones, was rebuilt in 1883 in the Early English style. It was a boy of this village who grew up to be the famous doctor, Sir John Floyer. He was one of the cleverest doctors of his time, the first to make regular observations of the rate of the pulse, a great advocate of the benefit of cold baths, and he is remembered especially because it was he who advised Dr Johnson's parents to send their son to be touched by Queen Anne to cure him of disease.

Hoar Cross. Majestic oaks, survivors of Needwood Forest, crown the hill above it, and a stately tower seen from afar beckons us to a picture of surprising beauty. Snug among its meadows and woodlands, the village has pleasant black-and-white and brick cottages, and in place of the old moated manor is a fine 19th century hall with many gables, domed towers, and tall chimneys, set in grounds beautiful with shrubberies and charming walks, formerly the home of the Meynell Ingrams.

Yet the supreme glory here is the 19th century church, which has been called the most beautiful modern church in England. In 1863 Hugo Meynell Ingram brought to the Hall as his bride Emily Wood, daughter of the first viscount Halifax, and, dying eight years later, left her his estates here and in Yorkshire. The young widow gave the rest of her life to building to him a shrine which was to be as lovely as art and wealth and devotion could make it.

Designed by George Frederick Bodley, one of the best of the Victorian architects, who worked on Liverpool Cathedral, the church, begun in 1872 and opened in 1876, is the work of a generation of building and the result is a masterpiece renowned for its architecture and sculpture, its craftsmanship in glass, metal, and wood. It is a building in rich red stone which, as the sun begins to set, glows with a dreamlike rosy loveliness. The deeply buttressed central tower, its embattled parapet 110 feet above the lawn, is a model of massive dignity.

Among the sculptures on the exterior are three portrait statues. On a buttress on the south side, St Chad has the head and features of George Selwyn, Bishop of Lichfield, who conducted the first service here. By the south porch is a figure of Athanasius reading a book, the head a portrait of the founder's brother, second viscount Halifax. On a column at the other side of the doorway is Bodley the architect, carved as St Basil. In the west chapel is a tablet to Bodley and his assistant Thomas Garner, and another, carved with a mallet, chisel, and other tools, to Robert Bridgeman, one of the craftsmen who helped to build the church.

In the churchyard, with its stone lychgate, its cross, its six dwarf yews, and one towering ash, is the tomb of the founder's brother, Frederick Lindley Wood, who, having helped to build the church, raised his sister's monument and adopted her name. He lies under a floral cross with four angels to guard him, a lifelike figure in his robes as High Sheriff of the county.

The outer aspect of the church arrests us by the dignity and restrained beauty of its lines, by its fine buttresses, and its great windows in tower, clerestory, and nave. The interior is a picture of old in new, of splendour and richness in which a little cathedral seems to have come straight from the 14th century. It needs but the mellowing of time to rank it with our supreme Gothic treasures. No slavish copy of a style, it reveals that joy in solemn loveliness, in exquisite form and colour which made mediaeval England so wonderful.

Arcades of beautiful arches rise from clustered pillars. The font has an oak canopy whose carving challenges comparison with the finest old craftsmanship. Exquisitely chiselled, it rises like a delicate spire almost to the full height of the arch beside it, with three tiers of what look like belfries with flying buttresses, ending in a lovely pinnacle crowned by a pelican on its nest. Doors open into this fine canopy, the interior of which is richly decorated.

The stone pulpit, its canopy like a crown, is entered through the thickness of a great pier, which has been pierced for the purpose. The stone reredos, splendid with carving, has a Crucifixion, about which are grouped 16 canopied angels holding the chalice, crown, and emblems of the Passion. On one side are our patron saints, George being a copy of the Donatello; on the other side are the British Saints Augustine, Columba, Anselm, and Paulinus, all wonderfully sculptured.

The beautiful chancel, its vaulted stone roof rich with bosses, is one great company of angels, saints, and martyrs. Sixteen angels seem to trumpet music from their niches on the wall; others carry sacred emblems, some sing, some swing censers, others appear to be sustaining the walls in place. Some serve by the tower arch, and they are on pillars and arches and in the windows, everywhere. The church is named after them, the Church of Holy Angels.

On either side of the altar are three carved seats under delicately chiselled arcades; and here is the bishop's carved oak chair. In the floor at the foot of the altar steps are the Meynell Ingram arms, lighted by the east window, with a central mullion in which, niche above niche, are delicately sculptured angels, the whole window framed in magnificent tracery under a deeply moulded arch. The glass, all designed by Bodley, fills every window in the nave, the chancel, and the five chapels with colour.

The woodwork is everywhere beautiful. Round the walls of the nave are 14 carved Stations of the Cross, almost the last work of two old master craftsmen in Antwerp. The screen, divided by the pillars of the tower, and extending in three sections across the church, has delicate iron gates in the centre. The organ, part of which came from Bangor Cathedral, is placed level with a chancel wall so as not to obscure the beauties of its setting, and is lavishly gilded and coloured. The Chantry Chapel has a lovely ivory Crucifix which Fra Angelico may have handled, for it came from the scene of his life and artistic triumphs, the convent of San Marco at Florence.

All this beauty and splendour is the common property of the village, which has here its own parish church, as free as if the villagers themselves had built and given all. Yet it is still a shrine, the crown and consummation of a woman's tribute to a man, and her thank-offering for her happiness in life. He himself lies in the Chantry Chapel, under a richly carved stone canopy; a splendid alabaster figure, he wears the uniform of the Staffordshire Yeomanry, over which is draped a military cloak, and at his feet lies one of his hounds.

Near him is the alabaster figure of his wife, who survived him 33 years. She lies under a massive carved oak canopy, on a sculptured altar tomb. The figure shows her serene and tranquil, as though conscious of a great task achieved. The head carved by Chevailleur and said to be a perfect likeness, rests easily on a cushion, with a drapery of lace falling over the shoulders; the hands are raised in prayer. The dog at her feet was modelled from the little animal which was long her cherished companion.

The Meynells were Meynells for centuries before adding Ingram to their name. They were in all the wars. They had a heroic representative at Crécy and Poitiers. Here they have an echo of the days in which they were at their doughtiest, and we may feel that nothing more beautiful than this was done by those craftsmen of old who had the generations and centuries in which to build, to better, and to make perfect.

Hollinsclough. This small village is delightfully positioned on the upper reaches of the Dove, looking across the open valley to the sharp cones of Chrome Hill and Parkhouse Hill, in Derbyshire. The charming church and school were built in 1840 under a single sandstone roof; they have a bell-turret and gables with tall pinnacles, and clear glass windows through which there are views of the enclosing hills.

Hopton. This small but attractive village stands on a sandstone outcrop, looking towards Stafford, and its lanes are deep cut into the rock. It has a little church, fashioned out of an 18th century barn, and a great history, for Hopton Heath, to the east, was the scene of the only big battle fought in Staffordshire in the Civil War.

On March 19, 1643, a Royalist force led by the earl of Northampton repulsed the Parliamentarians. Many of the slain, both Cavalier and Roundhead, were buried in the neighbouring churchyards of Sandon and Weston. Among the Royalists casualties was the earl of Northampton himself, who was surrounded when his horse was shot but refused to surrender and fought bravely to the end. The earl's son, the young Lord Compton, who was also wounded, wrote to his mother two days later, mentioning nothing of his own wounds but telling of his father's death. "Our loss is not to be expressed," he wrote, "for though it be a general loss to the kingdom, yet it toucheth us nearest. Pray, Madam, let this be your comfort, that it was impossible for anyone to have done braver than he did. Think that no man could more honourably have ended his life to be

97

partaker of heavenly joys. We must certainly follow him, but can hardly hope for so brave a death."

Horton. It stands on a hillside above the lovely Rudyard Lake after which Kipling was named, and it is the last resting-place of Staffordshire's own poet of the moorlands.

The church, mostly in the Perpendicular style of the 16th century, has restored 14th century nave arcades, a plain mediaeval font, and a carved screen of 1618 in the tower arch. On the chancel wall is a 400-year-old brass of John Wedgwood with his wife and eight children. The churchyard has an ancient yew over 20 feet round and a timbered lychgate of 1902. Here is a grey stone telling us (we need not believe it) that Mary Brooks was 119 when she was buried in 1787; and near by is the grave of George Heath, the poet they brought here nearly a century later, when he was only 25. He was born in the spring, and in the spring he died. As a boy he worked on his father's farm, but later he became a builder's apprentice, and it was while he was helping to restore this very church that he caught the chill which led to his death from tuberculosis. He was writing poetry when he was 20, and published a book of *Simple Poems* when he was 21, but his story is one of tragic unfulfilment, and sadness was the keynote of his work.

In his diary one day in May 1864 he wrote "Praise God for one more day", and on the following day he died. The grey stone cross above his grave has these few lines found among his papers:

> *His life is a fragment—a broken clue.*
> *His harp had a musical string or two;*
> *The tension was great, and they sprang and flew,*
> *And a few brief strains, a scattered few,*
> *Are all that remain to mortal view*
> *Of the marvellous song the young man knew.*

Ilam. With a rich heritage of natural beauty it is a wonderland of charms and interests. It has Saxon relics and a masterpiece of 19th century art; it was the birthplace of a famous play and the inspiration of an immortal book; it was the last home of a saint; it knew William Congreve the dramatist and the poet Charles Cotton, and it saw Boswell and Dr Johnson arm in arm, with the doctor disbelieving the evidence of his own eyes.

Spread out before it is the glory of Dovedale and the loveliness of the Manifold valley, and here adding mystery to beauty, the River Manifold, after an underground journey of several miles in dry summers, rises from the earth and hurries away to join the Dove a mile or so downstream. So lovely is this scene of the rebirth of the lost river that it bears the name of Paradise. Above the village rises the great hill of Bunster, sheltering the entrance to Dovedale and just reaching 1000 feet.

It was Jesse Watts-Russell who in the last century remade the Tudor Gothic hall, with towers and turrets and high twisted chimneys. Standing in fine timbered grounds above the entrance to the Manifold valley, it looks out across the river to the grandeur of the hillside woods beyond, itself a stately landmark in a picture of rare beauty, with a spring named after the saint in the church. The hall, now a youth hostel, and its grounds belong to the National Trust, the gift of Sir Robert McDougall, who has given us so much of Dovedale.

The village was rebuilt about 1840 by Jesse Watts-Russell while he was remaking the hall. At the heart of things, near the tree-shaded bridge spanning the Manifold, he raised in memory of his wife an Eleanor-style cross, 30 feet high, with four figures of women in its four niches, and added a fountain.

The interesting church is in the grounds of the hall, a veteran cedar growing by it, 15 feet round; the churchyard itself is as a garden, fair with yews, pines, hawthorns, and a thriving monkey-puzzle tree. Here are two lichened Saxon crosses of the 10th and 11th centuries. The earlier one, seven feet high, has figures on two sides and two birds beak to beak.

Much restored in 1884 by Sir Gilbert Scott, the church still has a wall with a blocked doorway, probably Saxon, the 13th century base of its tower, and a south chapel added in 1618. Its most ancient jewel is the wonderful font, so old that it is Saxon or Norman, the round bowl carved with curious humans and dragons.

A famous 13th century monument, in the south chapel, is the shrine and tomb of St Bertram, or Bertelin, whom we meet again at Stafford, and whose fame was so great that for long pilgrims from afar came here to lie stretched on his tomb, in hope of cure or consolation. On a 17th century alabaster tomb in the chapel lie Robert Meverell, in breeches and tunic with ruff and cloak, and his wife in a long flowing dress and a ruff. Kneeling on a wall-monument behind, with her four children, is their daughter, who was married to a descendant of Thomas Cromwell and related to a greater Cromwell, for her brother was the husband of Dorothy Cromwell of Hinchingbroke, aunt of the great Oliver.

One who was born early enough to know Lady Cromwell and her children, Robert Port, is buried in the chancel and has a generous inscription by Charles Cotton, one of Charles Lamb's poet heroes, friend and collaborator of Izaak Walton. It includes these lines:

> *Here, reader, here a Port's sad relics lie*
> *To teach the careless world mortality;*
> *Who while he mortal was unrivalled stood,*
> *The crown and glory of his ancient blood;*
> *Fit for his prince's and his country's trust,*
> *Pious to God, and to his neighbours just;*
> *A loyal husband to his latest end,*
> *A gracious father and a faithful friend;*
> *Beloved he lived, and died o'ercharged with years,*
> *Fuller of honours than of silver hairs;*
> *And to sum up his virtues, this was he,*
> *Who was what all we would but cannot be.*

On the north side of the chancel is the octagonal chapel added in 1884, with a vaulted stone roof supported by eight praying angels. Here is Sir Francis Chantrey's lovely white monument of 1826 to David Pike Watts, who is raising himself from his deathbed to murmur a last blessing on his daughter, the woman in whose memory the village cross was raised. She kneels, a graceful figure of wistful solicitude, looking up at her father as he lays his hand on her head. With her are her three delightful children. A little boy cranes his neck in order to see round the Bible, which, slipping from the pillow, obstructs his view of his grandfather; the youngest, overcome with grief, buries its head on the sorrowing mother's knee.

Another moving tribute of affection hangs under the arch to the south chapel—two old paper wreaths and two pairs of white gloves, which, with rustic piety and poetry, it was customary to leave in church after they had been used at the funeral of a betrothed girl. It was such a wreath as this that was allowed Ophelia in *Hamlet*, and comes into the scene in which Laertes denounces the churlish priest.

When the 17th century chapel was built round the 13th century shrine of the saint the hall and the park belonged to the Congreves, and here came William Congreve, a youth of 18, to recuperate after an illness. In a grotto in these grounds he wrote his brilliant but reprehensible comedy, *The Old Bachelor*, which established him as the first wit of the age. This comedy was among those singled out for censure when a little outlawed parson, Jeremy Collier, in his tremendous *Short View of the Stage*, scourged the Restoration dramatists in general and Congreve in particular. Congreve's defence that the play was written "to amuse myself in a slow recovery from a fit of sickness" brought Collier's retort, "What his disease was I am

Himley Church

The Market Hall at Longnor

The tomb of Emily Meynell Ingram in Hoar Cross Church

Chantrey's memorial to David Watts in Ilam Church

The Norman font at Ilam

not to enquire, but it must have been a very ill one to be worse than the remedy." The gallant little parson cleansed the stage at a blast.

Congreve passed majestic to his grave in Westminster Abbey while Samuel Johnson was a threadbare starveling at Oxford, 50 years before he sat down to write the dramatist's life, and to pooh-pooh the story of *The Old Bachelor* as the composition of an invalid. Johnson was himself strangely linked with this spot. When he was 68 he made Boswell accompany him here from Ashbourne, astonishing him in advance with his minute description of the history, romance, and grandeur of the scene.

They explored the grounds, they were shown the place where Congreve wrote the play, and they saw the river rising from its underground course. Johnson would not believe that it changed its course from the open air to passage underground, though, as Boswell wrote, they "had the attestation of the gardener, who said he had put in corks where the Manifold sinks into the ground, and had caught them in a net placed before one of the openings where the water bursts out".

Yet Johnson knew Ilam so well that the grounds of the hall had already inspired him to one of his most heroic achievements. When he was 50 and poor, and his mother lay dead, he wrote his only novel, *Rasselas*, in order to earn money for her burial and the payment of her debts, 45,000 words in the evenings of a single week. Here is his golden valley, which he transports to Abyssinia; without it there would have been no *Rasselas*.

It is interesting to remember that when Lord and Lady Cromwell lived at Throwley Hall, a 17th century house farther up the Manifold valley, they lent books from their library to Thomas Tomkinson, son of one of their farmer tenants here. He was a Puritan, but hearing of the teaching in London of Lodowicke Muggleton, who had founded a strange new religion, he joined them in denouncing Puritanism and all other creeds and became a Muggletonian.

Such was the name of the little community that came into being to preach, among other dogmas, that God left man to look after himself, and had made His last revelation to Tomkinson's cousin Reeve. A man of real ability, this farmer's son was the chief pillar of the Muggletonians, and among his writings was a poem of 26 stanzas entitled *Joyful News from Heaven, for the Jews are Called*.

Ingestre. Bounded by the Trent, the beautiful park embraces the stately hall and the fine church. Long the home of the Chetwynds, the hall passed to the Talbots, earls of Shrewsbury. Fire greatly damaged the Jacobean house in 1882, but the restored house, charming with its domed turrets and handsome bays, is like its predecessor. In this house, long famous for its gardens, Edward VII spent pleasant holidays, at times driving over to Alton Towers, the still more famous home then belonging to his host. The hall is now an arts centre for young students, administered by the county borough of West Bromwich.

Among precious documents destroyed in the fire were those relating the story of the church, which is believed to have had Sir Christopher Wren as its architect. The style of the building, its mastery of proportion and subordination of decorative to constructive detail, satisfy the experts that the church is Wren's. Tradition assigns the plan of the church to the architect of St Paul's, though the church was actually built for Walter Chetwynd. Beginning his work in 1673 and seeing it completed three years later, Chetwynd contrived that on the day of its consecration all the sacred rites, baptism, marriage, and burial, should be solemnised. He is buried amid his work, with an alabaster tablet to his memory.

There are many Chetwynd and Talbot memorials in the church, among the most notable being the marble tomb on which lies the bronze figure of Viscount Ingestre, who died in 1915 and is shown in the uniform of the Royal Horse Guards, with his streaming red-plumed helmet below. Lord Talbot, who died in 1849, lies on an altar tomb in his robes as lord-lieutenant; the 18th earl of Shrewsbury lies in an ermined robe, and another fine monument is to Lady Victoria Talbot, who died in 1856. The sanctuary window, with glass showing the Nativity and the two St Johns, is in memory of the 19th earl.

A charming plasterwork ceiling with fruit and flowers spans the roof of the nave. A fine oak chancel screen, carved with flowers and angels; and the canopied oak pulpit with fruit, flowers, and angels, were both carved by the great master, Grinling Gibbons. Cherubs, flowers, and fruit adorn the chancel's rich oak panelling.

Ipstones. A gem of the Staffordshire moorland country, it lies among grand scenery below the breezy ridge of Ipstones Edge. In the neighbourhood are many lovely old grey houses: Whitehough, a farmhouse built the year before the *Mayflower* sailed; Sharpcliffe Hall, long hidden in the trees; and Mosslee Hall, with a grand oak staircase made in Cromwell's day.

The church, made new in the 18th century, has a Norman tympanum with two fighting dragons. The finely carved oak pulpit, the lectern, and a grand screen, completely filling the space between the nave and the chancel, are all of the early 20th century, and the church has some frescoes painted during the First World War. Over the screen is Christ in Glory, the throne surrounded by a great concourse of angels and disciples, saints and prophets, while on the east wall of the 20th century chancel is an Annunciation. The east window has more saints in memory of John Sneyd, a 19th century vicar.

Many generations of his family were buried in this church, among them the John Sneyd who planted thousands of trees and beautified the rugged moorland hereabouts. Many of the larches, veterans of the noble army of ten thousand he planted here, are still thriving.

Elijah Cope, one of Staffordshire's poets, was born in this village, the son of a gardener who gave him the Bible as his only book of lessons. He grew up to teach woodcarving in the neighbouring villages, and became an authority on the folklore of the moorlands. He wrote many poems, and his *Elegy on George Heath*, another Staffordshire poet, was praised in a kindly letter from Tennyson. He died in 1917, but his simple charm and kindly character will long be remembered in these parts.

Keele. It was for centuries the home of the Sneyds, a fine old Staffordshire family. The church, where many generations of Sneyds have been baptised and buried, was rebuilt in 1870. It has a slender tower with a spire soaring 130 feet, and a fine iron screen to the memory of Henry Sutcliffe, rector here for nearly half of last century. The figures of the Elizabethan William Sneyd and his wife, which the previous church builders had left under the floor, were rescued after many years of oblivion and are now back on their altar tomb, battered but serene.

The grand hall of the Sneyds, rebuilt in 1861 by Anthony Salvin, the finest of the Victorian secular architects, became in 1949 the University College of North Staffordshire. This in turn was created the University of Keele in 1962, among the first of the new universities to be founded in Britain. It now has over 1600 undergraduates. Among the new buildings that have been erected in the beautiful park are the Library of 1962 (which has over 250,000 volumes), the fine Students' Union Building of 1963, by Stillman and Eastwick-Field, and the Chapel of 1965, by G. G. Pace.

Kidsgrove. To the north-west of the Potteries, this was once a colliery town, but it now makes electrical machinery and has textile-mills and chemical works. The Harecastle Tunnel, to the south, was built in 1777 by James Brindley, who lived near by at Newchapel, to carry the Trent and Mersey Canal through the watershed into the Trent valley, and was paralleled in 1827 by a second tunnel built by Thomas Telford, the great Scottish engineer.

King's Bromley. An enchanting village near the Trent, it has borne its proud name since Saxon days. Here the husband of Godiva had a house, and here he died a few years before the Norman Conquest, his body being taken to his church at Coventry. The Normans built here worthily, and although their church was reshaped in the 14th century and again in the 15th, when it was given a new tower and a clerestory, their south wall and one of their windows can still be seen. The church has a 17th century font and pulpit, some plain old stalls, and a fine modern reredos. There is a lovely screen with fruit and flowers and heads of monks, some of its carving being 16th century and some of it modern. In an aisle window are fragments of ancient glass showing a man and a boy with golden hair, a monk and a nun, and St Giles stroking a hart. The churchyard has a cross on a mediaeval base.

Kingsley. It is on a hill with the glory of the Churnet valley spread before it like a panorama. The refashioned church has kept the tower set up 600 years ago, with an old wooden sundial on the wall, and two windows by Burne-Jones under the ringing platform. In the nave is a tablet to the memory of brave Rowland Beech, who was killed while leading men to the rescue of others stranded in mine-shattered trenches near Ypres. By the churchyard gate are grim relics of the bad old days: a stone pillar with a ring to hold any village malefactor who needed a whipping, and blocks of stone to which the hapless beasts were fastened in bull-baiting days.

Kingswinford. Though it is growing rapidly as a dormitory village, it still has some pleasant corners and an old house or two to keep company with the ancient possessions in the church. This was mostly rebuilt in the early 19th century, using some of the old stonework, but it has several treasures, the oldest a remarkable Norman tympanum, over the vestry door on the inside, carved with a quaint St Michael thrusting his sword into the dragon's mouth. The saint has enormous wings and an air of detached aloofness, and the dragon looks only too ready to receive the sword. There is an old chest with exceptionally fine carving, and a Breeches Bible of 1605 with the famous verse telling how Adam and Eve "sewed fig tree leaves together and made themselves breeches". A brass plate tells of William Thomas Abbot, who was parish clerk for 56 years and headmaster of the school for 33; and on these walls we come across the name of Addenbrooke. One of this family, John Addenbrooke, was born here in 1680 and grew up to found the great hospital bearing his name in Cambridge.

The font, dated 1662, has a gilded modern cover by Sir Ninian Comper, by whom also there is a stained-glass window of 1935 in the south aisle. The tower was built in 1668. The steps and weathered shaft of a mediaeval cross are in the churchyard, and on an outside wall of the church is a simple memorial to Jim Horton, a seaman of HMS *Hood*, who was drowned in 1923 in an ice-bound pool while saving the lives of four choirboys.

In the Gothic church of 1851 at Wordsley, along the road towards Stourbridge, is a fine piece of craftsmanship made of alabaster and Caen stone. It is in the reredos, a sculptured group of the Wise Men and the Shepherds round the cradle, with saints and little angels under canopies at the sides, 29 figures in all.

Kinver. An expanding village of hills and views, it is beloved by those who come here from the Black Country. The church is perched high above the houses, and from it we get a magnificent outlook across the Stour, winding far below, and towards Dudley Castle on the skyline eight miles away.

The bold hill jutting out to the west is Kinver Edge, partly tree-covered and partly clad with heather. The property of the National Trust today, it was once the property of prehistoric men who lived in the Iron Age promontory fort on the summit. Of mediaeval origin are the dwellings in Holy Austin Rock and Nanny's Rock, rooms hewn out of the solid red sandstone and later made with the help of a few bricks into homes for several families.

The church is mostly a 14th and 15th century building, though the great brick arches in the south or Grey chapel are relics of the 18th and the north aisle was added in 1857. The rood-loft staircase, cut open and exposed to view, is thought to be Norman. The pulpit was carved in 1625 as a three-decker, but was altered in 1903. In a case in the south aisle is a charter granted by Charles I in 1627, freeing the people of Kinver from certain taxes.

The fine group of brass portraits on a tomb in the south chapel shows us Sir Edward Grey of 1528 with his two wives, seven sons, and ten daughters. The damaged figure lying in the north of Foley chapel is John Hampton, who died in 1472. A staunch Lancastrian, he was squire to Henry VI, ranger of Kinver Forest, constable of Chester Castle, and one of the trustees for the building of Eton College. He may have built the fine chapel in which he lies, and it is thought he was also the original builder of Stourton Castle, nearly a mile and a half away to the north. Now much modernised and called Stourton Hall, this was the birthplace in 1500 of Reginald Pole, the man who was a cardinal in Italy while England was Protestant, and came home to be Archbishop of Canterbury in Mary Tudor's fearful reign.

Reginald Pole was a younger son of Sir Richard Pole, who had links with the Tudors and married Margaret Plantagenet, the last of unblemished descent of the royal house. She was a niece of Edward IV, Henry VII having removed her brother from his path. Henry VIII gave her great estates, made her godmother and governess of the future Queen Mary, created her Countess of Salisbury, and helped with money and supervision the education of Reginald. From the outset Reginald was destined for the Church, and while still a youth was presented with various livings by the king; yet he became only a deacon, although Henry had marked him out for the archbishopric of York after Wolsey.

At first Pole seemed to favour the king's divorce, but, living abroad without fear, and realising that the divorce could not be attained without the separation of England from Rome, he sacrificed his prospects by writing a treatise vehemently condemning the proposal. Retiring to Italy, he was made a cardinal and sent to stir up Spain and France to invade England. His missions were fruitless except that they brought disaster to his family at home, where Henry beheaded his two brothers and then his mother for complicity in the plots he had set on foot.

Meanwhile Pole was dogged about Europe by would-be assassins in the pay of Henry. Sir Thomas Wyatt, the English ambassador in Spain, poet and gentle wit though he was, was long busy in Madrid for the murder of the hated cardinal. The Pope gave him a pension and a bodyguard, and sent him as mediator between the warring kings of Spain and France. The years passed on and Pole was still a refugee from his native land, though so great a figure in Europe.

Twenty years passed; Henry and Edward VI were dead and Mary was married to Philip of Spain before the cardinal again set foot in England. He had twice been proposed as the husband of Mary; he had twice narrowly missed being elected Pope, once by his own choice. Now he returned as the Pope's representative to preside over that scene at which Protestant England, through its Parliament, implored forgiveness of its sins and entreated him to readmit her into the Roman Church.

In the same week that Cranmer was burnt at the stake the

Haughton : Nicholas
Gravinar, 1520

Sandon
Hugh and Elizabeth Erdeswicke, 1500

Uttoxeter : Thomas
Kynnersley, 1510

Mavesyn Ridware : John and
Elizabeth Cawarden, 1485

Sandon
Hugh and Cecile Erdeswicke, 1473

Mavesyn Ridware : David
and Maud Cawarden, 1557

OLD STAFFORDSHIRE FOLK ENGRAVED IN STONE

Cardinal of England was made a priest, and in the choir of Bow church was consecrated Archbishop of Canterbury in the martyr's stead. When Philip finally left England he left Pole virtually in charge of the nation's affairs.

What part the new Primate actually had in the martyrdoms of Mary's reign is not known, but from the time of his becoming Mary's supreme adviser the persecutions increased in violence and horror. Towards the end he was superseded as legate and ordered to appear before the Inquisition on a charge of heresy, but the issue was left undecided. Mary Tudor died at seven o'clock on the morning of November 18, 1558, and he died at seven in the evening of the same day. It was Protestant England under Elizabeth that laid his body in state for a month at Lambeth Palace, and then bore it with regal pomp for burial in Canterbury Cathedral.

Lapley. It has something of a Saxon priory, founded in 1063, and something of a Norman church, and is a picture of rural beauty. It has also several fine houses, Lapley Hall, with tall chimneys, Lapley House, and Lapley Castle, as well as Lapley Court and Lapley Manor, two old timber-framed houses. It is the hall that has the remains of the priory, one traceried window still surviving from the Middle Ages.

The castle is a curious turreted and battlemented building, but it is Lapley House to which the romance of history clings. Although modernised outside, it has much that was here when the Commonwealth managed to gain possession of the house and the church. In 1643 the commander of the Royalist garrison at Chillington Hall, nearly four miles away, guided by an old servant, came marching at dead of night with his musketeers. Seven men scaled the walls, dropped in the midst of a company of startled defenders, overpowered them, threw open the gates, and stormed the house. They took captive also the Parliamentarians who were holding the church.

In the lime-shaded churchyard, from which there is a view towards the Wrekin, is part of an old cross, but it is the magnificent central tower by which our attention is riveted. The church, built by the Normans for the priory they found here, has still the base of the tower placed in position by these old masters; it was the 15th century which completed it as we see it, with its quatrefoil windows and a band of ornament below the stately parapet.

One deep-splayed Norman window is in the chancel, which has a notable 13th century window of five lancets, showing the first stage in the progress from plain masonry to elaborate tracery. The old Dutch font, sculptured with scenes from the life of Christ, including an admirable Nativity and Wise Men, is the mystery of the church, for nobody knows how it came here. In the chancel are 13th century sedilia and piscina, some mediaeval tiles and the engraved figure of a 14th century priest; and one of the county's three sanctus bells is here, apparently old enough for the unknown priest to have set it ringing.

On a wall in the nave are traces of a painting the old priest may have seen, but the beautifully carved priest's door, with four regal portraits and an angel trampling Satan underfoot, is later and is perhaps Dutch or Flemish work of the 17th century. There is 15th century oak in the chancel screen.

Leek. It lies on a hillside slope near the head of the Churnet valley, a delightful town in a setting of natural grandeur. The Capital of the Moors, it is faced on the north by the rugged range of gritstone outcrops called the Roches, like the turrets and battlements of huge forts raised by a race of Titans.

The Five Clouds, over 1500 feet high, outsoar the rest, but Hen Cloud, solitary and apart, is by its isolation the most impressive in its stark mass and mystery. The form of a section of the range is responsible each midsummer for apparent double sunsets, a rare phenomenon. On two successive evenings, June 20 and 21, the sun disappears, eclipsed by a flank of Bosley Cloud, and then, having continued its western way, reappears beyond another flank, and, slowly vanishing again, seems to set a second time.

Until the Dissolution Leek belonged to Dieulacres Abbey, a Cistercian monastery said to have been founded in 1214 by Ranulph, the famous sixth earl of Chester, who figures in Piers Plowman. He carried the sword at the coronation of Richard the Lionheart, was present at the crowning of King John, and stood by his deathbed and witnessed his will. He was at the coronation of Henry III. As a Crusader he built Chartley Castle, and was a national leader in war and statecraft. At first the foe and then the saviour of Hubert de Burgh, he died in 1232 and was buried at Chester, but his heart was brought here to the abbey.

Only fragmentary ruins of the abbey remain, about a mile north of Leek, but in the walls of a farm and its outbuildings are finely carved stones, bosses and gargoyles. Near the farm is a fine timbered house of 1612; and in the same area is a rocky hermitage, with traces of a fireplace, chimney, and doorway, where an anchorite once kept his solitary vigil.

It is believed here that but for the development of its industries Leek must have outrivalled Buxton as a health resort and beauty spot. Health and beauty it still has, and fortune has blessed it with famous silk manufactures, introduced by Huguenots in the 17th century. There are broad streets, a cobbled public square whose markets have been noted for centuries, and fine parks and recreation grounds. There are 17th century almshouses, some more modern, and an 18th century grammar school. The Nicholson Institute, built in 1887, with its domed tower, has a library and an art gallery, and museum with a rich array of fossils, birds, animals, and a magnificent collection of Burmese carving.

Leek has many 18th century houses with finely carved door cases, indicating a period of great prosperity, but the most interesting of the old houses is that in the Market Place, and now a shop, in which was born, in the year of the Great Fire of London, Thomas Parker, first earl of Macclesfield. The son of a lawyer, he was Chief Justice and Lord Chancellor, but in 1725, two years after founding the grammar school here, he was impeached for corruption and fined £30,000. He retired into private life but was allowed to be a pall-bearer at the funeral of Sir Isaac Newton.

A prominent feature of the town is the lofty clock tower in the Ashbourne road, the memorial raised by Sir Arthur Nicholson in memory of his own son and all the sons of Leek who fell in the First World War. Of white stone, it looks, as we catch sight of it from the top of Derby Street, like a smaller edition of the Campanile at Venice. The fine Butter Cross, 20 feet high, now in the cemetery, has an inscription telling that it was the gift of J. Joliffe in 1671.

St Edward's, the mother church of the town, is a splendid building, with eight pinnacles crowning the noble 14th century tower, in which 10 silvery bells make the town ring with their 14 tunes. In the churchyard, with its 17th century arched gateway, is the magnificent 12-foot shaft of a Saxon cross of the 11th century. A smaller Saxon cross, of the 10th century, still reveals its knotwork decoration, and in the south chapel of the church are fragments of carved Saxon stones from the original building, including part of a cross-head. The churchyard is famous for another stone with a story. Raised to the memory of William Trafford, who died in 1697 at Swythamley Hall, it is carved with a man, a flail, a sheaf, and the words "Now Thus", the legend being that Trafford, an ardent Royalist, when discovered at his home by Commonwealth soldiers, feigned idiocy, and, beating his corn with the flail, answered every question put to him with "Now thus, now thus", so escaping capture. A man with a flail and sheaf, and the motto Now Thus, make up the coat-of-arms of the de Traffords, a family of Saxon origin.

The church, approached through a 17th century porch, was

rebuilt by about 1320, after a fire had destroyed the previous church in 1297. It was restored in 1856 and the chancel was completely rebuilt in 1867 by G. E. Street, but the nave still has its magnificent timber roof, each cross-beam being made from a single oak. Late 19th century windows, including two fine rose windows in the aisles, contain stained glass glowing with colour, probably from the workshops of William Morris. The oldest treasure is a 16th century brass, in the north aisle, with portraits of John Ashenhurst, his four wives and 10 children. The alabaster font of 1867 is carved with scenes from the Bible, and the fine oak and walnut pulpit, of the same date, has the Twelve Apostles in canopied niches. A case in the south chapel contains the unique organ keyboard of 1750. This has the "black" keys made of ivory and the "white" keys of a dark wood. Here too are examples of the embroidery made at the School of Embroidery started about 1870 in Leek by Lady Elizabeth Wardle.

All Saints Church in Compton, built in 1887 in a late Gothic style by R. Norman Shaw, has an imposing interior, with a charming wall mosaic of St Peter, and, round an aisle window, a beautifully painted Annunciation, both by Gerald Horsley. The chancel panelling and the reredos were designed by W. R. Lethaby and painted by F. Hamilton Jackson. The ornate font of green marble dates from 1886.

Beauty and craftsmanship of the 19th century have been gathered, too, at the prominent Roman Catholic church, also in Compton, with its lofty spire, elaborate stone reredos, and colourful windows. One window, with a figure of Christ at a bedside, is in memory of Mother Mary Joseph, 49 years mistress of St Mary's School.

The parish church and some of the old houses must look much as they did when Charles Edward, the Young Pretender, came marching into the town on December 3, 1745, gay in his silk tartan and blue feathered bonnet, as Thackeray pictures him in *Esmond*. Failing to gain followers here, he marched the next day for Derby, returning in haste four days later to plunder the town on the retreat northwards.

It is interesting to remember the 34 ladies of Leek who made a wonderful copy of the famous Bayeux Tapestry, under the supervision of Lady Wardle. Beginning in 1885, they worked on it for 12 months, and their copy shows all the detail of the original tapestry—the life of the Conqueror, with 1512 embroidered objects (623 people, 202 horses and mules, 55 dogs, 505 other living creatures, 37 buildings, 41 boats, and 49 trees). The tapestry was bought by Alderman Hill in 1895 for £500 and given to Reading Museum.

Leigh. Several neighbouring hamlets share the same name and the same church with its mediaeval tower. The church itself was finely rebuilt in 1846, mainly in the Decorated style, by A. W. N. Pugin, and has treasure in its windows both ancient and modern. Among the old glass are figures of Christ and saints, kings and queens, and an unusual Crucifixion. In the 19th century glass is a picture of the Transfiguration, and figures of Enoch and Elijah, David and Solomon, all designed by Burne-Jones. In the south transept is a fine altar tomb with figures of Sir John Aston in the armour he wore 450 years ago, with his wife Joan in a tight-waisted dress and 14 battered children below. On the wall of the porch is a coffin lid engraved with a cross seven centuries ago.

Lichfield. Almost in the middle of England, this cathedral city has much for us to see that is lovely and of deep interest. It has one of the smallest yet perhaps the most graceful of our mediaeval cathedrals, standing on one of the earliest English sites of a Christian church. From its 16th century grammar school has gone out a group of boys whose names are famous in literature, law, the church, and the stage; and in one of its 17th century houses was born our illustrious Samuel Johnson, most famous man of letters of his day, creator of the first adequate dictionary of our language.

Far back in the remote days of history the city was called the Lych Field, Field of the Dead, from the tradition that thousands of Christians were martyred here by the Roman emperor Diocletian; and the first church was built in Saxon days by St Chad at Stowe, on the farther side of the pleasant pool which mirrors the cathedral. He came from Northumbria in 669 on a mission to Mercia, and by his preaching and his saintly life reconciled the Angles and Britons then living at enmity in the Mercian kingdom. He was the first bishop of Mercia; he transferred the bishopric from Repton, in Derbyshire and he died at Stowe in 672. As a shrine for the body of the holy man, his successor built a church where the cathedral now stands, consecrating it in 700.

Under the powerful King Offa, Mercia became the dominant kingdom in England, and in 787 Lichfield became an archbishopric, the head of a province that extended from the Thames to the Humber. But after 16 years it was merged again in the province of Canterbury. Of the Norman church built on the site by Roger de Clinton, nothing remains.

To the end of the 12th century we owe the lovely conception and proportions of Lichfield's cathedral as we see it. Between 1195 and 1208 the Early English builders replaced the Norman choir and transepts, in 1239–49 they raised the chapter house, and with the transformation of the nave (by 1285) and west front (by about 1293) the whole building had changed its severe and massive Norman character and assumed the lofty grace and elegance familiar to us all.

The lady chapel and presbytery were added in the 14th century, and thus the church remained until the unhappy days of the Civil War, when the cathedral was held by the Royalists and twice besieged before it was taken by the Roundheads. The interior was sacked and cruelly laid waste in 1643 and again in 1646 by the blind zeal of the victorious besiegers. It is sad beyond words to know that this gem of 13th and 14th century art, the first cathedral taken by the Parliamentary party, suffered more terribly than any other at the hands of wanton wreckers, who broke up the ancient carvings in wood and stone, destroyed or defaced the statues and monuments, and even carried away the roofs and the central tower, so that the first service here after the Restoration was in the chapter house, the only part sheltered from the weather.

But with the need came the man. The name of Bishop John Hacket, appointed in 1662, should live as long as the stones are left standing. He threw himself devotedly into the work of restoration, he toiled night and day to get subscriptions, and in seven years he saw the triumphant completion of his labours. For two and a half centuries little care was taken of this priceless building, but from 1856 each part was strengthened and restored, so that in 1908 it stood in its pride again, an almost perfect revival of its mediaeval beauty.

Lovely as the cathedral is, its charm is enhanced by its natural setting, for, though in the heart of the city, it is protected and isolated by its two pools, and in the quiet waters of the Minster Pool, just below the Close, are reflected the graceful proportions of its crowning beauty, the Three Spires known affectionately in all this countryside as the Ladies of the Vale. The central tower and spire, thrown down in the Civil War, were renovated and the summit cross replaced in 1950.

The west front is the cathedral's greatest glory. Within its arcades and panels are 113 statues, a wonderful gallery of carvings, all of the 19th century, except five at the top of the north-west tower. Above the figures of the Apostles is a group of English kings with St Chad in the middle. Above them are prophets, archangels, and figures from the Old Testament. Statues of saints and bishops adorn the towers, with a figure of Christ on the gable between them.

The doorways are equally rich in ancient and modern work. The porch of the central doorway has a 14th century figure of Christ, and on the outside of the porch is set out in carved detail the genealogy of

Christ in two lines, one from Abraham to the Virgin, the other from Adam to Joseph. In the north-west doorway are the Christian kings and queens of Saxon England, and on the other side is pictured the coming of Christianity, from the North with Aidan and St Chad, and from Rome with Gregory and Augustine. Much of the early iron-work of the doors was done by Thomas Leighton, the craftsman who made the exquisite grille of Queen Eleanor's tomb at Westminster.

The transept doorways have also a wealth of carving; in the north transept are the figures of a Tree of Jesse dating from the 13th century. Over the chapter house are the statues of famous churchmen; George Herbert, Richard Hooker, Bishop Ken (holding a scroll with the words of his great hymn, "Glory to Thee, my God, this Night") and Archbishop Laud, as well as Izaak Walton and Christopher Wren. Among the figures on the buttresses at the east end are some of Lichfield's famous sons, including Samuel Johnson and Elias Ashmole, who is holding a model of his Ashmolean Museum. Groups of Latin and Greek early Christian Fathers complete this unrivalled collection of statuary.

The first impression of the interior of this fine place is of its extra-ordinary beauty. It extends 370 feet from the west door to the lady chapel, in a fascinating series of arches. As we look at the fine proportions of the nave arcade, the exquisite capitals of the clus-tered pillars, the delicacy of the carved triforium and clerestory rising to the rich vaulting of the roof, we understand the words of Sir Gilbert Scott, the restorer: "I always hold this work to be almost absolute perfection in design and detail."

Detached from the great columns which support the central tower, 13th century pillars spring like slender trees from floor to vaulted roof. The transepts date from about 1220–40, but the stone vaulted roofs were put up in the late 15th century.

The nave pulpit and the choir screen of iron, brass, and copper were designed by Sir Charles Scott and are decorated with coloured marbles and enamels. The craftsmanship is very fine, especially the carved fruits of ivory, onyx, and precious stones. The design on a panel of the pulpit is St Peter preaching on the Day of Pentecost, and there are angels in bronze playing musical instruments on the screen.

The choir and its aisles are 13th century work; the presbytery was rebuilt in 1330–38. In the 19th century many layers of white-wash were removed from the walls, the built-up arches were opened out, and the plaster taken away from the stone carvings. The choir vaulting with seven-ribbed shafts is very fine. Three of the bays date from about 1200 and one pillar shows the blended influence of the 13th and 14th centuries. There are six 19th century figures of saints in the spandrels of the arches where earlier figures once stood.

The stalls and the bishop's throne were carved in 1860 by Samuel Evans, George Eliot's uncle, the original of Seth in *Adam Bede*. The carving is of delicate work enriched by wreaths of natural leaves; there are biblical scenes in the panels, and figures of the Apostles at the ends of the stalls. The pavement is laid in engraved tiles illustrating the life of St Chad, and kings and bishops who have had some connection with the cathedral. The reredos and the altar screen of alabaster and marble were designed by Scott. The reredos shows the Ascension with angels holding ivory trumpets. In the side arcades are 12 alabaster figures representing the noble army of martyrs in pairs of different ages, the last two turned to face the lady chapel instead of the choir. In the canopied sedilia of six seats are remnants of the vanished loveliness of the great 15th century screen.

In the Lady Chapel is a series of 19th century statues of 10 saints under ancient canopies: Cecilia with her organ, Werburgh with a model of Chester Cathedral, Priscilla with a lion at her feet, Faith with sword and rack, Catherine with her wheel, Margaret subduing a dragon, Lucy and her lamp, Agnes with a lamb, Agatha bearing a palm, and Ethelreda with a model of Ely Cathedral. The triptych on this altar was carved by the peasants of Oberammergau.

The 13th century chapter house, with its finely vaulted roof, is an irregular octagon, and the elaborately carved capitals of the central column show a different design on each of the four sides. One whimsical old sculptor has introduced various animals, including a cat and a rat, into the decoration over the chief seat.

In the library over the chapter house are valuable books and manuscripts. There is a copy of the Treacle Bible and of the Breeches Bible, a vellum manuscript of Chaucer's *Canterbury Tales*, and Dr Johnson's marked copy of South's *Sermons*, from which he quoted in his Dictionary. A carefully guarded treasure is the illuminated 7th century manuscript known as St Chad's Gospels, a unique copy consisting of 110 vellum leaves. At the sacking of the cathedral it was taken away for safety. A photostatic copy of this precious work is in a glass case in the Lady Chapel.

We find a picture book in stone in the wall arcade of the north choir aisle, where the artist has let his imagination wander as the strange medley of figures, foliage, birds, beasts, and grotesques came into being beneath his tool. There are joyous music makers on the bagpipe, harp, dulcimer, clarionette, and the pipe and tabor. One of the oldest parts of the cathedral is St Stephen's chapel, built about 1230, long used as an organ loft but now worthily restored. There is a record that Bishop Pattishull, who died in 1242, was buried before the altar, and in the restoration a stone coffin was found there.

The simplest and perhaps the most charming of all the restored work is the chapel of St Chad's Head, built after 1225 but left in ruins after the Civil War until 1897. It is reached from the south choir aisle by a narrow stair, and a 15th century stone gallery before the entrance was doubtless used for the exhibition of relics to pilgrims in the aisle below. The aumbry is here in which St Chad's relics were preserved. The restored work is perfect in its simple dignity, and wherever possible the stone vaulting and the ancient wood and iron have been used. The story of St Chad is told on the bosses and corbels; we see him sheltering the hart which fled to him for refuge, and in his cell surrounded by ministering angels at the hour of death. The alabaster reredos was carved by C. E. Kempe.

Remembering the glory of the old glass here we grieve that none was left from the years of desolation, but the famous 16th century Herkenrode windows are the glory of the Lady Chapel. These were the gift in 1803 of Sir Brooke Boothby of Ashbourne (in Derbyshire), who brought them from the dissolved Cistercian Abbey of Herkenrode near Liège, in Belgium. The precious glass, made about 1540, had been taken out and stored during the troubled days of the French occupation of Belgium in Napoleon's time, and Sir Brooke paid only £200 for the whole collection. The figures and groups are small and at first sight appear too crowded, and in these tall narrow windows it is difficult to trace the scenes and characters; but the wealth of colour is enough. Particularly lovely is the deep blue of the glass in the upper tracery. The subjects of the seven windows show the foundation of the abbey, with national saints, and scenes from the Life of Christ.

The two west windows in this chapel are filled with other Flemish glass brought from the Low Countries after the French Revolution, lying forgotten for many years in Christie's cellars. It had belonged to the Marquess of Ely, but was bought for the cathedral in 1895 and has a worthy place by the Herkenrode windows. One has a strangely beautiful design of the Fountain of Pity, in which the guardian angels of little children await them as they rise from the waters of baptism. The other, of equal mythical charm, shows the Falling Asleep of the Virgin, lying on a canopied bed surrounded by Apostles, who have assembled to watch the flight of her soul to Heaven. Two other fragments of the Herkenrode glass are in the choir aisles. In one, a crude mediaeval conception of the Trinity,

Lichfield Cathedral

The nave of Lichfield Cathedral

the Father, an old man in a tall hat, is holding the Son, and a weird kind of dove represents the Holy Spirit.

There is much 19th century glass in the cathedral. The Martyrdom of Stephen in St Stephen's Chapel is in memory of Canon Lonsdale, Chancellor of the cathedral for 51 years, who died in the beginning of this century. There is an alabaster figure of him here. The west window of the nave is in memory of Canon Hutchinson; it shows Michael, Joseph, the Virgin, and the Wise Men in the upper part, and below is a scene connected with each figure.

The men of the North Staffordshire Regiment who died in the Dongola Expedition and in the South African War are remembered in a window by C. E. Kempe. Another window by the same artist is in memory of Canon Curtis. A fine restored window with a Jesse tree by Clayton and Bell has taken the place of a poor 15th century window; by using many of the head stones which were found in the wall a beautiful reproduction of the original 13th century five-light lancet in the north transept has been given to the cathedral. The chapter house windows have scenes and figures connected with the early history of the Church.

Above the 17th century effigy of the good Bishop Hacket, carved in stone and painted, a window of 1901 shows the damaged cathedral after the Civil War, when the central spire had fallen and the roof was riddled with cannon shot. The magnificent 15th century window in the south transept has glass to some of the Staffordshire men who fell in South Africa. The striking design shows Christ on the Cross with angels around, and soldier saints below who have laid down their lives for truth and faith.

When we think of the monuments of Lichfield thought flies at once to the fairest of them all, Sir Francis Chantrey's masterpiece of the Sleeping Children, placed here in memory of the daughters of Prebendary William Robinson, who lost both during a fire in 1812. It has been aptly called the Snowdrop Monument, for the chaste beauty of the rounded limbs and girlish forms, lying clasped in sleep, reminds us of those fair and fragile flowers of the early year. Who can read unmoved the touching words which tell the loss of the widowed mother, who "in fond remembrance of their 'heav'n lov'd innocence' consigns their resemblance to this sanctuary in humble gratitude for the glorious assurance that 'of such is the Kingdom of God' "? We can well believe the story that Chantrey came here every year of his life to look again upon these sisters, one of his earliest inspirations. Another of his fine carvings is the stately kneeling figure of Bishop Ryder, who died in 1836; the perfect moulding of the head and hands clasped in prayer are of rare beauty.

The effigy by G. F. Watts of Bishop Lonsdale, who died in 1867, lies on a table-tomb with canopies which were part of the old screen of the Lady Chapel. Almost opposite in the north choir aisle is a striking bust by Epstein of Bishop Woods, who died in 1953. Among the earlier bishops in the cathedral is the 13th century figure of Bishop Patteshull and the 14th century figure of Bishop Langton, which was once jewelled, as the holes in the marble show. The alabaster figure of Bishop Selwyn, who died in 1878, is in a little chantry off the Lady Chapel. First Bishop of New Zealand and 90th of Lichfield, he was much loved in both parts of the world where he laboured, and on painted tiles behind the tomb are scenes from the story of his life. The canopies over the tomb where Dean Howard lies were part of a dismantled altar screen.

There are here three of those curious mediaeval monuments in which the head and feet were carved in a niche in the wall and a blank stone surface represented the part where the body should be. They are often nameless, but one of these is to the memory of Canon Strangeways. Another strange memorial is the 15th century tomb of Dean Heywode, in the north transept, only the lower part with his skeleton being left. The custom of the skeleton on the tomb was no doubt akin to the skeleton at Roman banquets, to remind mankind of the final decay of human life.

Several monuments in the cathedral are to distinguished soldiers. One of the earliest is a stone to Colonel Richard Bagot, one of the gallant defenders of the cathedral against the Parliamentary troops. He died fighting at Naseby. Admiral William Parker, the last survivor of the captains who fought with Nelson, is remembered by an altar tomb in the south transept chapel.

Many of the famous names of the city are remembered here. There are busts of Dr Johnson and David Garrick in the south transept chapel; in the south choir aisle is a medallion of Dr Erasmus Darwin, the grandfather of Charles Darwin; and under the south-west tower is a tablet to Dean Addison, father of the essayist. He lived in the house which is now the deanery. Anna Seward, known through her poems in the 18th century as the Swan of Lichfield, is recalled by a tablet under the north-west tower to her father, mother, and sister, the verses on it being written by her friend Sir Walter Scott. On the wall near by is a grateful tribute to Lady Mary Wortley Montague from a lady saved from the horrors of smallpox by Lady Mary's introduction of inoculation into England. There is a tablet to Gilbert Walmsley, a friend of Johnson and Garrick, registrar of Lichfield and a man of much benevolence.

In the peaceful Close a soft grass setting separates the Cathedral from the dignified 17th and 18th century houses which lie about it as a frame. Here in the beautiful Bishop's Palace, built in 1687, lived Canon Seward and his daughter Anna. She was much admired for her poems in the literary circles of her time, and also wrote a life of Dr Darwin. Gilbert Walmsley lived at the palace before the Sewards, and Garrick is said to have given recitals in the hall. When Bishop Selwyn came here on his return from New Zealand he built the palace chapel and placed in it some stained glass, one scene showing an incident in the Maori wars.

A pleasant walk from Dam Street, south-east of the cathedral, along the side of Stowe Pool, passing a willow descended from the tree Johnson loved so much, brings us to St Chad's church at Stowe, where the Saxon bishop set up his monastic cell in 669. Most of the present church was built in the 14th century, but in the south porch is an unusual trefoil-headed 13th century doorway. The church has a fine 14th century east window, with rich Decorated tracery, and a 15th century font. In the chancel are commemorated two friends who were closely linked with Samuel Johnson's life in Lichfield, his stepdaughter Lucy Porter and Catherine Chambers, the faithful servant of the Johnsons for many years. The tenderly worded inscription now on her stone was written by Dr Johnson:

My dear old friend Catherine Chambers, She buried my father and my brother and my mother . . . I humbly hope to meet again and part no more.

In the garden of a house next to the churchyard is the reputed St Chad's Well, built over the little spring where perhaps the saint came to drink and to baptise his converts. The timber canopy over the well was built after the War, the previous edifice having fallen into disrepair.

St Michael's churchyard, east of the city, near the Burton road, is one of the oldest and biggest in England. Tradition says that it was the central burial-place in Saxon times of the kingdom of Mercia, and there were burials here when there were only five burial-places in the country. The church was extensively restored in the 19th century, but has kept its 14th century tower, its 15th century east window, and its 17th century font. Here are buried the father, mother, and brother of Dr Johnson. Johnson wrote his great work *Rasselas* to pay for his mother's funeral and her few debts, and he composed the long Latin inscription on "the deep, massy, and hard stone" which lies in the central aisle of the church.

St Mary's, the chief parish church of Lichfield, in the market-place, was practically rebuilt in 1870 but still keeps its 14th century tower arch. Opposite is the bookseller's shop of Michael Johnson, who was churchwarden here, and the baptism of Samuel is recorded in the parish registers. The north chapel is the burial-place of the Dyotts, prominent in Lichfield history for centuries; the most famous of the sons was deaf and dumb and known as Dumb Dyott, but he was one of the stout defenders of the cathedral in the Civil War, and a shot from his musket killed Lord Brooke, the Parliamentary leader. When asked by Charles II to name his own reward, he requested that all his descendants of the name of Dyott should be brought by torchlight from the family estate at Freeford, three miles away, and buried at midnight in the chapel of St Mary's, and this custom was observed until the last few years of last century. This Dyott Chapel has a fine oak altarpiece with some 14th century and some Tudor panels.

St John's Hospital was founded in 1252 but rebuilt by Bishop William Smyth in the 15th century. It is one of the earliest English houses built after chimneys were introduced into domestic architecture. The eight tall chimneys form deep recesses rising from the pavement to the chimney-tops. Within the gates is a pleasant little garden tended by the old men, who rest in the sunshine on the seats of the stone terrace. The chapel has a stained window in memory of a warden of the hospital for 42 years, and there are fine old Corporation seats brought from St Mary's church over two centuries ago.

Three buildings in turn have stood near by on the site of Lichfield's old grammar school; the first from 1497 to 1577, the second until 1849, the third until 1903. Lichfield boys now go to a newer school in the outskirts on Borrowcop Hill, where the stone for the cathedral was quarried and where, legend tells us, three kings died in battle. The curiously maimed bodies of these kings form part of the city arms. The school-house has been carefully preserved as civic offices and the playground delightfully planted as a garden.

The school has a great record. It was the earliest provincial school founded after Eton, Winchester, and Wainfleet; and few small schools can show such a distinguished list of scholars. Three of the boys who sat on its benches are buried in Westminster Abbey: Johnson, Garrick, and Addison. Two became Bishops of Bristol, George Smalridge and Thomas Newton. Five contemporary judges had their first lessons in these walls—Chief Justice Willis, Chief Baron Parker, Mr Justice Noel, Chief Justice Wilmot, and Sir Richard Lloyd. John Hewlett, musician and antiquary, was a boy here, and another famous Lichfield scholar, Dr Richard Garnett, was Keeper of the Printed Books in the British Museum.

Another son of Lichfield who was to win renown, both as traveller and archaeologist, was Henry Salt, born here in 1780; by a strange chance he went to the school at Market Bosworth in Leicestershire, where for a short unhappy period Dr Johnson had been a tutor half a century before.

As Shakespeare's memory is honoured in Stratford-on-Avon so is Johnson's in Lichfield. In the marketplace are the statues of its greatest son and his biographer Boswell, who must always live through his admiring and faithful record of his friend's sayings and doings. Three scenes from his life are pictured on Johnson's statue: we see him as a little child taken to hear the preacher Dr Sacheverell in the cathedral, as a boy so much honoured by his school-fellows that they carried him on their shoulders, and as a man during a visit to his birthplace, when with the touching humility that only a great soul could possess he stayed bareheaded in the rain for three hours on the spot where his father's bookstall had stood, to atone for his youthful pride when he refused to take his father's place at the book-stall in Uttoxeter market.

This marketplace has seen strange and tragic sights. Three martyrs were burned alive at the stake in Mary Tudor's reign, and here a hundred years later came George Fox, founder of the Quakers; he was released from prison in 1651 and stood like a prophet on the snow-covered stones of the marketplace, bareheaded and barefooted, to denounce the city and its inhabitants.

It is to the generosity of an alderman of the city that Lichfield owes the preservation of Dr Johnson's birthplace. It was the book-shop of his father, and is kept as a museum and a memorial. The old shop window looks out on to one corner of the marketplace and the small rooms with high narrow windows abound with relics and reminders of the clumsy form, the mighty intellect, and the kindly heart of the man who spent here his early days.

We see his three-legged mahogany breakfast table and the big armchair in which he passed his last days. In the little panelled parlour with deep window-seats is the desk on which he wrote *Rasselas* to pay for his mother's funeral. We climb the staircase of wide oak boards and balustrade black and polished with age, and pass from silent room to room haunted by a thousand memories. Here is a collection of editions of his works, many of his manuscripts, some of his letters, and portraits at various times of his life. In the room in which he was born are some of the treasures he loved, his silver bib-holder, his teaspoons, and the silver pen which Edmund Burke gave him to celebrate the completion of the Dictionary; here are his shoe-buckles, his wife's wedding-ring, the walking-stick with which he used to tap the lamp-posts, and a precious teapot which gave him his countless cups of tea.

We can spend hours in wandering through the old town, where the places of interest are identified and described. At the former Three Crowns (since rebuilt and no longer an inn), next door to his birthplace, Johnson stayed with Boswell in 1776. In Dam Street is the site of Dame Oliver's school; she might well claim to be the grandmother of the famous Dictionary, for here little Samuel learned to read and spell.

The charming early 18th century Stowe House, beyond the Pool, was in turn the home of Thomas Day (who wrote the edifying story of *Sandford and Merton*), and of Richard Lovell Edgeworth, father of Maria Edgeworth. The Parchments, to the north of the pool and now converted into two cottages, was the factory started by Michael Johnson for the manufacture of parchment, in which venture he lost much of the profits he made as a bookseller. At the 18th century Stowe Hill lived Sir Thomas Aston, the father of three daughters Johnson much admired.

Adjoining the former Three Crowns is the birthplace of Elias Ashmole, described as "the greatest virtuoso and curioso that ever was known in England". He was born here in 1617; he went to the grammar school and sang in the cathedral choir. He was a devoted student of chemistry, astrology, botany, and other sciences. He gave a wonderful collection of rarities to Oxford, on condition that a suitable building was provided for it, and this was the origin of the Ashmolean Museum.

The Guildhall in Bore Street is on the site of the old Guild House which stood here in the reign of Richard II. It is partly of the 18th century, but was considerably rebuilt in 1846 and 1963. The Guildhall has some early 19th century glass which was formerly in the cathedral and the cartoons from which they were designed. Next door is a well-preserved timber-framed 16th century house.

Part of the walls of a 13th century friary and a Tudor fireplace have been preserved in the building of the Friary School, west of St John Street. It was converted into a house by the Sheriff of Lichfield in Queen Mary's reign, and here Johnson and Boswell visited their friends Moll Cobb and Miss Adey. In Bird Street, the extension of St John Street northward, are three interesting inns: the George, where George Farquhar stayed as a recruiting officer in 1705 (he afterwards made it the setting of his play, *The Beaux Stratagem*); the King's Head, where the South Staffordshire Regiment was raised in 1705; and the Swan, where Johnson lodged with his friends the Thrales in 1774.

Erasmus Darwin lived in the city from 1756 to 1781, in a delightful 18th century house near the entrance to the cathedral close. He was a doctor and scientist much in advance of his times. Among his friends were Rousseau, Watt, Wedgwood, and the Sewards, but unhappily he was never on friendly terms with the "18th century's greatest conversationalist", for it was said that, "wherever Dr Johnson was, Dr Darwin had no chance of being heard".

On the site of the Probate Court (now the city's museum) was the house where Captain Garrick lived, father of the celebrated David. The son was born at Hereford, where his parents were visiting, but the first 20 years of his life were spent here, and his mother's father was a lay singer in the cathedral. The house was pulled down in 1856. The museum has many reminders of the early days of the city, including the suits of armour which have an annual air when they are worn in procession on Whit Monday, a survival of the old Guilds. Here also are uniforms and trophies of the Staffordshire Regiment, whose barracks are at Whittington, south-east of the city.

In the pleasant park to the west of the cathedral is a statue of Edward VII sculptured by Robert Bridgeman, Sheriff of Lichfield in 1907. Behind it is a statue by Lady Scott of Edward John Smith, the captain who went down with his ship the *Titanic* in 1912, in the bitterest sea catastrophe of our century. He was a Staffordshire man, and we read on this statue that "he bequeathed to his countrymen the memory and example of a great heart, a brave life, and a heroic death".

In its Garden of Remembrance Lichfield has one of the most original and beautiful war memorials in England. The stone balustrade has a curious history. It was removed from Moxhull Hall in Warwickshire to Shenstone Court, Lichfield, and was bought by the town for this garden. When it was being set up one of the stones was found to be marked with the letter V, the mark used by the mason Vinrace who had built the bridge crossing the water at this very spot. The city arms are on an old stone built into one of the piers of the entrance gates. The garden is laid out beside the Minster Pool below the Close, and from it we have perhaps the finest view of the Three Ladies of the Vale.

Lichfield owes its original glory to St Chad, who died here in 672 and whose story comes down to us from Bede, who had his information from a monk trained here by the saint.

Chad was one of four brothers in the priesthood, two of them becoming bishops. He was partly educated in Ireland, which was then a sanctuary of learning, a light shining in the dark night of Europe's Dark Age. Wilfred, on being appointed to the see of York, went to Gaul for consecration, but was so long absent that

Oswy, King of Northumbria, nominated Chad in his stead. Mild and obedient, Chad went to Canterbury for confirmation in his office, but, the Primate having died, he was consecrated by two British bishops. He discharged the duties of his see with loving humility for the next three years, Wilfred approving his appointment and retiring to a monastery.

A new Archbishop of Canterbury deposed Chad because of the irregularity of his appointment, and reinstated Wilfred, but, delighted with the scholarship and saintly goodness of Chad, he appointed him bishop of the kingdom of Mercia, which then comprised an immense area. He established his see here, building a home not far from his church for himself and a small number of monks. Their time was devoted to prayer and good works. When he travelled about his diocese Chad went modestly afoot, until the Primate, recognising in him a holy man, begged and even commanded him to ride.

Bede had a vivid pen, and in his picture the saint moves and lives after 13 centuries. Chad died in 672, having predicted a week earlier the day and time of his death. The prophecy is attributed to divine revelation, but Chad was probably helped to his calculation by observing the course of the pestilence that was thinning out his little community and to which he himself had fallen a victim.

His body was first buried in his own church of St Mary, but in 1148 his bones were transferred to the present cathedral. While Bede was writing miracles were said to be wrought at Chad's tomb. His body lay in "a wooden monument, made like a little house, covered, having a hole in the wall, through which those that go thither for devotion usually put in their hand and take out some of the dust, which they put into water and give to sick cattle or men to drink, upon which they are presently eased of their infirmity and restored to health". So the legend ran and grew and led to the good man's canonisation. Chad clearly impressed his age as a man of great virtue, piety, and learning, and was an immense influence for good in a land still barbarous and largely pagan.

One of the sons of whom Lichfield has reason to be proud is Henry Salt, who helped to unveil Egypt's past. A doctor's son and trained to art, Henry Salt, born here in 1780, turned his gifts with brush and pencil to account by making a series of drawings for Lord Valentia, whom he accompanied to India, Ceylon, and Abyssinia, as secretary and draughtsman.

At 29 Salt was sent on a Government mission to Abyssinia to carry presents to the king, to promote friendly relations, and to bring back data. This led to his appointment, 13 years later, as British

From the castle here in 1403 Sir Robert Mavesyn rode out at the head of his retainers to join the forces of Henry IV at Shrewsbury, and at the same time his enemy Sir William Handsacre set forth to fight at the same place for the rebel Hotspur. The rivals met near here, where two ancient oaks are said to mark the site; they fought until Handsacre was slain by Mavesyn, who then continued his way to Shrewsbury to die in battle.

The church has a tower on which grim gargoyles have been keeping watch 500 years. Only one aisle, now the family burial-chapel, remains of the church which rose with them, the remainder being an 18th century rebuilding from old materials faced with brick; but the Norman font, after a century of exposure in the manor garden, is back in its place in the nave. In the chapel are floor tiles from the Conqueror's palace at Caen; it is fascinating to think that he may have trodden them before he and the Malvoisins set out for Hastings.

The chapel is remarkable for its monuments. The oldest is the canopied 12th century armoured figure of Hugo Mavesyn, founder of the church and father of its first rector; the next in age is a 13th century Crusader, Sir Henry Mavesyn, who served in the Holy Land and whose body was found wrapped in lead. In the chapel are seventeen alabaster slabs engraved with figures and heraldry, but only four are old; some were carved only in 1812.

Two engraved 15th century figures show Sir John and Elizabeth Cawarden, he in armour with huge elbow plates, she in a belted robe and a quaint round hat. Elizabeth was a daughter of the slayer of Sir William Handsacre. Her sister Joanna married the victim's son, and their daughter became the wife of Sir Hugh Davenport, who lies in engraved armour, with a big crested helmet and wearing long pointed shoes resting on a queer heraldic creature.

A bareheaded 15th century John Cawarden lies in armour with a lion at his feet; and David and Maud Cawarden rest under a 15th century canopy, he in a robe with wide fur collar, she in a girdled gown. Below are their four children. Interesting alabaster reliefs show the redoubtable Sir Robert Mavesyn, first slaying Handsacre, and then as he was on the day of his death at Shrewsbury; and another has John Mavesyn, who was killed while hunting. On the walls of the church are numerous hatchments and shields.

Mayfield. There are two villages here: Upper Mayfield, with many old stone houses, on a hill overlooking the Dove valley, amid a romantic countryside of glorious woods and fields, and Lower Mayfield, with the church and an old textile-mill, beside the river.

The five grey stone arches of the mediaeval Hanging Bridge cross the Dove to link Staffordshire with Derbyshire. It started life as a packhorse bridge; was widened for carriages 200 years ago, and again for motors in our own day; but still the 500-year-old arches stand.

The tower of the old church rises above the yews in the churchyard and the limes by the churchyard gate. The tower was built in 1515 by Thomas Rolleston and its door is scarred by bullets fired by the retreating Jacobites who came this way in 1745. The chancel and the aisle windows are of the 14th century, but the nave is far older, for its arcades and its finely moulded doorway are Norman. There are pews, altar-rails, an altar-table, and a pulpit superbly carved by craftsmen of Charles I's day. The octagonal font is dated 1510.

In the churchyard are an old cross, claimed to be Saxon, and a pathetic link with Thomas Moore, the grave of his daughter Olivia who was laid to rest here by her sorrowing parents in 1815. Between the two villages is the grey stone cottage where the poet lived for four years about the time of Waterloo, the home where he and his young wife Bessie spent many of their happiest hours. Here came the dawn of many of his hopes and fears. Here is the small garden where Bessie would pick the flowers to give away, and from these windows, with little Olivia in her arms, she would look across the road and watch her husband romping in the hayfield with little Barbara.

"I could not possibly have a more rural or secluded corner to court the Muses in," Moore wrote to a friend, and the Muses responded, for it was here, with his library of Eastern books massed round him, that he wrote his Oriental romance, *Lalla Rookh*.

It was in this quiet spot that he listened to the chimes of the church, sometimes called "the Cathedral of the Peak", across the river at Ashbourne, and immortalised their melody in these famous lines:

> *Those evening bells! Those evening bells.*
> *How many a tale their music tells.*
> *Of youth, and home, and that sweet time*
> *When last I heard their soothing chime.*

> *Those joyous hours are passed away*
> *And many a heart that then was gay*
> *Within the tomb now darkly dwells*
> *And hears no more those evening bells.*

And so 'twill be when I am gone
That tuneful peal will still ring on
While other bards shall walk these dells
And sing your praise, sweet evening bells.

The memory of those bells was both sweet and sad to him in after years, for they reminded him of Barbara, once frolicsome as a young kitten and now no more, and of the day when small Olivia closed her eyes for the last time, only a few months old.

Milwich. Its chief possession is a bell which was ringing here for Agincourt. It is the oldest dated bell in Staffordshire, and has been hanging since 1409 in the tower, which is mainly of the 15th century and has two other bells, of 1672 and 1703. The tower has shields in an ornamented border below the parapet. The remainder of the church has its mediaeval stonework hidden on the outside by the brickwork of 1792, and on the inside by the panelling put up in the 1880s to cover the walls. In the vestry is an old oak chest and in the nave is a battered font with arcading unfinished round its bowl, the work of a 13th century sculptor, but sadly mutilated.

Mow Cop. Its splendid hill, nearly 1100 feet above the sea, with magnificent views across the Cheshire Plain and far into Wales, belongs to us all, for it has been given to the National Trust. It is topped by a mock ruin of the 18th century, a prominent landmark; it is famous as the birthplace of Primitive Methodism, which, now merged in the parent body by the union of the churches in 1932, began here in 1807 as the result of the first English camp meeting, summoned by Hugh Bourne, a wheelwright of Stoke-on-Trent. Ten thousand Methodists held a service in 1937 to mark the handing over of Mow Cop to the National Trust.

An earnest local preacher, Bourne, who built a chapel at Harriseahead, to the south-east, from his own resources, had kindred spirits in a brother and in William Clowes, the champion dancer of Burslem. Seeking a return to a simpler form of worship, they called their sympathisers into the open air. Their first meeting was held on a May Sunday on this hill, and lasted 14 hours; similar gatherings followed elsewhere, and led to Bourne's dismissal from the denomination.

It was then that he and his friends formed the Primitive Methodist Church. Bourne continued to labour at his trade, but found time to conduct meetings all over the kingdom and in the United States, and before his death at Bemersley, an old man of 80, he saw over

5000 chapels established, with a membership exceeding 100,000. He is buried at Englesea Brook in Cheshire. It seems not a little surprising that the chapel here has no mention of this remarkable man.

Mucklestone. Fragments of Staffordshire's unknown past have been revealed here, near the Shropshire border, from time to time, for at a farm are two stones called the Devil's Ring and the Devil's Finger, both pierced in prehistoric days, and in the River Tern an ancient dug-out canoe was found earlier this century.

Old yews border the way to the church, which, though much rebuilt in 1883, has its finely proportioned 14th century tower and many ancient fragments in its walls. In the thirteen windows is a great gallery of glass by the best-known Victorian artist in stained glass, C. E. Kempe. One of the windows of the tower has figures of St George and the hapless Henry VI with his queen, Margaret of Anjou. From the battlements of this very tower Queen Margaret is said to have watched the rout of 10,000 loyal Lancastrians in the Battle of the Roses at Blore Heath 500 years ago.

Newborough. This small village, pleasantly situated in the heart of Needwood Forest, was one of three boroughs created in Staffordshire in the early Middle Ages, the others being Tutbury and Uttoxeter. The simple aisleless church, built in the Decorated style in 1901 by J. Oldrid Scott, son of the more famous Sir Gilbert Scott, has an unusual octagonal tower with a leaded spire. The east window, inserted in 1910, shows the ascending Christ with saints and angels, among them St Chad, who holds the cathedral at Lichfield, and St Werburgh, who holds Chester Cathedral.

Newcastle-under-Lyme. Although its years have been peaceful, this old market town first rose by the river as a place of defence. Eight hundred years ago the new castle was built by the great forest of Lyme, but castle and forest vanished long ago, and survive only as memories. With Simon de Montfort and John of Gaunt among its ancient lords, the town sent two members to Parliament for 500 years, and from Shakespeare's time was a famous educational centre. In 1932, the borough was greatly increased in size, doubling its area by joining hands with Wolstanton, Chesterton, and Silverdale.

The Guildhall, the old town hall, in the broad High Street, was built in 1714 and altered in 1854; the market cross near by was set up in 1820. The affairs of the town are now transacted at the new

Municipal Buildings, completed in 1967, in Merrial Street, to the north. The former civic buildings, of the late 19th century, in Ironmarket facing Queen's Gardens, have a clock tower with a lantern and a pinnacled dome, and statues symbolising Architecture, Painting, Music, and Literature. They are now used mainly for public meetings, concerts, and exhibitions.

The oldest thing in the town is the 13th century lower part of the buttressed and pinnacled tower of St Giles's Church, which has seen more than one building at its side. The present church, built in 1876, is the work of Sir Gilbert Scott, who, finding ancient tiles here, had them copied to form a tessellated pavement. There are two relics from the church of long ago, the worn stone figure of a man wearing a gauntlet and holding a sword, and the splendidly carved pelican lectern.

In Brampton Park, near the Wolstanton road, is the interesting Museum and Art Gallery, which has collections of textiles and Staffordshire pottery, and exhibits illustrating local history and natural history.

The town has cradled notable men in widely different fields. One of the most remarkable was Sir Nicholas Bagnal, son of a tailor-mayor, who educated him so well that he was admitted to the court of Henry VIII, and sent to fight in Ireland. A different career awaited Philip Astley, a cabinet-maker's son born here in 1742. Joining the Army as a youth, he became a magnificent rider, captured a standard at the battle of Ensdorff, and at the completion of his service received from his commanding officer a beautiful white charger, which he taught to perform. Developing into an un-rivalled horse-breaker and showman, he opened the first circus in England, which was for many years famous in London as Astley's Circus. Paying yearly visits to Paris, he lost his property there during the Revolution, but was compensated by Napoleon. In all he built 19 circuses in London, Paris, and Dublin. Of his many famous performers one was Belzoni, the strong man who left Astley to explore the Pyramids.

Two men closely connected with the fate of Charles I were associated with this place. John Bradshaw, who pronounced the sentence of death, was Recorder here, and one of the judges at the trial was Thomas Harrison, a butcher's son who left this town to become one of the most redoubtable of Ironsides. The son of a grazier and butcher at Newcastle, Harrison received an excellent education and left the practice of the law to join Essex's lifeguard at the outbreak of the Civil War. Passing from one Parliamentary force to another, he fought with increasing fame at Marston Moor,

K

Naseby, Langport, Winchester, and Basing, and in the second war at Worcester, where he conducted the pursuit of the flying Royalists with such thoroughness that few escaped. During Cromwell's absence in Ireland he commanded the entire military forces of England.

For posterity the chief interest in Harrison is centred on his action as one of the most rigid of Charles I's judges. It was he whom Cromwell entrusted with the dangerous task of bringing the king from Hurst Castle to London. The two men grew intimate, even friendly on the way! Yet no one was more active in drawing up the indictment and urging on the trial of the king than Harrison, and he was one of the signatories of the death warrant. After three months in the Tower of London at the Restoration of Charles II, he was the first of the judges brought to trial.

Unshaken, he defended himself with courage and ability. He declared that what he had done had been "as out of conscience to the Lord". He had never turned aside, even though it had caused him to be separated from wife and family and to suffer imprisonment. What had been done was done "in the name of the Parliament of England, by their power and authority", and "this Court, or any Court below the High Court of Parliament hath no jurisdiction of their actions". He maintained that the taking of the king's life had been ordained of God, that the king had "set up his standard against the people" and that his execution was no crime, but lawful. The sentence of death was unanimous, and on October 13, 1660, Samuel Pepys, who had witnessed the execution of Charles I eleven years earlier, wrote:

I went out to Charing Cross, to see Major-General Harrison hanged, drawn, and quartered, which was done there, he looking as cheerful as any man could do in that condition. He was presently cut down, and his head and heart shown to the people, at which there was great shouts of joy.

Newchapel. It is a mining village with a church on its hilltop looking south to the Potteries. The church was rebuilt in 1880 in a plain style as a memorial to one of our greatest engineers, the astonishing James Brindley, who is buried in the churchyard.

Turnhurst Hall, the house on the road to Tunstall where Brindley lived from 1765 until his death in 1772, was unhappily pulled down in 1929, but his name lives on in the neighbouring hamlet of Brindley Ford.

James Brindley was born at Tunstead, near Wormhill, in Derbyshire, in 1716, son of a wastrel farmer. He learned how to write his name and do simple sums, and after a wretched childhood apprenticed himself to a millwright who was something of an engineer. His master at first regarded him as a slovenly workman, but was soon glad to resign the control of the business to him, and Brindley ran the place, supporting the old man and his family with unswerving fidelity. Then he started a business of his own, and became the general utility man of the neighbourhood. If a machine broke down Brindley was sent for, and he never failed.

The illiterate millwright's fame spread wide, and he was called to Lancashire to pump a mine. He did the pumping, but had to obtain his power by a waterwheel 30 feet underground, and to carry water to it from the Irwell through a tunnel of 600 yards bored partly through rock.

The great opportunity came to Brindley at last through another remarkable man, the duke of Bridgewater, who heard of the untutored genius and called on him to build a canal, the first serious venture of the kind in England. It was to run from Worsley to Manchester, and to avoid waste from a system of locks it was to be on a level. This meant the boring of tunnels and the raising of embankments. Moreover, the canal had to be carried across the River Irwell.

Brindley thought matters out, formed his plans, and began. He went on, tunnelling here, embanking there, burrowing under Manchester at one end and under Worsley at the other, touching the coalfield at twenty points. The aqueduct was begun in July 1760; boats were crossing it in the next summer. Now the duke set him to link up Liverpool with Manchester, and Brindley did it—30 miles of canal carried over a course of infinite difficulty, including two rivers and two deep valleys, the first crossed by aqueducts and the second by broad and lofty embankments.

He had a genius for economy, for mastering difficulties by invention. It is impossible to follow him, through all his works, which gave England 365 miles of canals, a marvellous means of transport in the days before railways. He stimulated industry enormously, for he opened up coalfields which had been inaccessible and manufacturing sites which had laid idle.

England has never produced another man like Brindley. All the complex calculations for his engineering feats he worked out in his head. He lived only for his work. Once he went to a play and it completely upset him, confusing his ideas, he said, and unfitting him for business. Why did people want to bother with such things when there were canals to build? Canals were his grand passion. He told a Parliamentary Committee that nature had provided rivers to serve as feeders to canals.

When challenged by any specially difficult problem he would go to bed, and stay there wrestling with it. When he got up the problem was solved, and operations would begin. Rough and uncouth, he spoke like a genius, and Carlyle's picture of him is perfect:

The rugged Brindley has little to say for himself; the rugged Brindley, when difficulties accumulate, retires silent, generally to his bed that he may be in perfect privacy there, and ascertain in his rough head how the difficulties may be overcome.

The eloquent Brindley, behold, he has chained seas together; his ships do visibly float over valleys, invisibly through the hearts of mountains. The Mersey and the Thames, the Humber and the Severn, have shaken hands.

Norbury. Set in a beautiful countryside the village preserves records running back to two Saxon priests. It has a Gothic brick tower, built in 1757 by William Baker, to its otherwise complete 14th century church, which has a wide nave and a chancel with four stone seats, one perhaps originally a piscina. Over all are the great beams which have borne the high-pitched roof for 600 years.

Two 14th century possessions of the church are the founder's tomb and a brass portrait, the tomb, in the north chancel wall, showing Ralph le Botiller, cross-legged and in chain armour, with a red coat and shield, the fine brass, in the sanctuary floor, showing his wife in a cloak and veil. The founder was the central figure of a grim story. In 1302 he summoned the rector on a charge of stealing fish from the manor pond, but failed to prove his accusation. Three years later one of his servants murdered the rector, and it is thought Botiller built the church as an act of expiation.

The broken 15th century figure of a knight in armour, lying in the nave, is said to be Sir Edward le Botiller, and one of the two stone women in the chancel is thought to be his wife. On the south wall of the chancel is a characteristic early 18th century monument to the Skrymshers, who bought the Tudor manor. This passed in the reign of Elizabeth to Richard Barnfield by his marriage to the heiress. Their eldest son Richard, the poet, was born in 1574 at the manor house, which stood until the beginning of last century. Going up to Oxford at 15, Barnfield came to London, and, with wealth and scholarships to commend him, won the friendship of the leading poets of the age. It is considered certain that he was for some time in close touch with Shakespeare.

By a strange stroke of destiny the young poet travelled down the centuries shorn of his chief laurels, which were added to Shakespeare's, for from 1599 until our own day his sonnet, "If music and sweet poetry agree", and the ode beginning

> *As it fell upon a day*
> *In the merry month of May*

were always included in *The Passionate Pilgrim*, and ascribed to his immortal contemporary. Barnfield himself is buried at Stone.

At Norbury Junction, a favourite rendezvous of canal users, to the south-east, the Shropshire Union Canal is joined by a branch canal from Newport which ascends 15 locks in a mile and a half.

Norton Canes. In a coal-mining region between the Black Country and Cannock Chase, this village saw its church burnt down and built again in 1888. With its tower and its grey stone walls, all that was spared by the fire, the church has a red-tiled roof and a porch at the end of a row of dwarf yews. The war-memorial east window of 1927, by A. J. Davies, shows a radiant St James in a purple cloak, St John glowing in red, and a company of miners, some going down the pit and others dressed as soldiers. Here are two interesting memorials: a monument by a Stafford-shire sculptor of a woman mourning for Phineas Hussey, who died in 1833, and a brass inscription to William Collis who was rector for more than the first half of the 15th century. A mile and a quarter away to the south is Little Wyrley Hall, a 17th century gabled house with tall chimneys.

Oakamoor. A small place below a steep hill and amid the glorious scenery of the Churnet valley, it is proud to have had a hand in one of the greatest engineering feats of the 19th century.

Here is the factory of Thomas Bolton to which Sir Charles Bright entrusted the making of the core of the first Atlantic cable. It was the people at Oakamoor who made the copper core, which was twisted in seven strands to be afterwards sheathed and armoured and fashioned into the actual cable laid down. It was the people of Oaka-moor who made most of the 20,000 miles of wire which formed the copper conductor of the current and weighed 90 pounds to the mile. The factory produced this essential portion of the cable at a cost of £5 a mile, and we think the folk here, though the first cable was broken, must have been proud at that later day in 1858 when the first telegraphic message was flashed from continent to continent.

None could fail to be proud of being associated, however humbly, with what, at any distance of time, must be regarded as the tre-mendous feat of laying the Atlantic cable, a task accomplished in the face of heartbreaking disappointments and by the supreme resolve to gather every resource of discovery and invention to prevent their recurrence. The cable itself, begun in 1857, was finished in June and before the end of July was stowed partly in the British ship *Agamemnon* and partly in the American ship *Niagara*.

After the shore end of the cable had been landed in Valencia harbour the *Niagara* began the task of paying it out. For six days all went well, though slowly, and then, when 380 miles had been laid, the cable snapped and with it went £100,000, when the cost of preparations and postponement was reckoned. Next year, 700 miles of new cable having been made, the same ships renewed the attempt, meeting in mid-ocean and intending to pay out from there in opposite directions. Again there were breaks followed by splices, but at last, in 1858, Newfoundland and Valencia were connected.

Then to everyone's dismay the cable, owing to mistaken ideas on the part of its electrical engineer, refused to work. Lord Kelvin was called in and managed to get messages through. Communication was established amid wild rejoicings on both sides of the Atlantic and altogether 732 messages were sent between England and America. But the damage done to the cable was now beginning to tell its tale, and at the height of the rejoicings communication failed altogether on October 20 and the first Atlantic cable fell silent for ever. Not until seven years later was the first successful cable laid.

Okeover. It has the beauty of the Dove and the ancient house of the Okeovers in their stately park. The delightful hall, built about 1780, was altered in the 19th century and enlarged by the addition of a new wing in 1960. It looks down on a charming avenue of limes and elms, and in front are beautiful 18th century gates by Robert Bakewell, the great Derby ironsmith.

In this park the Okeovers have safely traversed the centuries as one of the oldest families in England. Not since William Rufus has the village known any but an Okeover as its manorial lord. When Charles Edward Stuart, the Young Pretender, came this way on his scurry to and from Derby in 1745, the head of the house was absent and the chaplain was in charge. A letter exists written by him to his master telling a rueful tale of outrages here by the Pretender's followers, who pillaged the house and church, picked the servants' pockets of their pence, robbed the parson of a treasured 1s 6d and his silver tobacco-box, and then, having threatened all with death, departed with the squire's horses and his saddles and bridles. Anything but a Bonnie Prince was Charles Edward to Staffordshire.

Near the hall is the church, with a 15th century tower looking down on a 14th century nave and chancel. It has a fine oak screen guarded by winged dragons, and memorials to the Okeovers, the most beautiful being a delightful angel holding a laurel for Mary Okeover, who died in 1764. Her husband soon followed her to the grave, and their inscription has the lines:

Thrice happy pair, in nuptial love so tied,
Whom death but for a moment could divide.

But the most famous of the Okeover memorials is a brass with a very queer story. Midway through the 15th century died William Lord Zouch, and his portrait was engraved on brass, showing him with two wives. When Humphrey Okeover died in 1538 his brass was stolen for him, the back of it being engraved with the 13 children of Humphrey and his wife. So matters stood for about three centuries, when the brass was stolen a second time, and in the end it came to light broken into 55 fragments. Mounted on oak these now hang in the nave, with a perfect figure of a woman in a big head-dress and a sweeping gown, and with several childish figures, but as for Humphrey Okeover, with whose death the crime began, he has vanished for ever. Yet he is not entirely lost to knowledge, for his portrait is in a window, and there he surveys other windows with other members of his family, and looks down on the shattered brass that knows him no more.

Oulton. In this quiet hillside village, about a mile north-east of Stone are pleasant features, the 17th century hall, with its brick and stone walls, and its yew hedge, and St Mary's Abbey, founded in 1624 for Benedictine nuns and moved here in 1853. The chapel, designed by A. W. N. Pugin, has an elaborate reredos with statues of SS Peter and Paul, and a large east window with the figures of six Saxon princesses.

Patshull. Church, great house, and cottages are all in its large and beautifully wooded park, which has pheasants on the lawns, and rainbow trout gleaming in a stream which feeds two lakes. The hall, made new in the 18th century, has been owned by three famous families, the Astleys, the Pigots, and the earls of Dartmouth, and is now a hospital. Near the church are two pillars with gamecocks set up by a gambling squire to commemorate the fact that, having lost the estate by one wager, he won it back by another; and another curiosity, in the churchyard, is a stone statue of a man in armour, with long curly hair, said to be the duke of Monmouth.

139

The secluded church, which has fine old yews about it, was designed in 1743 by James Gibbs, the follower of Sir Christopher Wren and architect of St Martin-in-the-Fields and St Mary-le-Strand in London. The domed tower and the north aisle were altered in 1874. On the chancel roof is a curious sculpture of St Michael, slaying his dragon.

The church's founder, Sir John de Astley, lies in armour on a 16th century table-tomb with his wife and charming figures of their 15 children. Sir Richard Astley, who died in 1687, is in Jacobean costume on a finely sculptured wall-monument above Sir John's tomb. He appears again in a panel at the head of his cavalry squadron, and at the side, seated on pedestals, are the mournful figures of his wives, Elizabeth and Henrietta.

Here was born and here is buried Sir Robert Pigot, who fought at Fontenoy; and here is a memory of the one ignoble Pigot, Robert's nephew Hugh. Baptised in this church in 1769, he entered the Navy, where his conduct was marked by an increasing severity which degenerated into tyranny. As captain of a frigate off the coast of South America he called to men up in the rigging that he would cause the last man down to be flogged, and in their haste two men fell to the deck dead at his feet. "Throw the lubbers overboard!" said Pigot, and that night the enraged crew mutinied and threw their pitiless captain overboard after them.

Framed on a wall is a wooden cross from the grave of Lord Guernsey, killed at the Battle of the Aisne in 1914. The 19th century iron chancel screen is gilded and decorated with roses, and the oak pulpit has cherubs with urns on their heads. There is a window with a trumpeting angel in memory of the famous Bishop Selwyn, and another to Bishop Lonsdale whom he succeeded, and in the sanctuary window is 19th century glass illustrating six of Christ's sayings.

Pattingham. Here on a day of long ago a man found a treasure hid in a field, a gold collar about four feet long, that may have been lost a dozen centuries or more.

An attractive village on the Shropshire border, it has much beauty. In the churchyard is an old yew about ten feet round, a fine cedar, a sundial on an ornamental pillar, and a Crucifix crowning a mediaeval cross. Above all rises the 14th century tower of the finely placed church, its spire, added in 1871, a lovely spectacle, unusual in Staffordshire. The massive north arcade was built by the Normans, and the chancel arch and spacious chancel were rebuilt during the Early English period. This has two sedilia or priests' seats (an unusual number), a piscina and an aumbry or cupboard. The font, much changed, has been here about 800 years; at it George Greenstreet christened the children for 53 years of last century. Near by is a rare stone book-rest, in the wall. On the south wall of the church are the oldest clocks in the village, two mass dials.

Penkridge. A small town of Saxon origin, in the wide valley of the Penk, it welcomed the coming of the railway and insisted that certain express trains should halt daily at its little station.

Pillaton Hall two miles away, which has been the home of the Littleton family for over four centuries, is now partly in ruins, and its moat is dry, but it has still its 16th century gateway with four little turrets, and a mediaeval chapel. Near the chapel lies a quern, looking ancient enough to have ground corn for generations before the Littletons arrived.

The stately collegiate church has a veritable gallery of monuments, a 15th century tower and 13th century arcades on lofty pillars. The nave and chancel are both 700 years old; the rest of the building is of the 15th and 16th centuries, the font is dated 1668. One of the most interesting things here is the 18th century iron screen, made in Holland and given to one of the Littletons by a Dutch settler in South Africa.

In the 19th century sanctuary window is glass with nine scenes from the life of Christ in memory of Edward Littleton, first baron Hatherton, who was buried in the chancel in 1862. He was a warm advocate of reform, and Chief Secretary for Ireland. In the chancel are six old stalls with carved misericords, and the sanctuary has a floor of coloured marbles. Eight angels from bygone days support the fine roof of the nave put up during a restoration in 1882, and there is old carving in two choir screens.

A monument in the vestry shows the last of the old manorial family, a 16th century alabaster portrait group of William Winnesbury with his wife and daughter in girdled gowns, caps, and veils. The earliest of the Littleton monuments (1518) is the incised alabaster slab of Richard, with a pouch and dagger at his girdle, the heiress he married, and their seven children, all of whom worshipped in the chapel Richard built on becoming owner of the hall. He is the last of the Richards; the heirs for about a dozen generations after him are Edwards, the younger sons Williams.

Sir Edward Littleton, who died in 1558 and lies on a tomb of coloured marble, is wearing armour and a necklace; and with him are two wives in close-fitting caps, and 10 children. The third

Edward, who died in 1574, has an elaborate Tudor tomb showing him with flowing hair and beard, wearing armour and a ruff, his wife and their 16 children with him. Most striking of all is the double-decker alabaster monument in which a 17th century Sir Edward and his wife kneel under canopies, with the next generation below them. The children of the two families are in panels, 26 figures in all.

The only memorial to the Williams of the family is a 17th century alabaster monument with a curious feature, for there are four Williams in the group. Father William kneels with his wife and their nine children; three of the sons are called William, but two of these died in infancy. On the monuments is verse of poor quality; but Penkridge finds compensation in the work of one of its own poets, Cecil James Tildesley, born here in 1877. His song on Cannock Chase has this joyous lyrical opening:

> *Oh have you seen, on Cannock Chase,*
> *The Birches, queens of silver grace,*
> *When Autumn's magic hand hath set*
> *On each a golden coronet?*

Truly there is something to charm the muse in this little town to which King Edgar issued a charter over a thousand years ago.

Penn. Across the common that was once part of the Royal Forest of Kinver we climb up to the church tower among the trees at Upper Penn. It is cased in red brick of the 18th century. In the churchyard are the steps of a mediaeval cross (with a modern shaft) and the base of a preaching cross said to have been set up about A.D. 1050 by Lady Godiva, Lady of the Manor of Nether Penn.

Part of the church is of the 13th century, but it was enlarged in 1845 and again in 1871, when the chancel was rebuilt. In the south aisle is a Norman font. Paving the sanctuary is a fascinating collection of tiles of unknown age. Similar to some known to be 600 years old in Westminster Abbey, they showed crowned figures, musicians, and bishops. A pathetic little memorial with no date was put on these walls by a mother "in memory of her lovely infant"; and the graceful sculpture of a woman by Flaxman is in memory of John Marsh of 1795, a Staffordshire magistrate.

One of the carved oak screens was put up in 1887 by a man who worshipped here for half a century; and the other is in memory of Sir Alfred Hickman, a well-known ironmaster and colliery proprietor who died in 1910. He advocated the development of the canal system from the Midlands to the ports of London, Liverpool, and Gloucester.

Ranton. Here, on Vicarage Farm, is a house with a priest's room and timber said to be 800 years old, while Ranton Abbey is a modern house near a noble tower among tall trees. The tower itself is about 500 years old, all that remains of an Augustinian priory founded here in the 12th century.

A yew about 14 feet round keeps company with the small 13th century church, which was restored in 1841, but has otherwise been little changed except for some 18th century brickwork round the chancel. The south door has 13th century nook shafts; the plain font is probably Norman. Two bells, which now hang in a war-memorial bell-turret, are believed to have rung the monks to service in the great days of the priory.

Rocester. It has lost a Roman camp and a Norman abbey. The camp was near a house known as Barrow Hill, and among the treasures found in its seven acres have been a brass spearhead, coins, and pottery. Of the Augustinian abbey founded in 1146 nothing is to be seen except green mounds in a field near the church.

Although this large village near the meeting of the Dove and the Churnet is very old, its church has not yet celebrated its centenary. It was rebuilt in 1872, except for the 14th century tower, which has a small spire. In the churchyard is the best-preserved cross in Staffordshire. About 20 feet high, with a beautifully clustered shaft ornamented with dog-tooth moulding, it is probably of the 13th century.

Rocester has large modern agricultural-machinery works and an old cotton-mill. This was built by Sir Richard Arkwright, the inventor of the spinning-frame, and was the first cotton-mill in Staffordshire, though it has since been enlarged.

Rolleston. Beautiful in the valley of the Dove, with Derbyshire just across the river, and preserving many old houses, it has woods and copses everywhere. High above it all rises the fine spire of the 14th century church.

Relatively a newcomer to the church is the oldest thing visible in the village, the great head of a Saxon cross, placed by an outer wall of the tower. This rich treasure was found forming part of the floor of a porch at Tatenhill Church, and an archaeological gem despised in one village has come to be the cherished prize of another.

Except for a modern aisle, a Norman doorway on the north, and a

Norman arch south of the nave, the church is entirely of the 14th century. The most surprising of the monuments is the alabaster figure in a chancel niche of Robert Sherebourne, lying as if asleep in the robes he wore as Bishop of Chichester for 28 of the most troublous years of the reign of Henry VIII. There is a statue of him in his old cathedral, but here he is, and beside him in a glass case is his episcopal seal which he gave to the church in 1503.

The earliest monument, in the sanctuary floor, shows the engraved figure of John Rolleston, a 15th century lord of the manor, lying in armour such as was worn during the Wars of the Roses, with a lion at his feet. By him is his wife, whose close-fitting gown is crowned by a hat like a flowerpot, and below the parents are their three children.

The strangest sculpture, on the east wall, is the 16th century alabaster Caldwell group. At the top kneel Thomas in a cloak and a ruff and his wife in a high-crowned hat and a ruff, and below, set between four columns, are their three solemn little sons, clad exactly like their father.

The long reign of the Rollestons ended soon after James I's began, when they sold the manor to the Mosleys, of whom Sir Edward, founder of that line, who died in 1638, is shown on a fine alabaster tomb, wearing the tunic, breeches, ruff, and long cloak of the period. Fine old glass in the Mosley chapel shows the Baptism and the presentation in the Temple.

Rudyard. In the heart of enchanting natural beauty, this small village is near the south end of Rudyard Lake, a reservoir nearly two miles long, built to feed the Macclesfield canal, opened in 1831. The centre of Staffordshire's little Lake District, it has glorious woods crowding down to the water's edge. It is a resort of week-end yachtsmen and a place of pilgrimage for lovers of beautiful things who come all the year round.

For some there is an invisible attraction, for the lake gave its name to one of the most famous writers of the late 19th and early 20th centuries, Rudyard Kipling. Among the leafy paths of this wonderland a few miles from the drabness of the "Five Towns", walked young Lockwood Kipling and Alice Macdonald, and here it was that he asked her to be his wife. So happy were they that when their son was born in India they christened him Rudyard in memory of this corner of Staffordshire that had meant so much to them.

Rugeley. A pleasant little town in the Trent valley, it looks to the wooded hills of Cannock Chase. It has engineering and clothing works, and a dominating power-station. Two men have made it notable, a good one and a bad one; and it has two churches that look at each other, a new one and an old one. The town also has an impressive Roman Catholic church near Lichfield Street, built in the 19th century, with a graceful tapering spire 150 feet high.

The old church became ruinous last century, and was deserted for its successor, but something has been saved from the wreck. Here still are the 14th century tower, one nave arcade with two very wide 15th century arches, and the 13th century chancel, which has a 14th century window, a piscina, and the stone seats for the priests for whom the doorway was built 500 years ago. There is a brass portrait of John Weston, wearing the long cloak and costume of Shakespeare's early days. Although reduced in size and with much of its glory vanished, the ancient church serves yet for worship.

The dignified new parish church, which replaces the ruin, was built in 1822 and is chiefly notable for its fine oak pulpit, carved with grapes, roses, and acorns as a setting for a figure of St Augustine. In the churchyard are the ashes of Thomas George Bonney, Rugeley's most distinguished son, who left the rectory here for Uppingham and Cambridge, to distinguish himself in mathematics and classics. A born student of nature, geology was his abiding passion, and during his vacations he explored practically the whole mountain systems of Europe, afterwards extending his investigations to the New World.

Entering the Church, he became lecturer in geology at Cambridge and London and President of the British Association. He was one of the pioneers of the microscopical study of rocks. He fired his students with an enthusiasm matching his own, and led them to study the rocks in all parts of the kingdom. Retiring after a quarter of a century in London to study and write in the quiet of Cambridge he spent his last 22 years there, and died in 1923, leaving a record of work and discovery which had made him famous.

Perhaps it is the bad man of Rugeley who is more widely known. His name is recalled by the most striking thing in the churchyard, a tombstone to John Parsons Cook, with the date 1855 and the statement that "his life was taken away". Behind that inscription lurks a terrible story. The man who took away the life of Cook was William Palmer, the Rugeley poisoner. Born in 1824 and educated at the grammar school here, he became acquainted with the nature of drugs as an apprentice to a Liverpool firm of druggists. He settled down as a doctor in a house opposite the Talbot Arms.

His practice being unremunerative, Palmer took to betting and racehorse-owning, seeking extrication from money difficulties by forging bills. In 1854 his wife, whom he had insured for £13,000, died with mysterious suddenness; and within a year his brother, whom he had insured for a similar amount, also died. On this occasion, however, a suspicious insurance company refused payment.

Palmer was by this time deeply in debt to a bookmaker, John Parsons Cook. Attending Shrewsbury races with Cook, he gave him poison and then conveyed him here, lodging him at the Talbot Arms. The poison did not kill him, and Cook summoned two other doctors, arranging that one should share his bedroom for the night. As Cook's medical attendant, Palmer was summoned from his house across the way, arriving immediately, ready dressed, as if he had expected a call. He gave the patient two more pills, and these effected his purpose, for his victim died in his presence.

The visiting doctor suspected no ill, but analysts from London declared that death was due to poison in the medicine Palmer had administered, and the coroner's jury returned a verdict of wilful murder against him. A hue and cry followed, for other people had died mysteriously after association with Palmer, but the police contented themselves with the exhumation of his wife and brother.

The case excited all Europe. *The Times* published an astounding article before the trial in London was reached, stating that Palmer had many partisans in Rugeley, adding: "The postmaster of the place is a spy in his interests, intercepts letters, and reports to him the contents. The very coroner of the adjacent country town, his judge, is for him as though he had been engaged as a solicitor for the defence, receives from him intercepted evidence from the other side, shrewd suggestions in his favour, and a present of game."

As astonishing feature of the 12-days trial was that, with all its resources, the prosecution was unable to identify the poison employed. Experts who attended the trial believed Palmer knew far more than his accusers about poisons, and had practised methods too subtle for them to penetrate. Palmer staggered on hearing the verdict, but instantly recovered. The execution was carried out in public at Stafford.

Rushall. There were stirring scenes in this suburb of Walsall in 1643 when Prince Rupert attacked the old hall, now sadly in ruins. It was bravely defended by the wife of Colonel Edward Leigh, but the Royalists made it their headquarters until they were driven out. A few of the cannon balls fired at the house can still be seen in the mediaeval walls. The Harpers defended the house in the Wars of the Roses, and their arms are still on the gateway.

The last of the Leighs to live at Rushall Hall was buried in the church in 1671. He was Edward Leigh, proud to his dying day of the way his wife had defended his house. He was a soldier, student of law, and a writer of books. The church, which was refashioned in 1854, has a font 700 years old.

Rushton Spencer. It is a remarkable church that we find here and a grim story that is told here. The story is of a young man buried alive—Thomas Meaykin, who was buried under a stone in the churchyard in 1781. "As a man falleth before wicked men: so fell I", we read, and the tale is that because Thomas was in love with his master's daughter her father had him drugged and buried alive at Stone. His friends, who are said to have opened his coffin and found him lying face downwards, brought his body to lie here in the place he had known as a child. The church stands alone on a hilltop high above the village, with noble firs and old yews about it; one of the yews is probably 500 years old.

The church, once known as the Chapel in the Wilderness, is unique in the county for having been built almost entirely of wood 600 years ago, though the timber was encased in stone in the 17th century and the high gabled dormer windows were inserted in 1848. A quaint little building, it has an 18th century timber-framed bell-turret, a roof of massive gritstone slabs covering nave and aisles, and a stone east gable of 1690. Inside are low beams with kingposts and a west gallery of 1719. The pulpit and squire's pew are of 17th century oak, and the massive font probably twice as old.

Some distance west of the church rises The Cloud, a gritstone hill nearly 1100 feet high, from which we look out over vast tracts of Staffordshire and Cheshire.

Sandon. It stirs our imagination by the beauty of the scene and the memories of the great. Its splendid park, home of the earls of Harrowby, with magnificent views along the Trent valley, of the Wrekin, of the Clent Hills, and of storied Chartley, is a little kingdom of great interest, embracing the fine hall of 1852–65 in the Jacobean style which replaces the Elizabethan house that was burnt down, the beautiful gardens, the interesting church, a lake, and at the end of an avenue of trees the moat, still wet, which long guarded the ancient manor of the Erdeswickes or Eardswicks.

The Erdeswickes were famous people in their day, but this place has links with other names which have outlived them all. Sandon has reminders of two Prime Ministers. The monument to Pitt was raised by his Foreign Minister, the first earl of Harrowby, who set up a column 75 feet high, modelled on the famous Trajan column. The other monument to a Premier is a Gothic shrine to Spencer Perceval, who was shot in the lobby of the House of Commons by a demented bankrupt. Not far from these memorials is a notable example of the work of the man who built the Houses of Parliament: it is the summit of the tower Sir Charles Barry raised at Trentham Hall, brought here when that great house was taken down early this century.

The 13th and 14th century church stands on high ground, with a 15th century tower looking down on eight stalwart yews. The south aisle is believed to have been the original church; the nave and the north chapel are 600 years old. There is mediaeval glass in the sanctuary, a Norman font and a curious square font of 1699 with figures at the corners, an altar table of 1644 and a Jacobean pulpit with a canopy.

The most famous possessions of the church are the monuments of the Erdeswickes, descendants of proud Normans. Hugh Erdeswicke is in his 15th century armour, with his wife in an ermined cloak, and their son Hugh, armoured but bareheaded, with his wife. Sampson Erdeswicke, who saw the red reign of Mary Tudor, lies with a dog at his feet, his wife in a long gown, and their five children. It was said of the next Hugh that he was "the sorest and most dangerous Papist in England"; here in this churchyard he struck a magistrate "upon the pate with his crabtree staff". All these Erdeswickes have alabaster tomb slabs with incised figures. On an immense monument is a second Sampson Erdeswicke, who died in 1601, in his red tunic and cloak, his two wives wearing long black dresses and white ruffs.

A pathetic story had the second wife, a Leicestershire heiress who first married Everard Digby and became the mother of a son who grew to manhood, a young giant in stature, full of promise. His widowed mother married Sampson and became a second time a widow, with only her son Everard Digby to comfort her. Everard turned Roman Catholic, and she turned too, and she had the agony of seeing him plunge into the murderous Gunpowder Plot which brought him to the scaffold. Sampson, with whom she kneels, settled down here to half a century of scholarly activity, the chief fruit of his labours being his treasured *History of Staffordshire*. He lavished time and fortune on this church, reglazing and restoring it, building his own tomb and monument, and painting the chancel walls with his family pedigree. His artistic record was lost, but in 1929, bright as the day they were painted, out from hiding came the old scholar's proud proclamation of the glory of the Erdeswickes.

Shugborough Park

The triumphal arch in the grounds at Shugborough Park

High House, in Greengate Street

STAFFORD

The Post Office, once the home of R. B. Sheridan

Here are all his pictures as he had them painted before 1601, genealogical trees rising from the tombs below, some of the trunks encircled with honeysuckle and vine. The ancestral trees being too small for all the heraldry of all the families he would commemorate, their shields are hung on branches or painted like stained-glass windows on the walls.

But the proud Erdeswickes are not all the pride of Sandon. There is a white stone near the porch in the churchyard which tells us that here lies the old vicar Walter Carless. Little was known of him, but much we know of his wife. She was Dr Johnson's first love and a cherished friend of his old age.

Ann Hector was a Lichfield girl, sister of one of Johnson's school-fellows. When the infatuation began and when it ended we do not know. Ann comes to knowledge late in the old scholar's life. In the course of a visit to Birmingham, where Edmund Hector then lived, Johnson, who was now 69, said to Boswell, "You will see, sir, at Mr Hector's, his sister, Mrs Carless, a clergyman's widow. She was the first woman with whom I was ever in love. It dropped out of my head imperceptibly; but she and I will always have a kindness for each other."

The same night he recurred to the subject as he and Boswell sat alone. "If I had married her it might have been as happy for me," he mused. And then, challenged on the subject, he declared that it was ridiculous to think that there was such a thing as only one woman for one man; things might work out very well if the Lord Chancellor, knowing all the circumstances, made marriages without the parties having any choice in the matter. There, however, we may assume that he was once more talking nonsense.

Ann's brother would have been proud of Johnson as his sister's husband. In youth he and two other boys used to call at Johnson's house in the morning, and, seating the young giant on his back, with one boy on either side as support, would carry him in triumph to school. He loved and venerated his old friend, and a few days before Johnson's death he wrote him an account of all he could remember of their boyhood, when Mrs Carless was Ann Hector, the gaunt young scholar's heroine.

Sedgley. Set on high ground at the edge of the Black Country, it has brick and fireclay works, collieries, and engineering works. Its dignified church, widely seen in this district where chimneys stand out above all else, was rebuilt in 1829, but has preserved memorials from an earlier church.

In the porch is a tablet to Michael Nickins and his wife, the only

L

surviving great-granddaughter of Sir Matthew Hale, a famous lawyer in the time of Charles I and the Commonwealth. He was counsel for Archbishop Laud in his impeachment, and prospered under both Royalists and Roundheads. Cromwell made him a Judge, and 18 years later Charles II raised him to be Lord Chief Justice.

Hereabouts in the 19th century were born two poets of county fame: David Bailey, a Shakespeare student long associated with Sir Isaac Pitman, and John Cornfield, a Radical reformer, a brickmaker, pawnbroker, and eccentric member of the Board of Guardians which sat at Dudley. John Cornfield was found drowned on his own estate, and left behind this verse among his writings:

> *So man comes forth a peevish April fool;*
> *In vain pursuits oft wastes his life away;*
> *Fain would he take from heaven its sovereign rule,*
> *And have unclouded sunshine every day.*
> *Forgets that summer's bounteous crops depend*
> *On winter's rigour and the stormy blast,*
> *That they who sow in tears till life shall end*
> *Shall reap with joy in summer-land at last.*

Above the town to the north-east rises the long ridge of Sedgley Beacon, commanding a view over the Black Country in one direction and of woods and fields in the other.

Seighford. Here lies a knight of the exciting Armada days, Sir William Bowyer, whose splendid tomb is one of the treasures of the church. Sir William, who died in 1593, wears armour; his wife is in a long gown and ruff, and with them are their six children, one in swaddling clothes.

Other things to see in this interesting church, rebuilt on a Saxon foundation, are the arches and massive pillars of the north arcade and the fine chancel arch, all Norman. The brick Gothic tower and the south side of the nave were built in 1754 by William Baker, but the tower rather curiously retains its 15th century pinnacles. The chancel is also of the 15th century; it has a huge arch opening to the north chapel (perhaps originally two arches) and a mediaeval window with portraits of the Virgin and Child, St Christopher crossing the river, a queen, a nun, a man, and a girl with golden hair, all nearly 500 years old. The finely carved pulpit is Jacobean.

Seighford, three miles from Stafford, is pleasant with its old brick cottages, and across the fields is seen the black-and-white timber-framed hall (now a hotel), with tall chimneys rising above noble cedars.

Shallowford. This quiet hamlet stands by the Meece Brook, and it should be a place of pilgrimage of all anglers, for here is Izaak Walton's farm. The brick-and-timber outbuildings are still much as he must have seen them, the black-and-white cottage still delightful. It was this farm that the kindly Izaak left to his native town of Stafford, stipulating that the rent should be used each year to apprentice two poor boys, provide a marriage portion for a servant girl, and buy coal for the needy.

His cottage was opened as a museum in 1924 and has unhappily been burned down twice since, but it has been built up again and refurnished carefully in a worthy effort to recapture the spirit of the angler's peaceful days. Here are all kinds of things fishermen delight in, old pictures of Walton's day, pictures of the fishing house where he and his friend Charles Cotton loved to idle, and the fireplace at which he sat long ago. How dearly Walton loved this corner of Staffordshire we know from one of his poems, picturing his life of contentment here:

> *Here give my weary spirits rest,*
> *And raise my low-pitched thoughts above*
> *Earth, or what poor mortals love:*
> *Thus, free from lawsuits and the noise*
> *Of Princes' courts, I would rejoice;*
> *Or with my Bryan and a book,*
> *Loiter long days near Shawford brook;*
> *There sit by him, and eat my meat,*
> *There see the sun both rise and set;*
> *There bid good morning to next day;*
> *There meditate my time away,*
> *And angle on and beg to have*
> *A quiet passage to a welcome grave.*

Shareshill. One of the strangest of feudal tenures is remembered in this parish, where an old hall and a church have the company of a windmill which, now sailless, was grinding corn when Charles II was king.

Hilton Park Hall, east of the Wolverhampton–Cannock road, was the home of the Vernons for four centuries and before that of the Swynnertons, lords of the manor long before the Vernons arrived, but is now the guest house of a Roman Catholic convent. In the large wooded park stands the lofty tower built in 1741 by Henry Vernon to commemorate the capture of Portobello two years earlier by his admiral kinsman.

In the hall was long preserved a mediaeval hollow brass figure, a man leaning on his knee, with a hand on his breast, known as Jack of Hilton. Under a feudal charter the lord of the neighbouring manor of Essington held his lands on condition that each New Year's day he brought here a live goose, and drove it three times round the central fire of the hall. Filled with water through a hole which was afterwards plugged, Jack of Hilton was placed in the fire; the water boiled and issued as steam from his mouth. The promenade with the goose had to be completed while Jack steamed, after which the bird was carried to a table, where its owner received from the lord of the hall his title deed to another year's tenancy.

The tower is all that is left of the 15th century church. The body of the church, in brick and stone, seems to be of the 18th century, and it has an unusual porch with bulbous pillars. The church has a battered heritage of its ancient treasure in two sadly worn and broken figures, kept on windowsills, one said to represent Sir Humphrey Swynnerton and the other his wife. He wears his armour, with a chain and pendant, she has her ruff; they are the last visible links with the ancient family from whom the hall passed to the Vernons.

Among the vicars here last century was William Havergal, one of the most gifted musicians the church has produced. From boyhood an organist, he was ordained when 23, but met with an accident which crippled him for years. During that time he found consolation in musical composition; he wrote anthems, services, and hymns; he brought about a re-birth of glory in church music. Frances Ridley Havergal, writer of many famous hymns, was his daughter, and after his death in 1870 she edited and published his work.

Sheen. For a lovely view of the famous Dove Valley and the surrounding limestone uplands we should climb Sheen Hill, to the north, with its rocky tor. In the church is a brass to A. J. B. Beresford-Hope, who rebuilt it, in the Decorated Gothic style, in the last century. He also built the school and the delightful vicarage with grey walls and windows of all shapes and sizes. In the school yard is a 15th century cross on five steps. The oldest stones in the church are in the north wall; outside the east window, exposed to the wind and rain, is the worn figure of a priest who ministered here 400 years ago, and outside the west end are some curious gargoyles.

Shenstone. This growing village, with many new houses of commuters from Birmingham and the Black Country, clusters round a hill above the Black Brook. On the windy hilltop, below two towers, is buried the last of Nelson's captains, Admiral Sir William Parker. He was a midshipman at 12, commanded his own ship when he was 21, and took part in the famous chase of Villeneuve, the man who lost Trafalgar. By 1812 he was rich enough to buy Shenstone Lodge (now a school, south of the village) where he lived for 15 years as a country gentleman, but he answered his country's call in 1827, and 14 years later sailed to China, where he captured many towns and won a knighthood. In the 30 years which followed he did much to establish a high standard of discipline in the navy.

The old church he knew was mostly pulled down in 1853, when the new church was built, but the 13th century doorway and the 16th century tower are here. The churchyard is a magnificent view-point, with a prospect towards Cannock Chase. The new church, in the Decorated style, has its own tall tower, an oak reredos with a panel of St George and the Dragon, and a wheel window in memory of the Admiral, who died in 1866. Near the vestry door is an interesting iron memorial to Catherine Browne, who died in 1704.

Stafford. Over 1200 years ago began the story of Stafford as we know it. Here St Bertelin, prince of the Mercian kingdom, renounced that kingdom and built himself a hermitage. Here Alfred's daughter Ethelfleda in 913 built fortifications against the Danes. Here one of the Conqueror's own kinsmen was feudal lord. Here came the Earl of Richmond on his way to Bosworth Field to found the Tudor dynasty, and here came Elizabeth I, receiving from the people the gift of a silver cup. We may still see a little of the town as Henry Tudor would have seen it, and a little more that Elizabeth would have known.

Old England lives on in Stafford's busy streets, Tudor days and the 20th century side by side. We walk the byways round St Mary's church, and above ancient doors and windows and modern shopfronts are blackened beams which have stood the rain and the wind 400 years and more. In Church Lane are several charming houses, among them two timber-framed buildings with overhanging upper storeys. In Mill Street, farther south, is a quaint little thatched and timbered dwelling, dated 1610 but now altered as a shop, and near by is a group of almshouses built about 300 years ago. In the thriving Greengate Street, the main street, heavy traffic passes between north and south, but all the bustle of wheels, all the miscellany of modern buildings, cannot take away the dignity of Stafford's finest old dwelling, High House, built in 1555. Proudly it stands four storeys high, with sturdy gables and splendidly timbered sides, a challenge to the meanness of some of its neighbours.

In this house Charles I stayed in 1642, while on his way to recruit more men at Shrewsbury. Here Prince Rupert displayed his skill as a marksman. Standing in what was then the garden, he took a shot with a horseman's pistol at the weathercock of the church; the bullet pierced the tail and the hole was plainly seen by all below. The king thought it a chance, but Rupert, taking aim again, pierced the cock's tail a second time. The cock now here replaced Prince Rupert's victim.

It was in the Civil War, when the town was loyal to the Stuarts, that the Parliament troops brought the walls of Stafford's Norman castle to the ground, so that nothing of it remains. Close by High House, now with shops in its lower quarters, are other old houses converted into shops, but having heavily timbered walls and gables. Charming it is to see the old architecture peeping out among the new. A few yards away is the Swan Hotel, an old inn with bow windows and a plastered front, and an air of coaching days. Dickens stayed here one night and called it "the extinct town inn, the Dodo", but George Borrow found it busier. Here this strange genius came as an ostler in 1852, after parting from Isopel Berners in Mumpers Dingle, and he tells about it in some of the most fascinating chapters in *Romany Rye*:

The inn, of which I had become an inhabitant, was a place of infinite life & bustle.

Travellers of all descriptions, from all the cardinal points, were continually stopping at it. Jacks creaked in the kitchens, turning round spits on which large joints of meat piped & smoked before great fires. There was running up & down the stairs, & along galleries, slamming of doors, cries of Coming, sir, & Please-to-step-this-way, ma'am, during 18 hours of the four & twenty.

Truly a very great place for life & bustle was this inn. And often in after life, when lonely & melancholy, I have called up the time I spent there, & never failed to become cheerful from the recollection.

In the same street is the brick and stone Chetwynd House (now the post office) where the Duke of Cumberland paused in 1745, in his pursuit of the Young Pretender, and Richard Brinsley Sheridan, the town's M.P. for 26 years from 1780, often stayed. The making of boots and shoes was one of Stafford's chief industries then, as now, and Sheridan made this witty toast about it: *May the trade of Stafford be trod underfoot by all the world.*

But let us go by the narrow way from Greengate Street beneath the timbers of High House. In a few strides we are confronted by Stafford's noblest church. St Mary's has an impressive octagonal tower, one of the few of its kind in England. The top is about 600 years old, the base older by a century. Very imposing is the 14th century doorway into the north transept, with its three orders of carving, ballflower and quatrefoil. The south transept, the south porch, and other parts of the church were altered during a considerable restoration by Sir Gilbert Scott in 1844.

Almost cathedral-like in its dimensions is this fine cruciform church. The tower rests on pillars of immense thickness. The fine nave and the aisles are probably 800 years old, the lofty chancel was built about 1300, and the clerestory windows are early Tudor. All the pillars in the nave differ in size and detail, and all the arches vary a little in width: these slightly pointed arches indicate the transition from the Norman style of architecture to the Early English. The nave has a rich timber roof of about 1500.

The font, one of the strangest in England, has survived eight centuries remarkably well. The great bowl is of irregular quatrefoil shape and has between its divisions four queer figures with a human resemblance in their faces and greatly attenuated bodies. Under the bowl crouch four massive lions, and round the base are four more animals grotesquely wrought. At this font Stafford's most illustrious son, Izaak Walton, was baptised. There is a white stone bust of him against a wall of the north aisle, and the face has the gentle expression we should expect. It is the only memorial to him in the town where he was born.

In the nave and chancel are hundreds of pew ends, and they are among the treasures of the church, all enriched with carving and all different, some with exquisite heads, others with elegant floral decorations. They are the work of last century. In one of the nave windows are a few fragments of 14th century glass, and the clerestory windows have panels with heraldry. Above the chancel arch are two angels with trumpets, painted 200 years ago, and other wallpaintings are to be found in the nave. The churchyard of St. Mary's has been laid out as a garden of Remembrance.

In the north transept is a splendid 16th-century tomb on which lie the alabaster figures of Sir Edward Aston, the builder of Tixall Hall and its gatehouse, and his wife Joan Bollys. He has lost his head and hands, but the lady is complete and exquisite, her head resting on an elegantly embroidered cushion. Round the sides are their eighteen children.

In the north transept, too, is a case of old relics. They include a

16th century pitchpipe used for starting the singing of the choir, and a fine black jack of 1750 with the names of the ringers of that year and of 1798 upon it.

Outside the west end of the church is the site of St Bertelin's chapel, excavated in 1954. Somewhere near this spot St Bertelin set up his hermitage, and around it the church would grow. The foundation stones, dated from about A.D. 1000, were restored. The wooden cross is a replica of a cross found five feet below the surface of the ground and perhaps the preaching cross of St Bertelin himself.

It is only a few steps, across Greengate Street again, to one of the greatest surprises in Stafford. Tucked away between modern buildings the tiny church of St Chad contains some of the finest Norman work in the county. The imposing arch over the entrance, with 16 grotesque beak-heads and zigzag carving, is a 19th century copy of Norman, part of the restoration by Scott, but inside we are in a building little changed since the Conqueror's day. The chancel arch is complete and practically perfect, an impressive sight. It has five orders of carving with hardly a blemish, and placed sideways down the columns are no fewer than 48 weirdly carved heads, no two alike. The nave with its massive pillars, the clerestory with its deep little windows, the arcade of simple arches and zigzag moulding, are all as their Norman makers left them. We look at the wall by the south-west pier of the tower and see a deeply cut inscription, made probably by the builder of the church; in it we read the name Odin, and the letters are almost as plain as on the day they were cut.

In the chancel is a series of small Norman arches with interlaced arcading, all finely preserved, discovered behind plaster some years ago. The men who made them may have made the splendid font, massively carved with grotesque heads in deep relief. We leave this small place feeling that we have truly stepped through the centuries; there are not many churches in England which give us a more complete picture of Norman times.

Born at Stafford in 1593, and apprenticed in London early in youth, Izaak Walton never forgot his birthplace, and was never more thankful to revisit it than when, after the Battle of Marston Moor, the party with which he was in sympathy sustained a crushing defeat. It was there, again, that he awaited the news of the Battle of Worcester, and was entrusted with the custody of Charles II's "lesser George" jewel.

The little shop in which he made his modest competence stood two doors west of Chancery Lane, in Fleet Street, hard by St Dunstan's Church, where Dr Donne, Izaak's friend, was vicar.

Through Donne he became acquainted with all the great church-men of the day. He married first a great-grandniece of Cranmer, and secondly the half-sister of Bishop Ken, author of such famous hymns as "Awake my soul", and "Glory to Thee, my God, this night". Walton was 19 when Shakespeare died; Michael Drayton was his "honest old friend"; he was familiarly acquainted with Ben Jonson; and he must often have encountered Milton, Pepys, and Evelyn, who, with Sir Thomas Browne, were among his contemporaries.

It was not until his sixtieth year that he published his *Compleat Angler*. There has never been anything like it. Amid the crash and thunder of the great staggering sentences of the 17th century rhetor-icians come these quiet enchanting tones, musing aloud in melody: jocund, happy, charged with poetry, a prose poet singing late and lone.

What a world of wonder and delight he creates as with his two comrades he stretches his legs from Tottenham Hill to Ware, resting in the rain to fish and shelter beneath the great honeysuckle hedge; buying with his catch of fish the favour of a buxom dairymaid who ceases milking her red cow to sing, at his request, "Come, live with me, and be my love"; and of the milkmaid's comely mother to "sing the second part, an answer to it which was made by Sir Walter Raleigh in his younger days":

> *If all the world and love were young*
> *And truth in every Shepherd's tongue,*
> *These pretty pleasures might me move*
> *To live with thee and be thy love.*

And so on to the inn, where they find a clean room, lavender in the windows, and twenty ballads stuck about the walls; where the hostess instantly roasts the chub that Piscator has caught and proves it, when they have said grace, worthy of the praise, "Trust me, 'tis as good meat as ever I tasted."

But Hertfordshire, then as now, had birds to gladden the air as well as fish to grace its streams, and we see how the monarch of them all impresses honest Izaak:

> *The nightingale, another of my airy creatures, breathes such sweet loud music out of her little instrumental throat, that it might make mankind to think miracles are not ceased. He that at midnight, when the very labourer sleeps securely, should hear, as I have very often, the clear airs, the sweet descants, the natural rising and falling; the doubling and redoubling of her voice, might well be lifted above earth, and say, "Lord, what music hast Thou*

157

provided for the saints in heaven, when Thou affordest bad men such music on earth?"

Here is the prose challenge of the 17th century to the melody and imagination of Keats and Shelley.

Walton's *Lives*, biographies of Donne, Wotton, Hooker, Herbert, and Robert Sanderson are unrivalled in their era. For more than 200 years scholars have been editing Walton and producing more and more sumptuous editions of his writings. He showers an added lustre upon historic Winchester, in the shelter of whose episcopal palace he passed his closing years and wrote his *Lives*. For all his apparent simplicity he was a punctilious artist; he gave two years to the writing of his life of Hooker, which runs only to some 20,000 words—a week's work for a journalist. His heroes shine the brighter from the spirit emanating from his personality and genius.

Stafford has made no richer contribution to the world than this gifted son of hers, who closed his creel in 1683, at the ripe old age of ninety.

Standon. Although its church was much restored about 100 years ago, it keeps its Norman doorway, its Norman font, and Norman stones in the base of its 16th century tower, standing amid yews and sycamores. The arches in the nave have rested on octagonal pillars for 700 years; they are taller on the south than on the north, and only the north side of the nave has a clerestory. In a recess in the chancel lies the broken alabaster figure of a priest, and on an alabaster monument in the south chapel are the engraved portraits of Francis Rose who died in 1500, his wife in a long gown, and their ten children. Ten old stalls in the chancel have misericords with roses and grotesques; and on one of the stalls is an inscription to William Thompson, who began singing here in 1860 and went on singing out of one century into another until he had been at it for over 50 years.

Stanton. A small village above the charming Titbrook valley, it has a little 19th century church looking out far over a lovely countryside, and a road taking us by a fragment that remains of Ouseley Cross.

The road by the cross brings us by a lovely dale to Ellastone, which gave George Eliot Adam Bede and Charles I one of his truest friends, Gilbert Sheldon, who was born here in 1598. He was the king's chaplain and constant attendant during the Civil War, and at the Restoration became Bishop of London, then Archbishop of Canterbury, and Chancellor of Oxford. A relentless opponent of Nonconformists, he was generous and helpful to individuals. During the Great Plague he stayed at Lambeth Palace while so many fled, and heroically sustained the sufferers. He lost the royal favour by an act of great courage, for he denounced the gross immorality of Charles II and refused him the Holy Communion.

Although a poor man's son, Sheldon gathered riches and spent them nobly, his benefactions representing over £350,000 of our money. His crowning work was the theatre at Oxford which bears his name. Built by Wren, it cost some £125,000 in modern currency, and was opened in 1669. In addition Sheldon laid out £10,000 on lands to support the fabric from their revenues. He died in 1677 and was buried at Croydon, in Surrey.

Stapenhill. Here by the Trent came Britons, Romans, and Saxons. About 30 skeletons were found in a Saxon cemetery many years ago, with urns, beads, iron knives, and spearheads, now in the museum at Burton, on the other side of the river.

The old church was refashioned in 1880, when it was given its prominent tower, inspired by the tower of Magdalen College, Oxford. The church has one heritage from its mediaeval days, a much-worn alabaster monument engraved with the portraits of William and Mary Dethick, he in the armour he wore in the 15th century, she in a close-fitting hat. Their eight children are with them.

Statfold. A few houses and farms, a hall, and its private church are almost all there is to see in this hamlet by the Warwickshire border. The hall, a big house which has been the home of the Wolferstans since the 15th century, has an octagonal turret said to have been built by Francis Wolferstan, a Jacobite and poet.

The small church in the hall grounds, long used as a mortuary chapel, has been restored for worship. The south door and two windows in the chancel are of the 14th century, and the west door and two little windows in the nave are of the 13th. The figures of two women have been lying under arches in the chancel for 600 years, one wearing a veil and one a bonnet, and in the east window is 17th century glass of unknown provenance.

Stoke-upon-Trent. The centre of the great china, porcelain, and earthenware industry, it has absorbed Longton, Fenton, Hanley, Burslem, and Tunstall. Arnold Bennett's "Five Towns" (there are actually six) were joined in 1910 to form the city of Stoke-on-Trent.

159

In this area are hundreds of potteries; their great firing-ovens were once as characteristic a feature as the oasts of the hop-gardens of Kent, but they have all been replaced by electricallyfi-red ovens. Here are buried potters who made English wares famous throughout the world, and the city seeks to be worthy of them. A fine building is the classical town hall with its stately columns, built in 1836. The College of Art, built in 1856, is the city's tribute to the memory of Herbert Minton; and the North Staffordshire College of Technology carries on the great tradition of Wedgwood, Spode, Copeland, Minton, and other local craftsmen.

Opposite the handsome King's Hall is the dignified war memorial, modelled on the Cenotaph in Whitehall. In the grounds of the Minton factory, in London Road, is a bronze statue of Colin Minton Campbell, three times mayor of Stoke and benefactor of his native town. But the proudest personal monument is that of the city's greatest son, Josiah Wedgwood, who welcomes the visitor at the station. Proudly regarding one of his own vases, he stands, a lifelike figure in bronze, proclaiming to all comers that here is the kingdom of the potters, while his townsmen have made him declare that he himself is its chief.

The story of Stoke is the story of a long and stirring struggle with difficulties, and of a splendid discontent which has inspired its potters to better their best, and to maintain the progress first attained when Wedgwood's genius inspired them.

There are several churches, the oldest (St Peter ad Vincula) rebuilt in 1839. In its churchyard is part of a Saxon cross, probably of the 10th century, decorated with knotwork. Here are erected two round arches on slender pillars, remnants of an arcade of the mediaeval church. In the churchyard is a tombstone with an astonishing inscription which says that Sibil and Henry Clark died in 1684, each aged 112. If it is true, they were born before the Armada came, lived through the days of Shakespeare's greatness, would shudder to hear of Charles I's execution, and would be amazed to learn that London was burning.

The chancel of the church is a gallery of remembrance of the great potters. Here on an alabaster tablet is a beautiful medallion of the prince of potters by a prince of sculptors, Josiah Wedgwood (who was buried here in 1795) lovingly depicted by the master hand of Flaxman, a veritable portrait of the man who raised the Potteries from primitive craftsmanship to a centre of high art; a noble figure, genius, philosopher, and true lover of his fellows. On the monument are carved two vases symbolising his life's work.

There is a bronze medallion to his favourite pupil William Adams,

PENKRIDGE : The engraved stone Monument of William and Katherine Winnesbury, 1523

of Tunstall, a skilled potter who fashioned some of the choicest work of the age (he died in 1805 and is buried at Wolstanton); and there is a simple memorial to William Taylor Copeland (who died in 1868), the commercial traveller who made known the works of Spode, was lord mayor of London, and brought immense wealth to Stoke.

Three Josiah Spodes are remembered here. The first founded the china works in 1770; the second revolutionised porcelain by introducing bone into it, and made the famous willow-pattern ware; the third has a marble monument with the figure of a woman weeping by a casket. Here also are memories of Herbert Minton, who, a child when Wedgwood died, was inspired by the example of his great predecessor to surround himself with the most gifted artists of his generation and to produce such porcelains, tiles, and mosaics as had never before been seen. Beginning with a staff of 50 rough-and-ready potters, he made his works 30 times as large in as many years, a veritable wonderland of art and industry.

In Church Street is the Spode–Copeland Museum, which contains early Spode and other pottery and also preserves an old "bottle oven" of the kind that was once a familiar sight in the Potteries but has now practically disappeared. All the interests at St Peter's are associated with this staple industry. Men who made the Potteries wealthy and their name famous through the world came to this church to worship. All were disciples of Wedgwood, all lit a lamp at the torch he had left burning. But for him there would have been no Spodes or Mintons.

Of all the arts of England, none is more native to the soil than the work of the Staffordshire potter centred in the six towns we now know as Stoke. It has often a sort of childish innocence of design, which owes nothing to foreign influences and which makes it in its way as characteristic of its country as Chinese porcelain. It can in no way be compared to that incomparable ware either in colour, design, or workmanship, but in its products may be traced almost as clearly the story of generations, even of centuries, of discovery and invention in glaze, decoration, and material.

Staffordshire ware travels all over the world today. It would hardly be possible to find a civilised dwelling in any continent without some of its cups and saucers or dinner plates or other articles of domestic use, and most of these have the attractiveness which is based on adaptability to use and correctness of design. Of late years decoration and design, after a lapse in Victorian days, have greatly improved, partly owing to the search for new ideas and partly because many of the beautiful old patterns have been revived.

It would be hard to decide when this antique beauty was at its best, for the work of the Staffordshire potter has taken many forms. It seems to have always been present, ever since England exchanged vessels of wood or pewter for pottery, and was probably there long before that, for in the history of any country the clay turned on the potter's wheel has led the potter to seek for new elegance and distinction. We need not suppose that it was at Stoke or Burslem, or at any of the Six Towns, that English pottery was cradled. It certainly was made widely elsewhere, and one of its new departures can be traced to Fulham and to the genius of John Dwight, the greatest potter England ever knew.

Before then Staffordshire had its own particular pottery, known as slip ware, which, though not confined to the Potteries, became identified with them because of the names of Ralph and Thomas Toft, who produced some of the finest pieces and left their name on their masterpieces. Any Chinese designer might be proud of one of the Toft dishes in the British Museum.

The new era in Staffordshire pottery came with John Dwight of Fulham who aimed at reproducing the substance and glazes of Chinese porcelain. His own researches never led farther than stoneware, one variety of which became known as the Staffordshire red clay, and in the hands of the brothers Elers, who set up a factory at Bradwell Wood near Burslem, was fashioned into teapots and cups with stamped and raised ornament. It was altogether as different from the everyday pottery of Staffordshire at that time as Josiah Wedgwood's elaborate models and patterns differed at a much later date from that of the other factories about him. It gave new impetus to the Staffordshire Potteries. Thomas Astbury and Joshua Twyford continued to make the red ware, introducing the first of those small Staffordshire figures which through two centuries remained the most characteristic art of the Potteries, though both art and craft flowed into many other channels.

Staffordshire was not to be left behind in the revolution brought about by the manufacture of English porcelain, but for the greater part the county remained faithful to its own earthenware, and made an advance in it which it has never lost and which remains the practice today. The fine white biscuit ware was dipped into a fluid glaze and subjected to a further firing. As the glaze contained white lead the process was accompanied by danger to the dippers, such as modern factory legislation has sought to eliminate.

The Potteries were to win a new renown in the days of Josiah Wedgwood who, while the rest of the world was making porcelain, raised Staffordshire's cream-coloured earthenware to worldwide fame. The perfection of this earthenware was Wedgwood's greatest achievement, but he will always be remembered for his untiring experiments in producing new forms, new colourings, and new designs, and for his lavish expenditure in employing English artists to decorate his pieces.

Contemporary with Wedgwood was Thomas Whieldon, one of those rare inventive craftsmen from whom new methods naturally flow. He gave Staffordshire the Whieldon ware, enriched with mottled and coloured glazes, which is one of its dearest possessions; and with him sprang into life again those Staffordshire figures which, even more than those produced by Chelsea or Bow or Worcester, represent a native English art in inspiration and modelling. Dainty is the last word one would apply to most of them, but they have vigour and life and humour borrowed from nowhere else.

Last in the survey of the Potteries is the name of Josiah Spode, who came in with the bone-ash porcelain, and whose Staffordshire factory was raised by his vigour and enterprise to a great position.

Josiah Wedgwood was born in 1730 into a family of potters, and owing to the death of his father was taken from school at nine and apprenticed to his brother. Illness maimed his right leg, and for the 25 years in which he was struggling for success he was constantly pained and hampered by his malady, which was not relieved until he submitted to amputation.

To a natural aptitude for his calling he added a passion for study and experiment, and by hard thinking and frugal living he was able to start a tiny business of his own and to apply art and science to the primitive methods then current. To improve his wares he had to revolutionise workshop practice, inventing new tools and teaching men to use them. In his quest of quality and beauty he nearly beggared himself with experiments in which his chemical combinations failed him, wrong temperatures ruined his pots, and kiln after kiln had to be destroyed.

Abundant success eventually rewarded his high courage and unflagging endeavour. He produced a beautiful cream ware which established him as the first potter of the age. It was used at Court; it was found in all aristocratic homes; it reached the Continent; it crossed the Atlantic; and eventually the Empress of Russia ordered a dinner service of it, the cost of which was 50 guineas for the actual ware and 40 times as much for its decoration.

Staffordshire pottery now became famous throughout the world. Wedgwood loved to be known as a creator of beauty rather than a mere vendor of pottery, and he had the fortune to see beauty pay. Wisely he spent his wealth and energy. He had a great share in

St Chad's Church, Stafford

The west front of Tutbury Church

The St Vincent mausoleum at Stone

Mediaeval figure of Christ
at Swinnerton

Pre-Conquest pillar in the churchyard of
St Peter's, Wolverhampton

promoting the Grand Junction Canal, uniting the Mersey, the Trent, and the Severn; and in making Staffordshire roads fit for Staffordshire commerce. He built great works and a great house for himself, made many families rich and happy. He left a fortune of half a million and the proud record of having achieved something notable in developing a love of elegant things.

Stone. It has a story which reads something like a Greek tragedy; it has been the nursery and sepulchre of saints; and here are buried a poet who knew Shakespeare, a sailor who saved us from invasion, and a bishop who helped to free Australia from a shameful chapter of its history.

It is possible that it might have averted the horrors of Culloden. When Charles Edward, the Young Pretender, burst into Stafford-shire in 1745 the Duke of Cumberland, seeking to give him battle, made his headquarters here at Stonefield. Charles went to Leek and from there sent out a messenger to his friends. The messenger got drunk by the way, and the chance of an encounter and a swift decision between the rival forces was thus missed.

It is possible also that Motley Pits, an old entrenchment here, may be the relics of defences thrown up in the Civil War, but it is also possible that they are of Saxon origin. Bury Bank, an encampment a mile and a half away near the Newcastle road, is said to be the site of the fortified palace of Wulfere, the 7th century Mercian king. Converted to Christianity, he married a daughter of Egbert and became the father of Werburgh, over whose grave rose the cathedral at Chester. Soured and shaken by incessant wars, Wulfere reverted to paganism; and because his sons clung to their faith he murdered them. Filled with remorse for what he had done, he pleaded before St Chad, who bade him stamp out idolatry from his kingdom; and he was faithful to his pledge. The scene of the tragedy is at the bottom of Abbey Street, where we may see the vaulted cellar of Priory House and the scanty remains of the ancient walls. They are all that is visible of the priory founded by Queen Ermenilda in memory of her murdered sons.

The new church was built partly on the site of the priory church in 1758 by William Robinson, who adopted the Gothic style. The chancel was rebuilt in 1887. The church is the patriarch of the town, for the town hall and the market hall are both of the 19th century. In the churchyard, where the chancel of the old church stood, exposed to the weather, is a 17th century altar tomb with William Crompton in Stuart dress, his head resting on a helmet, and his wife in a long dress and ruff.

In the family mausoleum, east of the church, is buried John Jervis, earl of St Vincent, Nelson's great leader, who by his victory over a Spanish fleet prevented its junction with the navy of France, and so averted the most serious threat of invasion of our shores since the Armada. Born at Meaford Hall (since demolished), not far away, he loved this place, and ordered that wherever he might die he should be buried here. As a token of his affection for the church he commissioned his friend Sir William Beechey to paint the picture which hangs above the gallery in the north aisle, of St Michael's triumph over Satan. The sanctuary window of the Resurrection marks the centenary of St Vincent's great sea victory; and a window of 1897 in the north aisle has figures of the martyred sons of the Saxon king, Wulfad and Rufin. The admiral's personal memorial, with a fine bust by Chantrey, is on the west wall of the nave. The oldest things in the church are the worn sculptures of a priest and a woman 600 years old, and next in antiquity is the 17th century brass, on the south wall, of Thomas Crompton, younger brother of William, in Jacobean armour, with his wife and their six children.

In the churchyard is buried Thomas Bakewell, a poor weaver who gave his life to the study of insanity and established a private asylum where, by humane and rational methods, he effected astonishing cures. A poet as well as a reformer, he sang of the moorlands, of his weaving, of the sorrows of the poor, and tenderly of animal life. He died in 1835, aged 74.

In the richly decorated 19th century Roman Catholic church, in North Street, is an altar tomb with the effigy of Bishop Ullathorne. Humbly born at Pocklington in Yorkshire, he was first a sailor, next a monk, and then went at 25 as chaplain to New South Wales, where he worked heroically among depraved and desperate convicts. After five years he returned home to write a scathing exposure of the terrible convict system, and, though his criticism aroused the indignation of vested interests in the colony, he helped to kill the idea of transportation and to make Australia a land for free citizens of the Empire. As Bishop of Birmingham he laboured for 38 years, dying in 1889.

The most illustrious native of Stone was the landscape painter Peter de Wint, who, beginning his career under John Raphael Smith, the famous engraver, won lasting repute by his portrayal of the rustic beauties of the north and eastern counties. Although he died in 1849 his fame abides, and all may see his work in the National Gallery and the Tate Gallery, in London.

But of all the names that come to us in Stone is one perhaps more enduring than all these—Richard Barnfield, the poet who knew

Shakespeare, who wrote poems which have come down to us erroneously attributed to Shakespeare himself. His home is gone and his grave lost, but here somewhere is buried this little-known immortal.

For two centuries and more the world read and loved two poems by this young squire, thinking Shakespeare himself had written them. Even today we find Richard Barnfield's work in most of the complete works of Shakespeare, in the group titled *The Passionate Pilgrim*. Few poems in that group, in fact, were written by the master himself, though they were given to the world as his in 1599. Who but the authors was to know of the theft? The sonnet which begins:

> *If music and sweet poetry agree,*
> *As needs they must (the sister and the brother),*

is in the perfect Shakespearean style, and the ode is a lyric worthy of Shakespeare both in its imagery and in its human touch.

The Ode opens with these often-quoted lines:

> *As it fell upon a day*
> *In the merry month of May,*
> *Sitting in a pleasant shade*
> *Which a grove of myrtles made,*
> *Beasts did leap and birds did sing,*
> *Trees did grow and plants did spring;*
> *Everything did banish moan*
> *Save the nightingale alone.*

The poet goes on to write about the sweet sad singer in lines which stirred Swinburne to hail him as "the first adequate English laureate of the nightingale" with none to take his place until Keats, who not only wrote the famous *Ode to the Nightingale* but, like Barnfield, was inspired by Spenser. The human note in the *Ode* reminding one of Shakespeare is in Barnfield's description of the true friend, who, he says, is not the flatterer whose words are easy, "like the wind", and who is no friend but in misery,

> *He that is thy friend indeed,*
> *He will help thee in thy need;*
> *If thou sorrow, he will weep;*
> *If thou wake, he cannot sleep;*
> *Thus of every grief in heart*
> *He with thee doth bear a part.*

This poem, which will keep Barnfield's name alive, was published with a few others in 1599, one being "Remembrance", in which he praised his four favourite poets (Spenser, Samuel Daniel, Michael Drayton, and Shakespeare). Though Shakespeare, who was ten years older, had already published some of his plays, Barnfield only praises him for his "Venus" and "Lucrece" perhaps because it was only Spenser's type of poetry that interested him. Though he was but 24 he had published two other books. *The Affectionate Shepherd*, an imitation of a poem by Virgil, and *Cynthia*, claiming that his Cynthia was "the first imitation of the verse of that excellent poet Master Spenser, in his *Faerie Queene*". The fact is that he imitated too much and never for more than a line or two let his own imagination catch fire. He wrote smoothly and had an intense love for all flowers, birds, and beasts: the countryside of Staffordshire is always in the background.

Born in Norbury Manor in 1574, he went at 15 to Oxford. The last we know of him as a poet is from his third book in 1605, but we do know that he lived the life of a country gentleman at Darlaston, near Stone, had a son, nursed a granddaughter, and died at the age of 53. It is strange that his poetry ceased at 25, and that there are known only five copies of his books published during his lifetime; but the strangest thing of all is that his name is remembered because a pirate publisher stole two of his poems and gave them to the world as the work of Shakespeare.

John Jervis, who took his title of Lord St Vincent from the scene of his chief sea victory, was born in 1735, eight years the junior of James Wolfe, with whom he spent some time at school. They met again in 1759 on the eve of an immortal event.

The son of a flinty-hearted lawyer who kept him miserably poor, Jervis made his way in the Navy from the rank of seaman to that of acting commander of the little *Porcupine*, and as such was selected to lead the boats carrying the troops for Wolfe's night attack on the Plains of Abraham. Before the flotilla set out Wolfe sent for his old school friend, and with a presentiment of impending death handed over to him his private papers and notebooks, his will, and the portrait he always carried of Katherine Lowther, whom he loved but who was later to become Duchess of Bolton. In the event of his death the portrait was to be brought by Jervis to England, set in jewels and returned to her. The part of Jervis in the voyage to the spot appointed for the landing at Quebec was executed with skill and courage, and he and Captain Cook share with Wolfe the glory of the deed and that day made Canada part of the British Empire.

During the recurring wars that followed Jervis steadily advanced by intelligence, valour, and industry, entering Parliament during peace, and returning to sea to win fresh laurels for his country and himself. Trinidad and other islands of the West Indies were among his contribution to the Empire during these world-wide combats. But we were then impoverished by wars and unable to maintain an efficient Navy in time of peace, so that ships and discipline alike deteriorated. The alliance of France and Spain made it necessary for us to quit the Mediterranean; a hostile fleet with 14,000 soldiers was prevented only by weather from invading Ireland; and plans were ripening for a descent by great French and Spanish forces upon our own coast.

That dream was shattered on St Valentine's day, 1597, when, in accordance with Jervis's expectations, a Spanish fleet of 27 ships of the line, heavily gunned, sailed from Carthagena with a view to joining the French fleet at Brest. Jervis was in the *Victory*, not yet famous; Nelson was in the *Captain*. Nelson, to whom Jervis was ever a hero, wrote, as the battle drew near, "Of all the fleets I ever saw, I never beheld one, in point of officers and men, like Sir John Jervis's, who is a commander-in-chief able to lead them to glory." Battle was joined off Cape St Vincent, and Nelson himself made it a resounding victory, sending the shattered vessels of the Spanish fleet scurrying to harbour, from which they emerged no more throughout the war.

Nelson shows us what Jervis had done with his fleet before the battle; history tells how he improved it afterwards, sternly repressing mutiny, mercilessly purging the Admiralty of corruption and jobbery, and firmly pressing on reforms that redressed grievances afloat and bettered the lot of seamen's families on land. He built Nelson's victorious fleets. A man of bitter humour but generous heart, he consistently defended Nelson's fame against the claims of Lady Hamilton and her creatures; and he was foremost in aiding Lady Nelson when she was in danger of being defrauded of her rights.

Jervis died in his 89th year, and it was by his own desire that his body was buried here, far from sea but in his native soil.

Stow by Chartley. The Normans gave the village its church, and their boldly carved chancel arch, a south doorway (both with zigzag ornamentation), a blocked doorway on the north, and a deeply splayed window in the chancel are still here to see. The priest's doorway and a doorway in the tower are of the 13th century; the tower itself is of the 14th century, and there are 14th century windows in the church.

The most imposing monument is an alabaster tomb with figures of Sir Walter Devereux, grandfather of Queen Elizabeth's favourite

Essex. He lies with his two wives. Sir Walter, who died the year Elizabeth was crowned, was Constable of Warwick Castle, saw hard fighting at sea, and served in Henry VIII's army against the French in 1544. He may have come to admire his monument, for it was made in his lifetime, showing him in his Garter collar, his head on a plumed helmet. His wives wear close-fitting hats, and round the tomb are six sons in armour and six daughters in the fashionable dress of the day. Over the monument hangs the helmet he wore. In the churchyard is a cross on an old base, and in the village are attractive cottages with old timbers.

Stretton. It is one of the two Strettons by the old Roman roads of Staffordshire; this one is near Watling Street. Here is the unusual sight of a canal crossing a road, the barges on the Shropshire Union Canal floating over an iron bridge of one arch built in 1832 by Thomas Telford.

The hall and the church are neighbours, the hall, in a park of tall and stately elms, sheltered from the churchyard by a row of old yews. Other fine trees enclose the church, which was largely taken down and built up again last century. Though much of the church is new the chancel is old and has a Norman priest's door and three deeply splayed Norman windows, one over a niche with a stone head which may have come from the old church. The east window has fragments of old glass, among them a Crucifixion and a saint's head.

Stretton. Now practically a suburb of Burton upon Trent, it stands by the Roman Ryknild or Ryknield Street. The spacious church, rebuilt in the Decorated style in 1897, has a big central tower, and north and south doorways crowned by statues of the Virgin and St Chad. The grey stone of the outside is rather sombre, but the interior shows a warm red sandstone.

Inside, the eye is drawn to the brightly painted and gilded roof, and the elaborate screen with flowers and fruit and 13 bosses, no two alike. The large font is of black and white marbles; the cover, a fine example of modern craftsmanship, has niches with eight Scriptural figures. There is a fine iron gate to a chapel, and the chancel has an east window of striking colours showing Christ in Majesty designed by Sir William Richmond, whose mosaics are inside the dome of St Paul's Cathedral in London.

Swynnerton. It has a great park with a fine 18th century house, attributed on grounds of style to Francis Smith of Warwick, and the home of the Fitzherberts, who have been here since the time of

Henry VIII. High up in a wooded countryside, it has a fair share of the treasures of our ancient past.

Standing by a fine chestnut tree is the tower the Normans began, crowned with a 16th century belfry and entered through a doorway carved with beaks of birds. The nave arcades have been here 700 years, the south chapel 600, and the south aisle 500. The beautiful oak chancel screen is by a Tudor craftsman. Under a canopy in the chancel lies a weathered knight thought to have been Sir John de Swynnerton, who was Constable of the Tower and died about 1254. A great sitting figure of Christ about eight feet high in the south chapel is so finely carved that it is believed it was brought to this church from Lichfield cathedral to escape destruction in the Commonwealth. It has lost an arm.

Swythamley. Its 19th century church stands in the beautiful deer park round Swythamley Hall, above the narrow valley of the Dane (the boundary with Cheshire) and below the gritstone moorlands. Wallabies introduced on the estate by Sir Philip Brocklehurst, began to escape in 1938 and these beautiful but timid animals are now to be seen running wild on the moorlands.

Over the moorland hill to the north-east is Ludchurch, or Lollard church, in a wild and beautiful countryside above the Dane valley. The "church" is really a remarkable chasm shut in by towering rocks hardly 20 feet apart at the top. Here, in this natural cathedral, with its moss and fern-covered walls overhung by trees, the followers of Wycliffe are said to have gathered and legend says that their singing betrayed a company of Lollards gathered here when soldiers were searching for them.

Talke o' the Hill. Its queer name is said to come from a Welsh word meaning a high place, a good name for this old mining village near the Cheshire border. In the heart of the village is a modern cross on five steps of the 13th century; and in the modern church are two old treasures said to have come from Little Moreton Hall, the famous house over the border. They are on brackets near the chancel arch, beautiful oak figures of Paul and John the Baptist.

The talk of the hill is often of tragic things, for the village has sad memories of four tragedies, two above ground and two below. In 1782 a disastrous fire destroyed many houses. Like a bolt from the blue came tragedy on another day in that same year, when nearly two tons of gunpowder which were being taken through the village exploded. Here one winter's day in 1866 a pit explosion took toll of over 90 lives, and another explosion in 1785 carried off 42 men and boys. Bitterly has this small place paid for our friendly English fireside.

Tamworth. Here flow two rivers, the Tame and the Anker, at the heart of a thriving market town, the sound of their mingling water running on like an ageless song. For a thousand years and more history has marched on the banks of these two streams, and we may stand on the castle walls built high on a mighty mound of earth and mark how the rivers join, and think of the pageant they have seen. Kings and queens come into it, a great statesman of the 19th century, and a boy who lived to find fame far beyond this town where he went to school.

The red roofs of Tamworth are below us as we stand on this proud height and look towards the massive and imposing tower of the church. All around us lies the green and fertile countryside beloved by Sir Robert Peel. No one who looks on this district, he said, no one who sees the extent of its woodlands, the delightful rivers that water it, enriching the spacious meadows that border them, can be surprised to find that in the earliest times it was the chosen seat of those who were the conquerors of the country.

It was in Saxon times one of the most important places in the Midlands. Here Offa, King of Mercia, built a great palace where now the stalls of the market stand, and surrounded the town with a trench of which a few traces remain. For nearly a hundred years the kings of Mercia dwelt secure in Offa's palace, until it was destroyed by the Danes. Then for 40 years the place lay desolate, until there came a woman of good courage, Alfred's daughter Ethelfleda, to rebuild the defences and start the erection of the castle. She finished her work, and in seven years was dead; she died here in 920, and from Tamworth her body was taken to Gloucester, where they buried her. She had seen this great mound raised to a height of 130 feet, with a space of 100 feet in diameter at the summit. She saw the great curtain wall rise, 10 feet thick and 20 feet high at the centre, containing some of the finest Saxon herringbone work. The passage of a thousand years has left its solidity unshaken, the regular precision of its stones unbroken, but most vivid is that chapter which saw the earl of Richmond encamped here four days before Bosworth Field, during his long eastward march from Milford Haven. The traditional site is two miles westward, not far from the village of Hopwas. In Shakespeare we read Henry's stirring speech heartening his soldiers on the plain near Tamworth:

> *Fellows in arms, and my most loving friends*
> *Bruised underneath the yoke of tyranny. . . .*

The walls of Tamworth Castle have work from Saxon to Tudor days. Most of the foundations are Saxon, and parts of the round keep and the tower belonged to the Norman castle of the Marmions. Within the curtain wall is the Tudor and Jacobean manor house of brick and stone. In the Tudor banqueting hall is a great window with oak mullions, one of the most striking features in this part of the castle, and still containing some Tudor glass. Overlooking it is the stone window of the minstrels' gallery. In the state drawing-room is a frieze of 55 panels of oak painted with the arms of the Ferrers family and other lords of the castle up to 1787; and in the oak room is a magnificent Tudor chimney piece most richly carved, with heraldic pillars and Corinthian columns, human figures and small panels showing Jupiter in a chariot drawn by eagles, a dragon at the foot of a tree guarding the golden apples in the Garden of the Hesperides, the punishment of Prometheus, and the fate of Adonis. There is a splendid Jacobean staircase with steps carved out of solid oak.

There are many pictures of historical interest and ancient arms and armour in these rooms. We see a collection of coins from Offa's Tamworth mint, and there are numerous mementoes of Sir Robert Peel. In front of the tower stands the Marmion Stone, a great weathered block, the base of a cross which stood perhaps six centuries ago on an ancient bridge across the Tame. Underneath the courtyard is the dungeon, with walls ten feet thick.

Tamworth's great collegiate church stands on the site where four other churches have stood since the middle of the 8th century. The north and south arcades of the central tower are Norman, and so is part of the south wall of the chancel. The church has a 14th century crypt, a chapel and tower of the 15th century, and a fine Tudor clerestory. The tower has a feature which has long been a fascination to architects, a curious double staircase, unique in England, mounting spirally, with 101 steps in one and 106 steps in the other. Both sets of steps are contained in a space little over six feet wide, and are so contrived that the floor of one is the roof of the other. One starts from an entrance in the churchyard and the other from inside the church, and both lead to the same landing on the roof.

The nave arcade has fine 14th century work, and the roof with its carved oak bosses is of the 15th century. Under 14th century arches in the chancel are two table-tombs with 14th century figures; one shows Baldwin Freville and his wife; the other, Lady Joan Freville. A third table-tomb of 1512, shows Sir John Ferrers and his wife with their ten children. Under a pointed arch in the north wall lies a figure thought to be Baldwin de Witney, the dean of the college, who rebuilt the church 600 years ago. In his dress the hood of the tippet is shown drawn over the head, and it is believed to be the only example in England of this way of arranging the vestments at that time. In the north transept is the mutilated figure of a warrior in chain mail, probably of the 14th century. Beneath the tower, in a pompous marble monument, we see another Sir John Ferrers and his son, both wearing Roman dress in the manner of 17th century statues.

The church has a remarkable group of three windows in the clerestory of the chancel, designed by Ford Madox Brown and made by William Morris. They show the marriage of Editha, patron saint of the church, to Sithric; Editha as an abbess with her nuns; the Conqueror giving Tamworth Castle to Marmion; and Editha striking one of the Marmions with her crozier in punishment for wrongs he did to the convent. In St George's Chapel are two windows designed by Burne-Jones, but not good examples of his work, though both were made by William Morris.

Tamworth has lost its ancient deanery, of which we see the fragment of ruined walls, and its old grammar school has a newer home in which the tradition of at least 600 years is nobly kept. The town hall, on weathered arches, was built in the first year of the 18th century by Thomas Guy, Tamworth's most famous schoolboy, founder of the London hospital which bears his name. It is the only direct visible link with him that Tamworth has. The almshouses he built in 1673 were rebuilt in 1913, a handsome group of buildings round pleasant lawns. In front of the town hall stands a bronze statue of the first Sir Robert Peel, father of the great statesman.

A surprise awaits every visitor to Tamworth who seeks the Spital Chapel, half a mile outside the town on the north. This little chapel of St James's Hospital, founded in 1285, is entirely hidden by houses and we reach it through a small iron gate as if entering a house. Odd it is to find this tiny place, still used for worship, overlooked on all sides by the windows of 20th century homes. We may come into it by a Norman or a mediaeval doorway, and it still has windows 600 years old. The best of all Tamworth's houses is perhaps the Moat, an Elizabethan house of brick with good gables on the Lichfield road.

Tatenhill. It lies among wooded hills and valleys, between Needwood Forest and the Trent. We come into its 700-year-old church through its original doorway and find it much as it has been through all these centuries. All through them this font on six attached pillars has been used. The tower is of the 15th century and there are 15th and 16th century windows in the nave. In the chancel is a sculptured monument from the days of Charles I showing a kneeling woman in a close-fitting bonnet and a long dress with a quaint figure of a child fast asleep in bed underneath. It is to Sir Henry Griffiths. Craftsmen of 1890 have carved St Michael killing his dragon on the oak reading-desk.

Tettenhall. With Wolverhampton close by, it stands on the edge of beautiful wooded country, with many old houses and a large green, in the centre of a growing residential district. Whoever reads the Anglo-Saxon Chronicle is familiar with it, for below Tettenhall Wood are barrows in which, it is said, mingles the dust of Danes and Saxons slain on that day a thousand years ago when Alfred's son Edward defeated the invaders.

Tettenhall College, a Nonconformist foundation of 1863, crowns a hill; at Barnhurst are the Tudor gateway and the grey-tiled dovecote which were once part of the home of the Cresswells; Wrottesley Hall has gone but the site recalls the thought that here had been a home of the Wrottesleys for 800 years, the estate having passed from father to son without a break while 34 rulers have governed our land.

A Hugh Wrottesley suffered with Simon de Montfort, another Hugh was with the Black Prince at Crécy and was one of the first Knights of the Garter. Chief of the 19th century Wrottesleys was John, second baron, a famous social reformer and amateur astronomer, who became President of the Royal Society and the British Association. George, one of his soldier sons, wrote the annals of four famous old Staffordshire families, his own, the Giffards, the Okeovers, and the Bagots. He was buried here in 1909. Many other Wrottesleys were buried in the church, which, with two fine yews in its sloping wooded churchyard, stands where the Saxon King Edgar built his church ten centuries ago. Nothing of his work remains for us to see, or of the church raised by his Norman successors, but the massive battlemented tower is 600 years old.

The mediaeval church was completely destroyed by fire in 1950, but by 1955 a spacious new church had arisen on the site. Built of red sandstone, this has unusual windows, inspired by the Decorated style of the 14th century, new stained glass, a fine timber roof and a remarkable font covered with mosaic.

In the churchyard lies an unknown man with a famous name, a native, William Pitt, who wrote in prose on agriculture and the history of the county, made merry verse about money, and was buried here in 1823, having lived through the days when his namesake was deciding the destinies of Europe.

Beyond Tettenhall Wood, near the Bridgnorth road is the handsome Wightwick Manor, built in 1887–93 for Theodore Mander, and partly timber-framed. Presented to the National Trust in 1937, it is furnished with original wallpapers and fabrics by William Morris and contains among its many treasures paintings by the Pre-Raphaelites, tiles by William de Morgan and some fine stained glass of Kempe illustrating William Morris's Earthly Paradise.

Tipton. In the midst of the Black Country, it is rich in coal and iron, and has a great variety of engineering and metal works. To some Tipton's chief possession will be the Parish Register, which is thought to be the oldest in the land. Much of it is beautifully written, and except for one gap it goes back to a day before Christmas in 1513 when (as we read) "Joane the daughter of Thomas Whitehouse was baptized".

This register (which the verger will produce if asked) had been kept for about 250 years when most of the old St Martin's was destroyed in a great storm. To get money for rebuilding the vicar of that time made use of a statute enabling him to apply through the Sheriff for aid from Parliament, and Parliament replied by authorising a levy. So towns from Brecon to Berwick-upon-Tweed were made to contribute to the building of Tipton church as it stands today.

Two interesting men we come upon at Tipton: Ben Boucher, a collier who wrote topical rhymes and sold them at a penny a sheet until he died in the workhouse in 1851; and Joseph Davies, who brought honour to this Black Country town during the First World War, winning a VC for his share in the capture of Delville Wood, while leading a company of Welch Fusiliers.

Tixall. With an abiding place in literature, it has stories to tell as sad, strange, and terrible as history affords. The small village has an obelisk 18 feet high, bearing the date of 1776 and the distances to Stafford and London. On the heath, to the north-west, are two barrows, Queen's Low and King's Low, burial-places of great antiquity. Much history is buried hereabouts.

The church, which gives the impression of being uncared for, was rebuilt in 1849 in the Decorated style. In the pretty yew-decked churchyard is buried Richard Biddulph, who served at the hall as steward to four generations of Astons. He was here while Drake was sailing round the world and while the Armada was being built and was sailing to destruction. He saw the rise and decline of that marvellous literary era which eclipsed the writings of antiquity. Spenser, Marlowe, and Shakespeare played their parts and went their way while he was here. Including Lady Jane Grey, he lived under seven sovereigns, and, born in the reign of Henry VIII, he died with Charles I on the throne. He was a young man when the superb gatehouse was built near-by to guard his master's home.

Through this gateway passed many famous men, among them three great writers. One was Michael Drayton, who makes the hall live on by a couplet in Polyolbion:

> *Trent, by Tixall graced, the Aston's ancient seat,*
> *Which oft the Muse hath found her safe and sweet retreat.*

The patron by whom the old poet was welcomed was the distinguished ambassador Sir Walter Aston, to whom Fletcher dedicated his pastoral play *The Faithful Shepherdess*. Prejudice and the Plague having denied the dramatist success, he appeals to Aston, "that noble and true lover of learning":

> *Among the better souls, be you the best,*
> *In whom, as in a centre, I take rest.*

Izaak Walton was a visitor in his turn, and presented the Aston of his day with a copy of his *Lives*.

The house succeeding that to which these immortals came has followed its predecessor to destruction. The Georgian hall was pulled down in 1927, and much of its material was used for the new church of St John at Stafford. But the famous gatehouse is at last secure, scheduled as a national monument. A Tudor masterpiece with domed turrets at its corners, it is remarkable for the fact that the windows of its three storeys have Doric, Ionic, and Corinthian columns.

There was a startling scene before the gatehouse in 1586, when commotion and terror marked the arrival of a gay cavalcade. It was Mary, Queen of Scots, riding by to a hunt, lured here by a trick after the Babington Plot. She was forced into the hall, a prisoner without attendants or even a change of clothes. For 17 days she was detained here, and as she left, a captive, poor villagers collected before the gatehouse clamouring for alms. "Alas," she cried, "I have nothing for you; I am a beggar too; all is taken from me."

So the gatehouse saw its first tragic chapter of history while it was still young; before it had run its first century events occurred here which beggared the most fantastic plays. It was the boast of Charles II, when imprisonment and executions over the pretended Popish Plot were rife and the whole country panic-stricken, that from first to last he "believed not one word of what was called Oates's Plot". Yet he held his hand while an innocent man was dragged from here to the Tower and his companions to the scaffold.

The hall to which the great gateway led for many generations was a stronghold of Protestantism following the Reformation, but had become a centre of Roman Catholic influence during Stuart days, and the infamous Titus Oates had no difficulty in involving its owner, Lord Aston, in the wholesale accusations with which he induced the country to believe that Protestantism was in danger, that the Roman Catholics were about to rise, murder the king, invade Ireland, and perpetrate a general massacre.

Lord Aston and his friend Lord Stafford were concerned with other Roman Catholics in Staffordshire in a secret movement aiming at the peaceful conquest of Protestantism by their alien Church, but at the hall was an unjust steward, Stephen Dugdale, a Roman Catholic of 38, who, privy to his master's secrets, absconded with a sum of money and, arrested as a Roman Catholic suspect, sought to save himself by fabricating a tissue of lies. Oates found him an able ally, who swore that he had been present at conferences and had read letters implicating Aston and Stafford in a plot to murder Charles II. He swore that he had been promised 1000 crowns and enrolment in the calendar of saints to secure the murder of the king. Aston was impeached and committed to the Tower, and not until seven years later, when Oates had been whipped at the cart's tail for perjury, did he regain his freedom. Afterwards he held Chester Castle for James II at the Revolution of 1688, then retired into private life and died here in 1714.

Lord Stafford was less fortunate. Son of the earl of Arundel, and a prominent Roman Catholic member of the House of Lords, he was accused by Dugdale of complicity in a Popish Plot, and finally Dugdale swore that in September 1678 he met Stafford as he came riding through the old gateway here, and that Stafford offered him £500 to assassinate King Charles. It was in vain that Stafford proved that Dugdale had originally sworn that there was no plot, in vain that witnesses swore to Dugdale's offering them heavy bribes to commit perjury against the prisoner, in vain that Stafford demonstrated that Dugdale's evidence was unsupported in a single particular. The panic-stricken country demanded victims, and the trial, lasting seven days in Westminster Hall, afforded the terrified capital a happy diversion. The aged prisoner was found guilty by 55 votes to 31, and in December 1680, protesting his innocence to the last, he was beheaded on Tower Hill, an outstanding sacrifice to mob terror.

Smitten with remorse, and imagining himself haunted by the ghost of the hapless viscount, Dugdale, the villain of the tragedy, sank into poverty and obscurity, and in 1683 died in a drunken delirium.

Trentham. Eclipse and tragedy are written across the scene, for a great palace is gone. Its superb park has become a popular resort, one of the fairest playgrounds in the county; but the splendour of Trentham, home of the dukes of Sutherland, is no more.

In this most beautiful corner of the Potteries, where the Trent flows by the site of a lost nunnery, stood the famous Trentham Hall of which there remain only the ballroom and one great hall, but with the grounds and their wonders open so that all who will may come. A house of 1633 rebuilt in 1838 by Sir Charles Barry, architect of the Houses of Parliament, the hall was famous. It is the Brentham of Disraeli's *Lothair*, and has been described not only by our romantic Prime Minister but by a Shah of Persia, who came here on a visit and put Trentham into a book. The magnificence of the scene, the boundless hospitality of his entertainment, all that went to make for his ease and happiness, conjured up in the mind of the Shah the thought of a nobleman grown too mighty near the throne, and he drew the Prince of Wales aside and asked him if he would not behead this man when he came to the throne! With unshaken gravity the prince replied that there were many other great nobles in the land and he could not undertake so formidable a clearance.

The kings and captains have departed, for Trentham was pulled down in 1911. The two great apartments left standing are the sole relics of the home which had housed the Leveson Gowers for three centuries; but the grounds, converted in their time from a waste of meadow lands into Italian gardens with no rival out of Italy, remain a joy for ever. Here is a glorious park with velvety lawns, hanging woods mirrored in a winding lake, the forest trees beyond, boats on the water and games on the greens, and all that makes life joyous under the open sky. Once the pleasure-ground of royalties and nobles, scene of all that was brightest in English society, it is now a pleasure-ground of the people, a compensation to the many for the loss of one stately home unwanted. One reminder of the old family remains: a stone column with an immense bronze statue of the first duke of Sutherland still crowns the hill.

The church had seen many changes before it was almost completely rebuilt by Barry in 1844. Standing on the site of St Werburgh's nunnery, founded about 680, it has the Norman pillars

179

which supported the roof of a priory established about 1100 by Hugh Lupus, earl of Chester. Two holes in a panel of the royal arms of 1634 over the north door are said to have been caused by bullets fired by Commonwealth soldiers who stabled their horses here. In the aisles are the trunk of a headless and legless knight, under a canopy, and a fine sculpture of Christ sitting at table in the house of Mary and Martha. On a marble tomb lies the lifelike figure, in a bonnet and a long cloak, of the second duchess of Sutherland, who died in 1868, and near by stands her husband in his ducal robes. Both monuments were carved by Matthew Noble in Carrara marble. On the wall are an alabaster tablet with 16th century portraits in brass of Sir Richard Leveson, ancestor of the dukes, and his wife and children, and an elaborate monument with a bust of Albert Sutherland Leveson Gower, who died in 1874. The oak screen was installed in 1633 and on the reredos is a fine painting of the Entombment by William Hilton, who died in 1839.

Trysull. The church is partly of the 13th century and partly of the 15th, and it has a good 14th century east window, but its best possession is the Tudor woodwork in the church. The screen, the pulpit, and the roof beams are all very good carving of the 16th century. The nave is unusual for having clerestory windows on one side only, and a low Norman arch is blocked up in an outside wall. The mediaeval oak chest is a fine piece of work, very long, with engraved iron bands; and some of the little heads and figures in the east window are 15th century glass. Above the vestry door is a carving of a bishop, possibly of the 12th century.

It is recorded here that in 1725 John Rudge left a pound a year to be paid to somebody who would send dogs out of the church and rouse the people who were sleeping. The Sleep Rouser would carry a long rod with a knob at one end and a fox's tail at the other; and he would tickle the faces of sleeping ladies with the fox's tail but the opposite sex he would deal severely with by using the knob.

From the red sandstone ridge called Abbot's Castle Hill, a mile and a half away, there are good views of the Shropshire countryside, the boundary running along the crest of this hill.

Tunstall. This is the northernmost of Staffordshire's busy pottery towns that make up the great manufacturing complex of Stoke-on-Trent. In Victoria Park is a clock tower in memory of two men of the same name divided by a hundred years: William Adams the potter, who finished his life-work in Trafalgar year, and a namesake

Weston Park

The orangery at Weston Park

Wetton Mill and Wetton Hill

of this century who also distinguished himself at pottery. On the tower are bronze medallion portraits of these two master potters.

It was here that another potter gave up the ambition of being a champion dancer and became the founder of Primitive Methodism. He was William Clowes, one of the most successful evangelists in religious history. Born at Burslem in 1780, he was a potter by trade. And as a dancer he was widely known before his conversion at the age of 25. He joined the Wesleyan Methodists, became a local preacher, and took part in open-air evangelist services called Camp Meetings, with Hugh Bourne and others.

The Camp Meeting form of service, usually held in a field, was officially forbidden by the Wesleyan Methodist authorities, but Clowes continued his connection with Bourne and his associates and was expelled. Between 1807 and 1811 the Camp gatherings were so successful that the nucleus of a new denomination was formed at Tunstall, where a chapel had been built. So rapidly the movement spread that both Bourne and Clowes lived to see the Primitive Methodists numbering more than 100,000 members.

Bourne was the organiser of the denomination and Clowes its orator. Clowes was a man of fine presence, with a magnificent voice, and a natural eloquence that kept thousands spellbound. He and his comrades took over the early open-air preaching of the Wesleyan Methodists and carried it on until the Salvation Army annexed it. He continued his work almost to the end of his 71 years, and the last nine years he had a pension of £25.

Tutbury. From the ruins of its castle to the ancient ford by the five-arched bridge over the Dove, every yard is charged with history. With a great Norman monument for background we seem to catch again the trampling of warhorses and the clang of armed men on the walls; we see men flee here for refuge and flee again to save their lives; we see kings and princes come and go; we hear the sighs of a captive beauty who has been Queen of France and Scotland, and was proclaimed by the Pope and the French as Queen of England too.

In the broad main street is a fine old inn, the Dog and Partridge, with a timbered front which seems to have known little change in 500 years, and in the churchyard are the stocks. But imagination is content with the hillside church looking down on the town, and the castle ruins looking down on the church.

Treasured and cherished as the gem it is, the church, with its immensely strong low tower, rose as part of the Benedictine priory founded about 20 years after the Norman Conquest by Henry de

Ferrers. His son Robert, the first earl of Derby, a great figure at the Battle of the Standard, completed the work, something of which is in the present church. The deeply recessed west doorway, one of the finest examples of Norman art in England has seven orders or arches of carving, the innermost but one believed to be the earliest use of alabaster for an arch in any English church. The whole is crowded with magnificent carvings of human figures, strange animals, and beak-heads. Above the doorway is a Norman window flanked on either side by blind arcading, and the rich Norman south doorway has a tympanum carved with mounted men and dogs who for over 800 years have been hunting a colossal wild boar.

The interior does not disappoint our high expectations. Two splendid Norman arcades rest on columns about six feet thick, some of them clustered, some with scalloped capitals, and above these the pillared arches of the Norman triforium have become the clerestory. The west wall of the nave is a noble picture of Norman sculpture, with zigzag decorating the splendid doorway and interlaced arches, and there are three fine Norman windows in the 13th century aisle. The choir of the great church and all domestic buildings of the priory were destroyed at the Dissolution in 1538 and nothing of them remains. The present apse at the east end of the church was added in 1868 by G. E. Street.

Above the wonderful church, romantic on the skyline, the ruins of the castle are grouped about a large enclosure bounded by an earthern rampart supporting an embattled wall and surrounded by a deep dry moat, except on the side which falls steeply towards the river. On the Norman motte or mound is an 18th century "folly" built to resemble a ruined keep. The gatehouse at the north-east corner of the courtyard is a work of the 14th century; the rest, including the two towers and the range of state apartments, is of the 15th century.

The castle first rose in Saxon days, but was rebuilt in the Conqueror's time by the founder of the church, whose grandson was punished in 1174 for rebellion against Henry II by the destruction of his fortress. It was rebuilt soon after, but another earl of Derby, fighting on the side of Simon de Montfort, was defeated and disgraced, and the castle again destroyed in 1266, when the estate passed to a son of Henry III, another of whose sons, Thomas of Lancaster, raised the castle to its crowning military glory.

Thomas lost his fortune here and his head at Pontefract; and some 40 years later the most famous duke of Lancaster, John of Gaunt, came into the possession of the castle. Even he was not safe within its walls, but in 1385 had to fly for his life on hearing that Richard II was marching with murderous intent upon him. At Gaunt's death Richard seized Tutbury, and the estate has ever since remained Crown property. It was leased by Elizabeth I in 1569 to the sixth earl of Shrewsbury, who brought here in custody Mary, Queen of Scots. His wife, the redoubtable Bess of Hardwick, declared that there was a love intrigue between the prisoner and the earl, but Mary wrote complaining of her accommodation, declaring that she was "in a walled enclosure, exposed to all the winds and inclemencies of heaven, the greater part of it rather a dungeon for base and abject criminals than for a person of my quality". Allowed £52 a week for the maintenance of his prisoner and her companions, Shrewsbury said the sum "did not pay for victuals alone", as may have been the case, seeing that her retinue included "5 gentlemen, 14 servitors, 3 cooks, 4 boys, 3 gentlemen's men, 6 gentlewomen, 2 wyves, 10 wenches, children, a number of good horses, and grooms".

Shrewsbury supplied her with plate and rich hangings, and a visitor, who described her as "wearing black hair though given to hair of other colours on other occasions", found her apparently contented with embroidery, and much at home with the Shrewsburys. In spite of the vigilance of her janitors, she maintained a busy correspondence in cipher with the duke of Norfolk, to whom she was secretly engaged. After his arrest the letters she wrote here were conveyed to him in empty beer bottles with marked corks, which went in unsuspected with the full bottles carried into his cell in the Tower.

Mary's second departure from here, in November 1569, was taken in haste; she returned for five months in 1570; and she was here again in 1585, ill. Her lodging was an old hunting lodge of timber and plaster in the castle yard.

Little more than half a century was left to the castle when, on December 21, 1585, Mary rode away for the last time. The Stuarts made it their headquarters when hunting in Needwood Forest, but the end approached with the Civil War. Here Charles I came to hide and rest for the last time after Naseby; not until the following year, when his cause was hopeless, did the castle surrender. Then, warned by experience, the Ironsides destroyed it, leaving for us these old walls, and the gateway by which kings and princes, priests and soldiers, and a pitiless woman of bitter sorrows had so often come and gone.

Uttoxeter. It looks down a sloping mile of Staffordshire to where the River Dove divides it from its neighbour, Derbyshire. Its revenues were given to Windsor and the chapel of the newly founded Order of the Garter when the Staffordshire men came home from Crécy. An old market town, it was created a new borough in about 1225 by the earl of Derby, and it now has large agricultural-machinery works.

It has memories of a strange philosopher, of the surrender of a duke and his beaten army, of a gallant admiral, a famous lady, and our greatest talker. The philosopher was Thomas Allen, born here in 1542, and educated at Oxford, where he became one of the foremost mathematicians of the age, friend and correspondent of the greatest spirits of his era. But he was an astrologer, and men accused him of wizardry, declaring that he practised black magic to bring about the marriage of his patron the earl of Leicester to Queen Elizabeth I. His servant asserted that spirits mounted the scholar's stairs as thick as bees, but in spite of this he escaped the perils of a credulous age and died in his bed at 90.

One of the most sensational scenes in the life of the town was in August 1648, when the first duke of Hamilton, next in succession to the Stuarts for the Scottish throne, came here with all that was left of the army of 20,000 with which he had started from Scotland to strike a last blow of Charles I. Always a muddler, never trusted by either side, he had rounded his luckless career by allowing himself to be hopelessly defeated by Cromwell, and fled here from Preston. He surrendered to Lambert, and while his soldiers were imprisoned in the church, where they played havoc, Hamilton was sent to Windsor. There he saw Charles leave for London for his trial and death, and his own execution followed three months after.

The town gave its name to the peerage conferred on Alan Gardner, its most illustrious sailor son, who left here in 1755, a boy of 13, to spend the greater part of the next half century fighting our battles at sea. The lady whose name is cherished here is Mary Botham, a daughter of Uttoxeter folk, who married William Howitt in 1821. Although her mind was exercised in writing or editing about 100 books, she never forgot that on the day William took her to the altar she wore her first silk gown, "a very pretty dove colour", with bonnet to match, and a soft silk shawl.

The parish church still has the tower under which men came to thanksgiving for the victory at Crécy. It was part of the fine church built between 1325 and 1350 by Henry Yevele, son of a freeholder of Uttoxeter. Yevele, the designer of the naves of Westminster Abbey and Canterbury Cathedral, had been called "the greatest English architect". The church itself was, unhappily, rebuilt in an imitation Gothic style in 1828. Under the tower are two alabaster tombs: one of 1555 with the engraved figure of Thomas Kynnersley in armour (half the tomb, with the figure of his wife, is missing), the other with a lady in a flowing robe and veil, of about the same date. Below her effigy is a cadaver or skeleton that was formerly part of another tomb (it is the skeleton of a man).

A rare servant of this church was Thomas Lightfoot, vicar for 36 years of the 17th century. There is no memorial to him, but he lives on in the fame of his son John, the Hebrew scholar. There is a memorial to Henry Abud, the iron screen under the tower being in memory of his 48 years as vicar. In the north aisle is a remarkable war memorial in the form of an alabaster reredos.

For centuries the town has been famous for its markets, and it is in the marketplace that we find the most appealing of all its monuments. Here, copied from a famous statue in Lichfield marketplace, is shown an aged man with bowed head, the skirts of his coat swept by the wind, a picture of grief and remorse. It recalls one of the most moving events in the life of Dr Johnson.

Upon a bitterly inclement day when men in the full vigour of health were glad to seek shelter, an aged giant, strange in gait and given to convulsive shudderings and strange rolling of the head, lurched into the marketplace of Uttoxeter, came to a halt at a certain spot, bared his head to the storm, and stood like one transfixed. The time was about 1780, and the strange old figure in the marketplace had come from afar to make atonement for a petty rebellion against a father's will committed sixty years before.

It was Dr Johnson and he told the story of his pilgrimage on the occasion of his last visit to Lichfield, his beloved native city. True to his habit of recruiting new friends, he had this day taken to his heart a young clergyman, Henry White, who lives in our literature merely because the Doctor talked to him on this day and told one of the strangest little stories of his strange and chequered life. Johnson discoursed of his boyhood and of his relations to his parents, and said that he could not in general accuse himself of having been an undutiful son. Then he went on in his inimitable easy stately way to tell this famous anecdote:

Once I was disobedient; I refused to attend my father to Uttoxeter market. Pride was the source of that refusal, and the remembrance of it was painful. A few years ago I desired to atone for this fault; I went to Uttoxeter in very bad weather, and stood for a considerable time bareheaded in the rain, on the spot where my father's stall used to stand. In contrition I stood, and I hope the penance was expiatory.

A thousand visits to Uttoxeter could not dim the mental picture of that scene. All about this country old Michael and his son Samuel used to ride and walk intent on the sale of second-hand books.

Perhaps shame rather than pride dictated the son's refusal to go to the Uttoxeter stall. The elder Johnson was a victim of melancholia, which could only be kept within bounds if the old man kept continually riding about the countryside, for he was liable to mental breakdown during physical inactivity.

He had a workshop for the repair of his books and the making of parchment, a detached building which gradually became ruinous. Half of it, to the rear, fell down for want of money to keep it in repair, yet its owner was no less diligent to lock the door each night, although he knew that anyone who chose could walk in at the back, where the wall had fallen.

That was the father whom Johnson disobeyed and to whose memory he made reparation when he himself was 70 years of age.

Wall. The Romans built here a town and posting station, and called it Letocetum. It flanked their Watling Street, crossed not far away by Ryknield Street. Then danger to the Eternal City called the legions home, and Letocetum, a prey to invading Saxons, fell into ruin.

Alfred used the road as a boundary between his kingdom and that of the Danes, but heeded it not as a place of strength and comeliness. The wonders we see here were as nothing to our ancestors. Not all was lost, not all fallen; Camden wrote of it in the 16th century as taking its name from its Roman walls; Plot, the 17th century historian, described its Roman pavements; and there are 18th century records of a military barricade of great oak trunks standing erect in close order.

Slowly the soil covered up the remainder, while much was carried away to make roads, houses, and farms. In the last century the church with its tower and its little spire rose on the hill, a landmark in the beautiful country round. When this was completed the village bethought itself of the imperial city under its feet, and dug for it. Three excavations were made during last century, and more extensive and scientific excavations have been undertaken in the present century. The results will be lost no more, for the site is scheduled as a national monument.

Here are Roman baths ranking with the best in the country, marvellously preserved by the soil which so long hid them. There the hot bath, the tepid bath, and the cold bath. The furnace is perfectly revealed with its floor of splendid Roman cement intact, there are evidences of three floors having existed at different times in the Roman era. There is a wide step worn smooth by Roman sandals, and the remains of a niche in which was a statue. There are foundations of the walls which enclosed the exercising-grounds; and near by is the site of a Roman villa which, having been explored, is now again buried.

Here dwelt the Romans to whom Nero was lord of the world; here were Romans who trembled at the name of Domitian. Coins of both these tyrants circulated here. Not all is lost of the citizens of that proud Empire, for in the museum near by is a black urn, still charged with the bones and ashes of some lordly Roman of that long ago. Roman tiles abound, and there is part of the flue which once conveyed hot air from the hypocaust, which we see still wonderfully preserved. But the baths are the most impressive relics left of a Staffordshire ruled by the consuls and legions of Caesar.

Walsall. An ancient town on the edge of the Black Country, it looks north and east to scenes of unspoilt beauty, proud of its roll of fame and proud of its achievements. Bringing the country into the town, it is rich in open spaces and recreation grounds (it has hundreds of acres), chief among them being the Arboretum, beautiful with trees, shrubs, flowers, and lakes. Reedswood Park is an example of what can be done to make an ugly country beautiful, for it is a paradise won from the dumps of disused mines, one of the county's created wonderlands.

Long the capital of the saddlery trade, where horses were bitted and buckled and harnessed in all the trappings of utility and splendour, Walsall found its main industry menaced by the mechanical transport of our time and turned its leather-work to account in equipping cars, and its bit and buckle foundries into factories for steel structures of all kinds. It has coal and iron at its door.

There is honest pride in the wide main thoroughfares of Walsall, in the Renaissance-style Town Hall of 1902 and other municipal buildings, and in memorials to men and women who have served it or distinguished it. Twentieth century Walsall seeks to better its streets as 18th century Walsall bettered its manners. John Wesley recorded that he had an unhandsome reception here in 1743, but 20 years later found the town changed, for "God hath tamed the wild beasts, or chained them up!"

Jerome K. Jerome has a tablet at Belsize House in Bradford Street, where in 1859 he was born into the family of a preacher who was also a mine-owner, and a Nonconformist mother who remembered being pelted with mud and stones for going to chapel in Wales. Floods ruined Father Jerome's mine, and the boy suffered from miserable poverty, but he educated himself and made the English-speaking world laugh with his delightful story of *Three*

Men in a Boat. So it was with his autobiography, which is full of laughter and tears, and ends with the solemn testament of a Christian who has fought the good fight and is assured of his goal. He died in 1927, Walsall's most gifted literary son and one of England's merry gentlemen.

It was a younger son of the town, Lieutenant S. N. Webster, who won the distinction of being the first man to travel at more than four miles a minute. He won the Schneider Trophy for England by flying at 4.69 miles a minute, the greatest speed attained by a human being at that time. Walsall's proudest monument to warlike valour is the bronze bust (outside the Central Library in Lichfield Street) of Seaman Carless, who won the VC in a naval engagement in the First World War while serving as a gunner. In spite of a fatal wound he helped to remove stricken men to safety and to lift a shell for his gun; then, falling, he struggled to his feet again, cheered on the men, sank down, and died.

The war memorial is a white stone cenotaph in Bradford Place, but thought for the living has been blended with memories of the dead, and three playing-fields, an addition of 500 acres to the town's open spaces, are part of the gift of remembrance. It is the valour of peace which is expressed in another monument at Walsall, valour which prompted a gentle woman to face death a hundred times. The monument is F. J. Williamson's delightful statue of Dorothy Pattison, the immortal Sister Dora. She stands at the Bridge in bronze on a red granite pillar, with four panels of scenes from her work. We see her in nursing uniform, holding a roll of surgical bandages, her scissors hanging from her belt, her fine face a blend of courage, humour, and benevolence, looking as Walsall saw her last century, the Florence Nightingale of the town.

Memorials of Sister Dora are in the fine Art Gallery, built in 1965 in Lichfield Street, and in the Central Library near by is an interesting museum of leathercraft and other Walsall trades.

High above the town, and seen for miles around, rises the spire of St Matthew's Church on its hilltop, with superb views from its churchyard towards the Wrekin, Barr Beacon, and Cannock Chase. Of the 15th century church we see the tower and the chancel, which has an unusual vaulted passage underneath. The nave and aisles, rebuilt in 1821 by Francis Goodwin, have slender pillars carrying nave arcades made of cast iron and tracery of cast iron in the windows. The graceful spire was rebuilt in 1951.

The oldest monument, worn and mutilated, is that of Sir Roger Hillary in 14th century armour, who has come back to the church after being put out into the churchyard and later serving as an ornament at Rushall Hall. On an alabaster wall-monument is a medallion bust of William Purvis, who served for 24 years in the 17th Lancers, fought in the Crimea and the Indian Mutiny, and returned to his birthplace, to tell of that tragic ride in 1854 when he charged with the Light Brigade, and was one of that little host which came back through the valley of death.

Under the chancel arch is a carved screen of 1913 with a Crucifix between a pathetic Madonna and St John, reaching from the rood to the height of the arch. But it is the old woodwork, brought here from Halesowen Abbey, in Worcestershire, which is most charming. There are eight splendidly carved poppyheads, among them an eagle with three bodies and a demon's head whose hair is like flames. There are 18 grand old choir-stalls, with richly chiselled arm-rests and misericords, a splendid series of carvings including an angel, grotesque animals, a jolly little man, all head and no body, a musician who has been cheerily blowing away for 500 years, a centaur looking one way and shooting his arrow another, and an athlete who seems for ever seeking to leap over a pole.

Most appealing of all in the church is the sanctuary window in memory of Walsall's good angel, Sister Dora. The daughter of a rector of Hauxwell in Yorkshire, Dorothy Pattison wanted to join Florence Nightingale in the Crimea, although at the time she knew nothing of nursing. But her father disapproved of her ideas, and not until she was nearly 30 did she leave home to teach in a Buckinghamshire village school.

Soon she joined the Sisterhood of the Good Samaritan, taking the name of Sister Dora. The Town Council of Walsall had asked the sisters to open a hospital for industrial accidents; the sister in charge fell ill, and Dora, with very little training, had to take over the work. Smallpox broke out. Epidemic followed epidemic, and she was taxed to the limits of her tremendous endurance. She spent her hours of rest nursing in their own homes those who had none to care for them.

The discipline of the sisterhood could be strict to the point of inhumanity, as Dora found when she was refused permission to visit her dying father. In the end she left the sisterhood, went on with her nursing, and took charge of the work of a hospital here. She did the work of an army, and always gaily. "Make you laugh?" said one of her patients. "She'd make you laugh if you were dying." Dora studied anatomy, and could perform minor operations skilfully. As eye accidents were frequent in Walsall she went to the Ophthalmic Hospital in Birmingham to learn about their treatment. She was deeply religious, and combined her work with prayer.

"Sister, save my arm. It's my right arm!" pleaded a healthy-looking workman hurt by a machine. The doctor shook his head gravely, and said "Amputate," but suddenly Dora felt strength in her; she did what a nurse is supposed never to do—she opposed the doctor, who was furious. For three weeks she strove; the man's name was forgotten and to the whole hospital he became Sister's Arm. He was saved, and on every spare Sunday the workman would walk 11 miles to ring the bell and enquire after Sister Dora. "Just tell her that *her* arm rang the bell," he would say.

At last she was attacked by cancer. Nothing could be done for her, so she went back to her wards and continued dressing wounds, serving meals, washing up, cracking jokes, so that her patients, seeing her radiance, caught a new enthusiasm for living. To the end she hid her suffering from them.

Waterfall. It is up on the lonely limestone uplands, taking its name from a queer trick of the River Hamps, which is not far off and sometimes vanishes underground through crevices.

Although the church was mostly rebuilt in the 19th century, it has kept its wide and curiously distorted Norman chancel arch and a Norman doorway, both adorned with chevron, and the windows have been refashioned in the Norman style. The plain screen and panelling in the chancel are Jacobean.

The charming valley of the Hamps was once traversed by a narrow-gauge mineral railway, carrying limestone, which, starting at Waterhouses on the main Leek–Ashbourne road, ran down the valley and up the Manifold valley to Wetton Mill and Hulme End, but the rails have been taken up and the trackway converted into a delightful route for walkers and cyclists.

Wednesbury. A large town playing its part in the age of iron and steel, with locomotive and other engineering works, yet with a memory older than Christianity in England still lingering in its name. It is said that on this hilltop where St Bartholomew's church now stands was once a heathen temple to Woden, the great Norse god, the god who received heroes into Valhalla and had two ravens to keep him posted with the news of the day. It is believed, too, that Wednesbury is the place referred to in the Anglo-Saxon Chronicle as the scene of a fierce battle between Saxons and Britons in 592.

The 19th century Christian temple on the hill is a fine place, its interior is enriched with a wealth of decoration. And there are ancient treasures, too. The lectern, older than the Reformation and believed to be unique in England, is a gilded fighting cock made of plaster on an oak pedestal. The great picture shielded by curtains is a Descent from the Cross by Jean Jouvenet, a French artist of the 17th century. Several of his big canvases are in the Louvre, among them another Descent from the Cross. The carved oak pulpit of 1611 is one of the finest in Staffordshire.

On the sanctuary wall are the kneeling figures of Thomas and Eleanor Parkes of 300 years ago, with six children below them. On an altar tomb lie the figures of Richard Parkes (who died a few years later) and his wife Dorothy who gave the church a beautiful chalice. Carved here with a huge head, Richard was "much wanted, and lamented when he died". On the wall is a memorial to Isaac Clarkson, a 19th century vicar who served for 35 years. The apse and transepts were built in 1890–1908 by Basil Champneys, and the church has fifteen stained-glass windows of this period by C. E. Kempe.

Wednesfield. With the making of keys prominent among its present-day industries, which include the making of traps, chains, tubes, and other metal objects, it goes back in history a thousand years to the day of a fierce battle between Alfred's son Edward and the Danes. The Danes were heavily defeated by Edward with his army of Mercians and West Saxons, and their two kings Halfdan and Ecwils perished in the battle. The pleasant classical red-brick church standing today in the town centre was built in 1903. It is the second rebuilding of an 18th century ancestor; the previous church, rebuilt in 1843, was burned down in 1902.

Weeford. Hereabouts in 1700 was born a forerunner of Sir Richard Arkwright. He was John Wyatt, a distant kinsman of Dr Johnson, and a mechanical genius who narrowly missed fame. In 1738 he patented the first machine to spin by rollers moving at different speeds. His machine, worked by donkeys, was set up in a cotton-mill in Birmingham, where the first two hanks of cotton to be spun without hands are still preserved for us to see. Ingenious as his invention was, it was not as satisfactory as Arkwright's spinning-jenny, which superseded it. Yet Wyatt was not entirely a failure as an inventor, for he first brought to perfection the compound lever weighing machine of the type still used at railway stations. He was buried in St Philip's churchyard at Birmingham in 1766.

The small village where he worked as a carpenter is in a hollow close by the Black Brook south of Watling Street. The aisleless

Gothic church, standing by a farmyard, was built in 1802 and given a new chancel in 1876. In the transepts are interesting windows: one has portraits of Christ and the Four Evangelists holding books and quills, in memory of Robert Cowpland, 46 years rector last century; the other has 18th century French glass showing Pilate washing his hands, and was brought from the duke of Orleans' chapel near Paris during the French Revolution.

West Bromwich. Any beauty in these parts must fight the grime of a thousand chimneys, yet West Bromwich, which has metal industries of all kinds and is especially famous for its springs, tubes, and castings, has also a possession of astonishing beauty as well as a church with much that is interesting.

Oak House, to the south-west of the town centre, is a treasure of which any Tudor gentleman would have been proud. How it escaped the slum-building century we do not know, but here it is, restored by Alderman Reuben Farley and given by him to the town, a picture in black and white nearly 500 years old, with lovely gables, an unusual lantern turret, and clustering chimneys. In front is a charming flower garden, and behind (where the house is faced with brickwork of about 1635) is a rich lawn. Inside, we can wander about its panelled rooms, upstairs and down, looking at the beautiful period furniture and enjoying the atmosphere of this wonderful old house. A marvel it is for a Black Country town to possess in its midst. Out of gratitude West Bromwich presented Alderman Farley with the freedom of the Borough in a casket made out of some old timber from Oak House.

The parish church is on high ground north-east of the town centre. It was largely rebuilt in 1872, but a good deal of its tower is 14th century work. The oldest thing to see is a little Norman pillar built into the wall among some old tiles under the tower. The font is of the 14th century, and in the nave is a massive old chest, 7 feet long, carved out of a solid block of oak. The figures on the tomb in the south chapel are Ann Whorwood of 1599 and her son Field Whorwood of 1658.

By the side of his mother Field looks a giant, yet he can scarcely have been as tall as another son of West Bromwich, of whom it is said that a hole was made in the ground for him to stand in so that he should equal his fellows. He was Walter Parsons, a blacksmith who became a porter of James I and won fame as a strong man. Without undue exertion he could pick up two hefty yeomen of the guard, carrying them wherever he pleased, one under each arm, no matter how they struggled. The story is told that a foolish man who once insulted him in the street found himself hanging by his waist-band from a hook high up in a butcher's shop.

In Hall Green Road, some distance north of the church, is another fine old house, the mediaeval timber-framed manor house, built round a courtyard. It has been well restored and is now an inn.

Weston-on-Trent. This village lies in the broad Trent valley, near the busy road to Stoke, and its oldest inhabitant is in the churchyard by a little brook, a yew which was a sapling when Queen Elizabeth I was young, has been cut down, but is growing again. The church has bells in its tower which have been ringing longer still, for both are said to be of the 15th century. The splendid tower itself was built about 1220, and has on three sides a pair of lancet windows set in an arcade of four sharply pointed arches. Much of the church is 700 years old, but the clerestory and chancel are of the 19th century, and so is the oak pulpit with its flowers and angels. The registers record the burial of Civil War soldiers who fell at Hopton Heath and were interred in the churchyard near the old yew.

To the west of the village runs the Trent and Mersey Canal, and beyond this is the 17th century gabled hall of grey stone, now restored and converted into flats.

Weston-under-Lizard. This delightful model village stands by Watling Street, near the Shropshire border. Its great house, Weston Park, the home of the earl of Bradford, overlooks a charming lake in one direction and faces out over beautiful terraced gardens and a large deer park landscaped by "Capability" Brown in the 18th century. The graceful house was built in 1671 for Lady Elizabeth Wilbraham, who was almost certainly her own architect, and is one of the finest examples in England of the Restoration period. It contains elegant furniture and tapestries, including a set of Gobelins tapestries from designs by François Boucher, as well as portraits by Holbein, Van Dyck, and Lely, and other fine paintings and works of art. In the 18th century the house passed to the Newports, earls of Bradford, and then in 1762 to the Bridgemans, who were created earls of the second creation in 1815. A portrait of Sir Orlando Bridgeman shows him with the bag of the Great Seal of which he was keeper in the reign of Charles II and which is in the house. Disraeli was a frequent visitor at Weston Park and here are many of the letters he wrote to Selina, wife of the 3rd earl of Bradford.

The church, adjoining the house, with old yews and cedars about it, has long been famous for its monuments. Much restored in 1701 by Lady Elizabeth Wilbraham, it has 14th century stones in the chancel and a 15th century tower with three bells that were ringing before the Reformation. The finely carved oak pulpit is curious for its heavy canopy and its elaborate 18th century ornament of flowers and vegetables, a rare combination.

In the Bradford chapel are several alabaster monuments to the Bridgemans, earls of Bradford. There is a cherub with a laurel crown above a casket in memory of the first earl, who died in 1825, another monument to the second earl, who died in 1865, and one to his wife, who is lying on a couch with three angels hovering over her. It was this Lady Bradford who figured in the life of Disraeli after the death of his wife. He never seemed to be tired of the company of Lady Bradford, or of her sister Lady Chesterfield at Bretby in Derbyshire. Once he wrote from Bretby to Lady Bradford expressing his great regret that he was imposing himself as an invalid on the home of Lady Chesterfield. She was a dear angel, he said, who was more than kindness to him as he sat in silence musing over the past, and he added these human words in his letter to Lady Bradford:

I have had at least my dream, and if my shattered energies never rally, which is what I must be prepared for, I have at any rate reached the pinnacle of power and gauged the sweetest and deepest affections of the heart.

A painted marble monument with a ship in full sail, in the nave, is in memory of Richard Bridgeman, who served in the Navy and was killed in the air in East Africa in 1917. A window near the west end, commemorating the fifth earl of Bradford, who died in 1957, contains medallions of 17th century German glass.

In the sanctuary are two of England's small group of oak monuments, both showing cross-legged knights in armour with their feet on lions. One is perhaps Sir Hugh Weston of 1305 and the other his uncle Sir John Weston, who is thought to have accompanied Edward I to Flanders. During the journey he is said to have been entrusted with royal jewels, and here he has a purse hanging from his belt. The Westons lived here until about 1349, and among the old glass in the windows are fragments of 14th century shields showing their arms. They are in the east window, with small kneeling figures of a Sir John Weston and his wife.

Wetton. This high-lying village has many old limestone houses, some of them Tudor, and some of the most glorious country in

Staffordshire round about it. Far below flows the River Manifold, but its romantic natural possession is Thor's Cave.

In the churchyard, north-east of the 19th century church, is buried a beloved village schoolmaster, explorer of the cave in the last century. He was Samuel Carrington, who shared with Derbyshire's antiquarian Thomas Bateman all his excavations on the uplands. They found Roman remains at Borough Hole, they opened prehistoric graves, they sought and found rich treasure in Thor's Cave. The stone on the schoolmaster's grave has shells and fossils carved on it, and the Weston Park Museum in Sheffield has some of the things they found, part of a collection of Stone Age, Bronze Age, and Roman antiquities which is one of the best out of London. The old tower of the church is probably of the 14th century and the font in which the schoolmaster would be baptised has been here several centuries.

Whitmore. Here was born a country boy who was to spend most of his days in the East End of London; he was Samuel Stone, born at the rectory in the year the Victorian Era began. He would be baptised in the battered old font the Normans made, for his father was rector at this attractive church. Rebuilt in 1676 and much renewed since, it has a timbered porch with a timbered gable above, and a timber-framed bell-turret borne on wooden posts.

In the chancel is an alabaster tomb on which are engraved the portraits of Edward Mainwaring in armour and his wife in the long flowing dress that women wore in the days before the Armada. With them are three children and their dog.

Very pleasant is this birthplace of Samuel Stone the poet, for the Meece Brook flows through the village. The charming 18th century Whitmore Hall is reached from the church by a splendid avenue of limes; and to the south are the fine woods of Swynnerton Old Park. Samuel grew up to be a scholar and a poet, and it is the pride of this village that when it sings "The Church's One Foundation" on Sundays it is singing a hymn with a worldwide fame, written by one of its own boys.

Willenhall. Lying between Wolverhampton and Walsall, it has an old-established lock-making industry and iron and brass foundries; and a museum of locks was opened in the Central Library in Clemson Street in 1961. Amid all this is a church of some interest rebuilt in 1867, thanks to the energy and generosity of the vicar, G. H. Fisher, who was here for 57 years. A cornerstone of the transept is inscribed to his memory. The church has attractive woodwork and two memorial tablets, each with its human appeal. One is to Dr Richard Wilkes of 1760, the last of a family who had lived here for 300 years, and the other to Mr William Hall, who died suddenly in a railway carriage. The tablet is placed over the pew he occupied for half a century.

But for those with imagination there is more than this in Willenhall. For those who can forget the large new housing estates all around, and the Birmingham Canal running through it, there is the piece of waste land that was Mumpers Dingle in George Borrow, the Dingle where Lavengro fought the Flaming Tinman. It is a mile north of the town centre, and they still call the bridge over the canal Dingle Bridge.

Halfway between Willenhall and Walsall stood Bentley Hall, the home of that Colonel John Lane who was buried in the family chapel in St Peter's church at Wolverhampton. From the hall on a September morning in 1651 a king of England set out as a humble member of a little procession, making an escape which was to change the course of England's history. Bentley Hall was pulled down in 1927, but the historic site is marked by a cross.

At Bentley Hall lived Jane Lane whose quick brain and undaunted courage enabled Charles II to escape from his enemies after the Battle of Worcester. Charles, disguised as a yokel, had spent three days and nights wandering from hiding-place to hiding-place, including a whole day up an oak tree at Boscobel. On September 8, five days after the battle, Charles sent his devoted friend Lord Wilmot to Bentley to ask Colonel John Lane to help him to escape to London.

Now it so happened that the Colonel's sister Jane had arranged to pay a visit to her sister Mrs Norton at Abbot's Leigh near Bristol. She had already secured from the Governor at Stafford the necessary permission to travel, which included a manservant and her cousin Henry Lascelles. Jane at once offered to take Charles as her servant in order that he could reach Bristol and take a ship out of England.

That night Charles arrived and changed his green threadbare coat and ill-fitting breeches for the grey suit of a serving man. He had already shorn off his dark curls when he donned a very greasy old grey steeple hat without lining or hat band at the beginning of his flight.

Next morning at daybreak Charles, assuming the name of William Jackson (one of Colonel Lane's tenants), brought Jane's horse out of the stable and helped her on to the pillion seat behind him. John Petre and his wife, her relatives but not in the secret,

Whitwick Manor

The parlour at Whitwick
Manor

The Civic Hall

WOLVERHAMPTON

The Market

mounted a second horse, proposing to accompany them as far as Stratford-on-Avon, while Henry Lascelles, who was to escort them the whole way, mounted a third.

The little cavalcade proceeded without any adventures until they sighted some cavalry near Stratford. The Petres were terrified and in spite of Jane's remonstrances turned aside. But Charles and Jane and Henry quietly jogged their way through soldiers and town without a challenge.

That night they spent at Long Marston in the house of John Tomes, a kinsman of Jane, where the king was bullied by the cook because he did not know how to wind up the roasting jack. On the following night they stayed at Cirencester, and next day they rode through Bristol to the Nortons' house beyond it. The first man the king saw was one of his own chaplains watching a game of bowls being played on the green before the door, but he was unrecognised, and took Jane's horse round to the stable and waited events.

Jane, in the meantime, interviewed Pope the butler, told him that her manservant William was still weak from ague, and so secured him a good bedroom. Now Pope had been a trooper in the Royalist Army and recognised him, but he proved a real friend, trying to find him a ship and meeting and warning Lord Wilmot, who refused to disguise himself, not to come to the house, but to meet him at Frank Windham's house at Trent, near Sherborne.

But Mrs Norton had fallen ill and it was difficult for Jane to leave. Her ready brain quickly devised a plan. She had a letter delivered to her purporting to come from home and stating that her father was desperately ill and needed her. So off they set again, "William Jackson" this time riding singly with the luggage, and they came to Trent where Jane and her cousin Henry Lascelles bade farewell to the king and returned to Bentley.

Jane's travels, however, had only begun. It somehow leaked out that a lady had aided Charles, and so, disguised as peasants, Jane and her brother tramped across England to take ship at Yarmouth for the continent. Charles went to meet her and sent her to live with the Princess of Orange. He gave her a gold watch and other presents and at the Restoration Parliament voted her a pension of £1000 a year. She then married Sir Clement Fisher, of Great Packington in Warwickshire, and lived until 1689, spending her pension freely.

Wolstanton. We come uphill from Newcastle to a wide green and to a church with a fine spire, and meet a knight of Elizabeth's day. He is William Sneyd of 1571, lying in alabaster on a canopied tomb. Dressed in armour and a ruff, he rests his head on a helmet, his wife Anne by him, and with them their 15 children, the five boys wearing armour as if to protect their ten sisters. Anne is shown without hands, and it is said that in her lifetime her husband cut her hands off because she was lazy.

The church was rebuilt in 1858, except for the 14th century tower, which has a peal of eight bells. Seven of these were brought from Trentham in 1704 at a cost of 9d per pound of metal. In the south aisle is a tablet to numerous members of the Adams family, including William Adams, the potter, who is buried here and whom we meet at Stoke. In the churchyard, north-west of the church, is a flat tombstone recalling the "Wolstanton murder"; it is that of Sarah Smith, who was poisoned in 1763 at the age of 21.

Wolstanton is on the site of a Saxon settlement older than Newcastle or Stoke, but it now has modern colliery buildings. From the hilltop we look over the busy Trent valley to the churches of Hanley and Burslem.

Wolverhampton. The capital of the Black Country, the biggest town in Staffordshire after the Potteries, and the centre of an immense iron industry, Wolverhampton has a thousand years of history behind it. It has a multitude of workers in nearly two hundred trades, and it has on its borders a delightful countryside in which its workers can take their pleasures. As he walks through its streets the traveller is probably set wondering by the sight of the name of Fold—Molyneux Fold in North Street, Farmers Fold in Victoria Street, Pountney Fold in Dudley Street, Bennet's Fold in Salop Street, and more. It is the town's way of remembering the time when its situation in the middle of the Midlands made Wolverhampton the natural market for the sale of wool. Here the wool was gathered for sending to the Continent to be made into cloth, and the wool was stored in barns or warehouses, each warehouse having a yard into which the sheep were driven. Here came merchants from the ports of London and Bristol to make their bargains. The years have rolled on, and no more are the sheep in their Wolverhampton fold, but the names remain to remind the busy folk of this industrial town of the days when the world was a quieter place, and shepherds with their flocks were familiar figures in their streets. Now there is a change indeed, and Wolverhampton is among our most progressive towns, no longer with sheep in its folds, but with ironworks and other manufactures.

To walk through the streets of this town is to feel that behind it is the spirit of moving forward; to go through its vast workshops and see the building of buses and cars, of locks and safes, of electrical machines and automatic devices, of tubes and boilers and tanks—and to see coming into being the countless things that belong to this age of wheels and cranks and pulleys and levers, is to feel that we are touching industry at a thousand points. To be taking a holiday here and running into the country round—into Worcestershire and Shropshire with all their charm—is to realise that Wolverhampton, though of the Black Country, is not in it. It has a marvellous range of lovely places within its reach.

For centuries before the Black Country became black this was a place of importance, and if there were nothing else to prove it there would be the splendid church of St Peter, this great centre-piece of a town, standing proudly on a hill where Christians have been worshipping for at least ten centuries. Reached by a flight of steps and set among trees, it is an attractive spectacle.

Something of the air of a cathedral it has, with a splendid 15th century tower rising up from 13th century arches. The lofty nave with its double clerestory windows is of the 15th century, and the chancel of 1860 (by Ewan Christian) is a copy of the 14th century style. Wherever we look about us there are things old and beautiful to catch the eye. The oldest of them was perhaps already ancient when Christianity came, and tradition says that men who had made a bargain came to shake hands on it through this holed stone. Near by is the Dane's Cross, the carved but weathered shaft of a churchyard cross, probably of the 9th century. The porch has a vaulted roof, and a room above in which the priest slept, his duty being to say very early mass for merchants and travellers. The interior of the porch is finely carved in oak in memory of Sir Charles Mander, who died in 1929. The western gallery of the nave is a good piece of Jacobean carving, put here in 1610 by the Merchant Taylors Company for the use of the grammar school boys. The old oak misericord seats were brought here from the ruined monastery of Lilleshall in Shropshire.

Two remarkable examples of carving in stone are the font and the pulpit. The octagonal font bowl was brought here at the Restoration to replace one destroyed during the Commonwealth. Carved with flowers and foliage, it stands on a 15th century pedestal with eight little figures of saints under arches. At the font were baptised the three daughters of Button Gwinnett, a Gloucestershire man who had been married in the church in 1757 to Ann Bourn of Wolverhampton. He emigrated to America while it was still a British colony and was one of the signatories to the Declaration of Independence.

The 15th century pulpit is a veritable treasure, unique in Stafford-shire and taking a high place among the stone pulpits of England and with a remarkable staircase. With all its sides beautifully decorated, the pulpit here is attached to a pillar of the nave. A fascinating lion sits guarding the steps, and there is a tradition among the choirboys that the animal will yawn if the preacher goes on over half an hour.

The north transept chapel with its carved oak roof was built before the Reformation. In it are a 16th century alabaster tomb, with the figures of Thomas and Katharine Lane, and the wall-monument (by Jasper Latham) to Colonel John Lane of Bentley, who died in 1667. With his famous sister Jane, he helped Charles II to escape after the Battle of Worcester and hid with him in the oak at Boscobel. The nation paid the cost of this monument, Parliament granting £1000 for it.

Cut off by 15th century screen work, the 14th century south transept chapel holds the memorials of the Levesons, an old Wolver-hampton family. John and Joyce Leveson were buried here in Elizabethan times, and there is a fine bronze statue of Sir Richard of 1605, showing him in armour. It was carved by Hubert Le Sueur, whose figure of Charles I at Charing Cross is one of the finest sculptures in London and has been called one of the most impressive equestrian monuments in the world. As a boy of 18 Sir Richard Leveson fought against the Armada, serving as a volunteer in the *Ark Royal*, the biggest ship in Elizabeth's navy. In 1600 he was Admiral of the Narrow Seas commanding a fleet sent to look for Spanish treasure ships, and within two years he had destroyed Spanish ships in Kinsale harbour and engaged others off Lisbon, wrecking two galleys and bringing ten back to England. For his exploits they made him an admiral for life, but he died when he was only 35, a fine sailor of the breed of Drake.

In the chancel windows are panels of old Flemish and German glass, once in the church of St Mary, now demolished, and inserted here in 1959.

On the walls of St Peter's are sculptured portraits of the first MP and the first mayor of Wolverhampton; and there is a tablet in the north aisle to William Walker, who as a chorister of St George's Chapel at Windsor sang before Elizabeth I; he was organist here. Most fascinating of all, an 18th century tablet in the porch tells of another musician, Charles Phillips, "beloved by all for his absolute contempt of riches and inimitable performance on the violin". Born in Wales, he fiddled his way through Europe and met with both kinds of fortune, and on his death Dr Wilkes of St John's College, Cambridge, wrote for him this epitaph:

Exalted Soul, thy various sounds could please
The love-sick Virgin and the Gouty ease;
Could jarring Crowds, like old Amphion, move
To beauteous order and harmonious love.
Here rest in Peace till Angels bid thee rise
And join thy Saviour's Consort in the Skies.

Boswell tells us that Garrick once repeated this epitaph to Dr Johnson, who, with a shake of his head, said, "I think, Davy, I can produce a better." Then, stirring his tea awhile in a state of meditation,
he produced these lines:

Phillips, whose touch harmonious could remove
The pangs of guilty power or hapless love:
Rest here, distress'd by poverty no more,
Here find that calm thou gav'st so oft before:
Sleep, undisturbed, within this peaceful shrine
Till angels wake thee with a note like thine.

A typical piece of 18th century England is St John's, to the south
of the town centre. Built in 1755–60 to the designs of William
Baker, the church has a most attractive classical interior. There
are two old carved chairs in the chancel, and the altar painting is a
copy made by Joseph Barney, a Wolverhampton man, of Rubens'
Descent from the Cross. The organ is the work of that great 17th
century organ-builder Renatus Harris, and has a story of its own.
In 1682 the Temple Church in London decided to have a new
organ, and commissioned both Harris and his famous rival Father
Smith to set up instruments for trial. Both did so, and an exciting
contest it must have been, for the immortal Purcell was one of the
players. The Benchers could not agree which was the better organ
and decided to call in Lord Guildford, Lord Keeper of the Great
Seal as arbitrator. He died before he could make a decision and
was succeeded by the infamous Judge Jeffreys, who pronounced
in favour of Father Smith. The rejected organ of Renatus Harris
was installed in Christ Church Cathedral, Dublin, where it remained until 1750. It was stranded in Wolverhampton in 1752,
while on its way back to London and was bought for £500 for St
John's, where the richly carved case is well in keeping with its
surroundings.

The grammar school is now in its fifth century, for it was founded
in 1512 by Sir Stephen Jenyns, a Wolverhampton boy who grew up
to become a wealthy Merchant Taylor and Lord Mayor of London
in 1508. His school was moved in 1874 from the heart of the town

to a fine new home in Compton Road, in the western suburbs. From time to time since then new buildings have been set up in its grounds, and now Lord Mayor Jenyns would no longer recognise the little grammar school in these fine buildings that have grown up.

The Wolverhampton and Staffordshire College of Technology, founded in 1933 (and now incorporating the National Foundry College, established in 1948) and the College of Art are among the town's many educational centres, the technical college housed in a building with a sculptured relief of Science and Industry on the front of one wing. The Central Library, in Garrick Street, was a pioneer in providing students with a separate room where they may study in peace and comfort. The town has also 200 acres of parks and playing-fields, West Park being among the loveliest in the Midlands, with its flowers and shrubs and trees, and the swans on its lakes. Here, on a fine site, stands the statue of Charles Pelham Villiers, one of the remarkable public men of the 19th century. He lived through the whole of it except the first and the last two years, and for over 60 years sat in the House of Commons for Wolverhampton.

But while Wolverhampton is zealous in its care of the citizens of tomorrow, it by no means forgets its citizens of today, and it has a group of public buildings worthy of any town of its size. In Victoria Street a small black-and-white timber-framed house with a big leaning gable has been allowed to remain as a worthy fragment of the past, but elsewhere out-of-date buildings are constantly being replaced by new and better ones, and streets are being widened so that Wolverhampton's people may keep moving with the times. The Town Hall, west of St Peter's, is a Renaissance-style building of 1870, extended in 1902; the Civic Hall, in a more modern style, was built in 1938. Queen Square, the recognised centre of the town with its banks, shops, and business premises and its equestrian statue of Prince Albert (by Thomas Thornycroft), seems to embody all the solid qualities of the Midlander; and it is certain that the practical-minded Wolverhampton man, who may claim that his manufactures are in every corner of the world, thinks first and foremost of utility. But that he has also a warm regard for the arts and crafts is shown by the Grand Theatre of 1894, in Lichfield Street, where plays, opera, and ballet are performed, and the splendid Art Gallery and Museum, also in Lichfield Street.

This fine building, opened in 1885, is adorned outside with sculptured panels in which scores of figures represent Painting, Sculpture, and Science; and inside are galleries with collections of sculpture, English enamels, and early Staffordshire pottery. Among the paintings are pictures by Romney, Gainsborough, Lawrence, Turner, David Cox, and George Morland. In Bantock Park, in the south-west suburbs, is a branch museum with collections of porcelain, ivories, and Japanned ware, and exhibits illustrating local history and industry.

At a time when England was in a panic, and many atrocities were being committed, two priests of Wolverhampton were martyred for their share in the bogus plot discovered by the wretched Titus Oates. One, named Gavan, was beheaded along with two other priests and the aged Lord Stafford; the other, William Atkins, a poor paralysed man of 80, was dragged from his bed, taken to Stafford, and condemned to death. Someone relented, and the sentence was not carried out; the old man was shut up in Stafford gaol and allowed to perish there.

We may wonder if any coin of precious metal ever caused such strife as the rejected halfpence of William Wood, a prosperous ironmaster of Wolverhampton, where he was born in 1671. We owe him gratitude for the preservation of our old woods and forests, for he was the first man ever seriously to attempt the substitution of coal for wood in the smelting of iron. He had a stake in the country, mining iron and copper in 39 counties and receiving the exclusive right to furnish Ireland with halfpennies and farthings for 14 years.

At that time 23 pence were coined from a pound of copper for England, and Wood was allowed to make a pound of copper yield the equivalent of 30 pence for Ireland. That might have passed, but it was learned that the patent had in reality been granted by George II to the duchess of Kendal, to whom Wood had had to pay £10,000, in addition to annual bribes to people about the Court.

All that Ireland needed was small change to the value of £15,000, but Wood was authorised to foist upon her over £100,000 worth, his reward being an estimated annual profit of £4000. A fury of indignation was excited, including denunciation by the Irish Parliament; protests that the coins would involve Ireland in a loss of £150 on every hundred pounds of copper coined; declarations that the money as issued was debased even beyond specification. Then Swift took up the cudgels for Ireland in the famous Drapier's letters; and, in the character of a Dublin draper, predicted the ruin of his country by Wood's small coins. A grand jury refused to return a true bill when a prosecution was instituted against Swift; instead, the jury indicted the persons who had accepted the coins. All Ireland, led by Swift, the Chancellor, and the Archbishop of Dublin, was up in arms, and so fierce and protracted was the storm that Wood's licence had to be cancelled, and the patentee consoled with a pension of £3000 a year. This he received for only three years, for he died in 1730.

It was at Wolverhampton that one of the most proficient villains in history, the notorious Jonathan Wild, was born about 1682, his parents being worthy people. He grew up to the trade of a buckle-maker at Birmingham, married, deserted his wife and child, and left for London, a competent workman, with a mind of unusual audacity and organising faculties.

His life in London soon brought him to prison for debt, and during his four years' confinement he made the acquaintance and learned the secrets of many of the worst criminals. At length released, he entered into an infamous partnership with a woman of notorious life, and converted an inn in Cock Lane, Cripplegate, into a depot for the reception of stolen property.

But he soon out-distanced all other criminals. He employed thieves of both sexes and sent to prison or the gallows those who would not work for him. He mapped the metropolis into areas and appointed thieves for every area—special depots for robbery with violence, pocket-picking, and burglary, down to petty thefts in houses by girls whom he had placed in service. His plan was to act as broker between thieves and victims, restoring the product of the robberies he had planned to the owners for handsome rewards, and paying the robbers a moderate commission. All the criminals were at his beck and call.

Advertising widely as a restorer of property and as thief-taker, Wild owned several warehouses for the storage of his plunder, engaged a staff of skilled jewellers to alter and disguise stolen jewellery and watches, and kept a sloop to transport to the Continent goods too dangerous for sale in London.

As self-appointed thief-taker he set up an office, wore a handsome livery, and carried a staff heavily tipped with silver. An Act of Parliament was passed to declare the receiver equally culpable with the thief, but he went triumphantly on, planning robberies, receiving the goods, and sending to the gallows those who rebelled or whom he feared. He had a run of many years but was at last laid by the heels, and in May 1725 was hanged at Tyburn, with a record of villainy and treachery far transcending the wildest fiction.

Wombourn. With its grey 15th century spire, crowning a red sandstone tower a century older, this is the only church in England dedicated to St Benedict Biscop, who is said to have introduced glass windows into England. The rest of the church is of the 19th century, with two good possessions.

In the south aisle is an alabaster tablet carved with the Good Samaritan and brought here from Italy in 1720 by Sir Samuel Hellier, very quaint in its perspective of the winding road from Jerusalem to Jericho. In the north aisle is the monument to Richard Marsh of 1820, a medallion portrait and an expressive weeping figure of a woman sculptured by Chantrey.

About half a mile away, beyond the Wolverhampton road, stands The Wodehouse, in attractive grounds. It is partly Jacobean and partly much older, and has among its treasures a carving of an Elizabethan figure called the Silent and Good Woman, with these among the lines below her:

> Be frugal, ye wives, live in silence and love,
> Nor abroad ever gossip and roam.

St Benedict Biscop, whose memory is enshrined in this village, was born in 628, and at 25 renounced the world and went on a pilgrimage to Rome. Two years later he went again, and the Pope, knowing Benedict to be "a man of wisdom, piety, and nobility of mind", appointed him to conduct to England Theodore of Tarsus, the new primate. After two years as an abbot at Canterbury Benedict was in Rome again, this time buying books. He brought them to his native Northumbria and showed them to the king. Perceiving his learning and zeal, the king gave him some land at the mouth of the Wear on which to found a monastery.

Here at Monkwearmouth Benedict started to build, and within a year there stood a church which was the wonder of all Britain. Benedict adorned it with the most beautiful pictures and ornaments he could find, and for the first time there was a church in this country worthy to be compared with those on the Continent. He was the first Englishman thus to consecrate art to the service of religion.

Ten years later he founded another monastery, this time at Jarrow, and made a last journey to Rome to gather together a library. On his return he found that the plague had carried off a great number of his monks, and the only survivors at Jarrow were the abbot and one little scholar. The little boy was the Venerable Bede, who, when he grew up, was to write a life of St Benedict, telling us most of what we know of him. With his usual energy Benedict soon collected a new company of monks, but his end was near. In 703 he died, leaving behind him a tradition of vigour and beauty long to be felt in these islands.

Wootton. A quiet stone village in the shelter of the Weaver Hills, its claim upon the traveller is its big house, Wootton Lodge, a stately Jacobean mansion; it has lost its handsome Wootton Hall, where a book was written by a man who set the intellectual world on fire, Jean-Jacques Rousseau.

Wootton Lodge, standing a mile away in a park rich with timber, was built for Sir Richard Fleetwood, who moved in here early in the 17th century, leaving the family house of Calwich Abbey (about two miles away) to his son. He was allowed to put on the escutcheon over the great doorway the heraldic symbol of the Red Hand of Ulster, for he was one of the squires to whom James I sold baronetcies in return for money for the Ulster Army.

Sir Richard's old home rises abruptly from a wedge-shaped rock at the head of a wooded ravine, with magnificent views from its noble windows and from the flat roof with its delightful open parapet and chimneys which from a distance look like pinnacles. Built about 1607–11, it has been attributed to Robert Smythson, who designed those two remarkable houses: Hardwick Hall, in Derbyshire, and Wollaton Hall, in Nottinghamshire. There are few statelier houses in the county than this, approached by a bold flight of steps on the only side that does not descend precipitately to the stream. Admirably placed for fortification, it was the boast of Sir Richard that none could take it, yet, when Parliament's guns were raised on the spot still called Cromwell's Battery, it surrendered in less than two days, and Sir Richard and his two younger sons and 70 other prisoners were roped together and taken to Derby.

Not far off stood Wootton Hall, the handsome house which was built as the home of the Davenports. It was to an older, smaller house of the Davenports on this site that there came in 1766 one of the strangest visitors entertained in this country, Jean-Jacques Rousseau, who was then 54 and just entering on that phase of dementia which was to develop into madness and death.

The most famous man in Europe, Rousseau had already done his work, with books which had shaken Europe after centuries of slumber. Intensely gifted, but governed less by the head than by the heart, he had attacked culture as the evidence and the cause of social degeneration. Putting into practice his cry for the defiance of convention, he had already deposited his five children in a foundling hospital.

His greatest work of all, the *Social Contract*, represented society as founded by agreement, with the head of the State as the people's mandatory, not their master. With gaps of obvious absurdity in his philosophy, he was nevertheless a new and thrilling voice, and is still regarded by many as having enunciated principles which constitute a Magna Carta for mankind. His teaching set Europe aflame; he was the prophet of the French Revolution, as Napoleon was its sword.

Then, Europe having become impossible for him, he fell in with his friend's suggestion and came to England as a refugee, to be received like a prince and to have several houses placed at his disposal. He chose old Wootton Hall for its seclusion, insisted on paying £30 a year rent to its owner and his staunch admirer, Mr Davenport, whose servants were left to wait on him, and here he settled down with his French housekeeper, Thérèse Le Vasseur.

For a time he delighted in the beauty of the countryside, but gradually the peace he had sought drove him nearly mad. He was filled with the embittered suspicions of a hunted animal, seeing enmity and treachery in his friends and deadly foes in his neighbours; even the servants (to whom he could express his wishes only by signs) he suspected of wishing to poison him.

The simple village folk of Wootton encountered with fear and wonder this wild figure who would walk their lanes in a long black gown and a gold-tasselled velvet cap, his arms often filled with wild plants, for his one absorbing passion here was botany. It is said that at a spot known as Twenty Oaks he would sit to write the unjust and bitter letters which estranged David Hume from him. The only neighbour he made a friend of, in fact the only one who could speak French with him, was the taciturn bachelor Bernard Granville of Calwich Abbey. Here that wonderful woman Mary Delany, Bernard's sister, met Rousseau and was alarmed at his gallantry to her favourite niece Mary Dewes.

But all the time his French housekeeper, hating the English solitude, continued to aggravate his fears of persecution, and when, after rather more than a year, she told him that she had found the cook mixing cinders with the food, it was the final straw. He rushed away, leaving his trunks with the keys dangling in them and his rent money on the table. He was next heard of at Spalding, where he wrote to the Lord Chancellor appealing, in this friendly country, for a cavalry escort to guard him to the coast. He fled to Dover, where a storm which delayed his sailing was regarded by him as the special interposition of a malevolent Providence. He reached France in May 1767 and England knew him no more—except as all the world knew him, by his works, the influence of which has been abiding and profound.

Wychnor. This is a community of scattered farms rather than a village. Its flitch of bacon is not so well known as Dunmow's, but everyone hereabouts has heard of it, and a wooden flitch still hangs in the hall of Wychnor Park, a house hidden by trees. It is said that John of Gaunt granted the manor to the Somervilles on condition that they would always give a man who had been married a year and a day a flitch of bacon if he would swear that he and his wife lived happily together.

By three firs on a little hill above the pleasant meadows of the Trent stands the church, looking over to Alrewas and upstream to Cannock Chase. It has an Elizabethan brick tower, walls mainly of the 14th century, with fine square-headed and traceried windows, and fragments of old glass are in the windows.

Yoxall. It was the home of a famous booklover and the scene of a campaign against slavery. Thomas Gisborne lived for 60 years at Yoxall Lodge, which has now vanished. A saintly man who wrote books and poems, he was a great friend of Wilberforce, who often visited him here. Wilberforce was here with his friend Thomas Babington in the autumn of 1790, both devoting their time to a report on slavery. Another visitor at the Lodge has given us this peep of the month they spent here:

Mr Wilberforce and Mr Babington have never appeared downstairs since we came, except to take a hasty dinner, and for half an hour after we have supped; the Slave Trade now occupies them nine hours daily. They talk of sitting up one night each week. The two friends begin to look very ill, but they are in excellent spirits, and at this moment I hear them laughing.

Over 50 years before Wilberforce came to Yoxall Lodge Thomas Astle, the famous expert in ancient writing, was born here. He wrote a valuable book on the *Origin and Progress of Writing*, and gathered an amazing library. From his relative Philip Morant, the Essex historian, he inherited a fortune and a library of old books and manuscripts, and for the rest of his life he went on adding to this collection till he had the finest private library of manuscripts in England. His books were bought by the Royal Institution for £1000, but he had thought too much of his precious manuscripts to allow them to be dispersed. They went first to the Marquess of Buckingham, who built a library for them at Stowe, and eventually they were sold to the British Museum for £45,000. Among the greatest treasures were King Alfred's Psalter, the Wardrobe Book of Edward II, and a beautiful volume of Anglo-Saxon charters.

The village, above the meeting of the Swarbourn with the Trent, has many attractive brick and timber-framed houses. It was once the home of Izaak Walton's grandfather, has an old vicarage with a tiny oak-panelled room thought to have been a hiding-place. The church was made new last century with the aid of Lord Palmerston, who helped to pay the cost. On the south side is a late Norman doorway, and the Gothic tower is of the 17th century. There are two modern screens, one under the tower with old fragments, and in the north aisle is a monument with marble figures of the Elizabethan Humphrey Welles and his wife, he in a long cloak, she in a close-fitting cap and tight-waisted dress. In the south aisle, in his naval uniform, a sword at his side, is the effigy of Admiral Henry Meynell, who died in 1865 and is buried at Hoar Cross.

APPENDIX

Places of interest open to the public

(* Indicates National Trust Property)

Alton: Alton Towers, gardens open daily, Easter to mid-October.

Blithfield: Blithfield Hall, open Good Friday to early October on Wednesdays, Thursdays, Saturdays, Sundays, and Bank Holiday Mondays.

Brewood: Chillington Hall, open May to August on Thursdays.

Bushbury: *Moseley Old Hall, open March to November on Wednesdays, Thursdays, Saturdays, Sundays, and Bank Holiday Mondays and Tuesdays.

Great Haywood: *Shugborough, open March to October daily except Mondays, but including Bank Holiday Mondays.

Sandon: Sandon Hall, gardens only open on Sundays from April to mid-July and in early August.

Tamworth: Tamworth Castle, open all the year daily.

Tettenhall: *Wightwick Hall, open all the year on Thursdays and Saturdays, also May to September on Wednesdays and all Bank Holiday Mondays.

Weston-under-Lizard: Weston Park, open Easter to mid-September on Wednesdays, Thursdays, Saturdays, and Sundays (Sundays only in April), and on Bank Holiday Mondays and Tuesdays.

STAFFORDSHIRE TOWNS AND VILLAGES

In this key to our map of Staffordshire (which appears at the front of this volume) are all the towns and villages treated in this book.

Abbots Bromley	F7	Cheddleton	D3	Hollinsclough	F2
Acton Trussell	D7	Church Eaton	C7	Hopton	D6
Adbaston	B6	Clifton Campville	H8	Horton	D3
Aldridge	F9	Codsall	C9		
Alrewas	G8	Colwich	E7	Ilam	F3
Alstonfield	F3	Croxall	G8	Ingestre	D7
Alton	F4	Croxden	F5	Ipstones	E3
Armitage	F8				
Ashley	B5	Denstone	F5	Keele	B4
Audley	B9	Dilhorne	D4	Kidsgrove	C3
		Draycott in the Moors	E5	King's Bromley	F7
Barlaston	C5	Drayton Bassett	G9	Kingsley	E4
Barton-under-		Dudley	D11	Kingswinford	C11
Needwood	G7			Kinver	C12
Baswich	D7	Eccleshall	C6		
Bednall	D7	Elford	G8	Lapley	C8
Betley	B4	Ellastone	F4	Leek	E3
Biddulph	C2	Endon	D3	Leigh	E5
Bilston	D10	Enville	C11	Lichfield	F8
Blithfield	E7	Etruria	C4	Longdon	F8
Blore	F4			Longnor	F2
Blymhill	B8	Farewell	F8	Longton	D4
Bobbington	B11	Fazeley	G9		
Bradley	C7	Fenton	C4	Madeley	B4
Bradley in the Moors	E5	Flash	E1	Maer	B5
Bramshall	F6	Forton	B7	Marchington	F6
Branston	G7			Mavesyn Ridware	F7
Brewood	C8	Gailey	D8	Mayfield	G4
Brierley Hill	D11	Gayton	E6	Milwich	D6
Broughton	B6	Gentleshaw	E8	Mow Cop	C3
Brownhills	E9	Gnosall	C7	Mucklestone	A5
Burntwood	F8	Great Barr	E10		
Burslem	C4	Great Haywood	E7	Newborough	F6
Burton upon Trent	H7	Grindon	F3	Newcastle-under-	
Bushbury	D9			Lyme	C4
Butterton	F3	Hales	A5	Newchapel	C3
		Hammerwich	F9	Norbury	B7
Cannock	E8	Hamstall Ridware	F7	Norton Canes	E9
Castlechurch	D7	Hanbury	G6		
Cauldon	F4	Hanley	C4	Oakamoor	E4
Caverswall	D4	Harlaston	G8	Okeover	G4
Chartley	E6	Haughton	C7	Oulton	D5
Chasetown	E9	High Offley	B6		
Cheadle	E4	Himley	C11	Patshull	B9
Chebsey	C6	Hints	G9	Pattingham	C10
Checkley	E5	Hoar Cross	F7